*Woolfian Boundaries*

# *Woolfian Boundaries*

### Edited by Anna Burrells, Steve Ellis, Deborah Parsons, and Kathryn Simpson

Every effort has been made to trace all copyright-holders, but if any have been inadvertently overlooked, the publisher will be pleased to make the necessary arrangement at the first opportunity.

Copyright 2007 by Clemson University
ISBN 978-0-9796066-1-8

Published by Clemson University Press in Clemson, South Carolina

Editorial Assistants: Julie Gerdes and Kara McManus

To order copies, please visit the Clemson University Press website: www.clemson.edu/press.

**Front cover illustration:**
*The Window*, 1918
Oil painting by Bloomsbury artist Roger Fry
Courtesy of the University of Birmingham Collections
and by the kind permission of the copyright holder.

# Contents

Ruth Gruber • *Forward* .................................................................................................vi
Anna Burrells, Steve Ellis, Deborah Parsons, Kathryn Simpson • *Introduction* ...............ix

Suzanne Bellamy • *Textual Archeology: An Australian Study of Virginia Woolf in 1942*..... 1
Amber K. Regis • *"From all this diversity…not a riot of confusion but a richer unity": The Limits of Self-Representation in Virginia Woolf's* Orlando: A Biography .................... 8
Deborah Gerrard • *Brown-ness, Trees, Rose Petals, and Chrysalises: The Influence of Edward Carpenter's Mystical Evolutionary Socialism on the Writing of Virginia Woolf, with Particular Reference to* The Years ........................................................ 15
Katie Macnamara • *Mapping Woolf's Montaignian Modernism* ........................................ 22
Jim Stewart • *Woolf and Andrew Marvell: The Gendering of Modernism* ........................ 30
Ben Clarke • *"But the barrier is impassable": Virginia Woolf and Class* ........................... 36
Helen Southworth • *"Outside the magic (and tyrannical) triangle of London-Oxford-Cambridge": John Hampson, The Woolfs, and the Hogarth Press*............................ 43
Lara Feigel • *Buggery and Montage: Birmingham and Bloomsbury in the 1930s*............... 51
Alyda Faber • *"The shock of love" and the Visibility of "indecent" Pain: Reading the Woolf-Raverat Correspondence*.................................................................................. 58
Susan Reid • *Killing the Angel in the House: Virginia Woolf, D. H. Lawrence, and the Boundaries of Sex and Gender*.................................................................................. 65
Randi Synnøve Koppen • *Real Bodies and the Psychology of Clothes:* Three Guineas *and the Limits of Sartorial Reasoning* ..................................................................... 72
Ian Blyth • *Woolf, Rooks, and Rural England* ............................................................... 80
Richard Espley • *Woolf and the Others at the Zoo*......................................................... 86
Christina Alt • *Pests and Pesticides: Exploring the Boundaries of Woolf's Environmentalism*...... 93
Jane Goldman • *"Ce chien est à moi": Virginia Woolf and the Signifying Dog*................. 100
Bonnie Kime Scott • *Virginia Woolf, Ecofeminism, and Breaking Boundaries in Nature* ...108
Emily Kopley • *Woolf's Transformation of Providential Form in* Mrs. Dalloway ........... 116
Thaine Stearns • *Pilfering Modernism's Image: Woolf and Those Other Londoners*.......... 121
Ben Harvey • *Borderline Personalities: Woolf Reviews Kapp*.......................................... 127
Elizabeth Wright • *Performing the Self: Woolf as Actress and Audience* ........................ 138
Wendy Parkins • *"Whose face was it?": Nicole Kidman, Virginia Woolf, and the Boundaries of Feminine Celebrity* ........................................................................ 144
Maggie Humm • *"Memory Holes" or "Heterotopias"?: The Bloomsbury Photographs* ...... 150
Tara Surry • *"Over the boundary": Virginia Woolf as Common Seer* .............................. 157
Elisa Kay Sparks • *"The evening under lamplight…with the photograph album":* To the Lighthouse *as Family Scrapbook* ..................................................................... 164

Melba Cuddy-Keane • *Afterword: Inside and Outside the Covers: Beginnings, Endings, and Woolf's Non-Coercive Ethical Texts*................................................................ 172

*Notes on Contributors* ................................................................................................. 181

# *Foreword*

## by Ruth Gruber

On October 15, 1935, Virginia Woolf invited me for tea at 52 Tavistock Square, her home in London. I spent the day walking up and down the street in Bloomsbury. I was going to meet my literary idol. In May of that year, with the daring of youth, I had sent her a trade paperback of my doctoral thesis on her work, published by the Tauchnitz Press in Leipzig. I had written it three years earlier, at the age of twenty, as an American exchange student at the University of Cologne.

Professor Herbert Schöffler, Head of the English department at Cologne, asked me to work for a PhD. I told him it was impossible. My fellowship, given by the Institute of International Education, was designated for one year only. Moreover, there was no mention of pursuing a doctorate.

Schöffler smiled benignly. "I have a special reason," he explained. "I love Virginia Woolf's writings, but my students don't know English well enough to analyze her work. You are the only English speaker on our campus. A doctorate has never been done in a year, but maybe you can do it."

Even then my philosophy was "Dream dreams, have visions, and let no obstacle stop you." I had to work fast to complete the two German requirements for a doctorate: to write a thesis and to pass the oral exams. I had never read Virginia Woolf before, but Professor Schöffler gave me a stack of her books in light-green hardcover, each one noting on the title page: "Published by Leonard & Virginia Woolf at the Hogarth Press, Tavistock Square. London." Downtown in the bookstores I found two additional works by her, published for English-speaking tourists by Tauchnitz in the days before television. They were *Orlando* (quickly to become my favorite) bound in a bright-red hardcover, and *Mrs. Dalloway* in a tan paperback.

Soon I was jotting impressions in the margins of each book, captivated by Woolf's literary innovations, her vivid descriptions of the conflict between poets and critics, and the equally vivid conflict between women as creators and men as destroyers.

In the summer of 1932, with the thesis finished, I stood for the orals. Sweat poured down my face; my knees trembled as three inquisitors interrogated me. Among the questions that Professor Schöffler asked was a pivotal one: "You called Virginia Woolf's novel *The Waves* a 'rhythm of conflicts.' What did you mean?"

I managed to pull out of my brain sentences still fresh from my thesis. "It's the struggle between light and darkness. It is the law of polarity, of conflicts as irreconcilable as night and day, of poets versus critics, that reverberates through all her writing. It is her final solution to the problem of style and the riddle of life. No truth is absolute, no style is supreme. We live our lives in a polarity of conflicts."

After half an hour, Professor Schöffler ushered me out the door and told me to wait. Soon he reappeared, shook my hand, and announced: "You have received the doctorate *mit sehr Gut*. It is the equivalent of your *magna cum laude*."

The Virginia Woolf thesis was to chart the course of my life. In 1935, after its publication, I asked Woolf if I could interview her for another book I was planning to write on the subject of Women under Fascism, Communism, and Democracy. In response to my letter, Virginia Woolf generously invited me for tea.

At 6:00 pm on the designated date, I arrived at her home and rang the bell. Leonard Woolf greeted me and brought me into the living room. Virginia lay on a rug before the fireplace. She was an elegant figure of grace and beauty, dressed in a long gray silk gown, with gray shoes, gray stockings, gray hair, and a silver cigarette holder, through which she blew gray smoke.

Leonard shook my hand and escorted me to an upholstered armchair inches away from her. "This is strange," I thought. "I've come to sit at her feet, and now she is lying at mine."

He then seated himself at the far end of the room. His face was long and egg-shaped, with soft cheeks that seemed to have no bones. His eyes sank beneath thick black brows, and his hands moved erratically with a nervous tremor. Despite his distance from us, I had the sense that he was hovering over Virginia, brooding and protective.

The housekeeper brought in a tray with delicate cups already filled with tea. There was nothing to nibble on. No sandwiches, no cakes. I was so afraid that my trembling hands might drop the cup that I carefully placed it on a small end table and never touched it again. Virginia and Leonard had no such fear.

I was too awed to speak, but she finally placed her cup delicately on the floor and opened the conversation: "I looked into the study you wrote about me. Quite scholarly."

"In your letter," she continued, "you wrote that you are a journalist and are planning to write a book. I don't know how I can help you. I don't understand a thing about politics. I never worked a day in my life."

I was startled that at this stage in her life she did not consider it was work to publish ten books, countless essays, and many brilliant reviews. Also, nearly everyone in her Bloomsbury circle, especially Leonard, was deeply involved with the political issues of the day.

A long silence ensued, during which I waited for Virginia to speak again. Curled up before the fire, she smoked dreamily, looking into the flames.

Returning from wherever her reverie had taken her, she finally broke the silence: "We were just in your Germany."

Why did she call it *my* Germany? I had written her from my home in Brooklyn and my accent was decidedly American. But I did not interrupt her.

"We were driving through on holiday," she said. "Our car was stopped to let Hitler and his entourage pass. Madness, that country."

"As a student in Cologne," I ventured at last, "I went to hear Hitler speak at a huge rally." Leonard moved his chair closer to us.

"The place was filled with men in brown uniforms and high boots, who waved flags emblazoned with swastikas," I continued. "They went wild, screaming and waving their flags as Hitler entered, surrounded by bodyguards. He climbed to the podium and began to rail against America, and especially against Jews. His voice terrified me. It seemed to come not from his lungs but his bowels."

"He has a terrifying voice," she agreed. "There is such horror in the world."

"But what strikes me so forcefully in your books is hope," I replied. "The hope that women will help end the horror of war and create peace."

"Once," she said, "we had such hope for the world."

The words rang in my head. *Such hope for the world.*

❧

Nearly seventy years later, in the summer of 2004, I reconnected with Virginia Woolf when one of my assistants discovered three letters Woolf had written me in 1935 and 1936. Thrilled with the discovery, my editor, Philip Turner, announced: "Stop everything you're doing. Remember, you wrote the first doctoral thesis on Virginia Woolf's work. I'm going to publish it in its entirety, including these three newly discovered letters and also her diary entries about you."

The book, entitled *Virginia Woolf: The Will to Create as a Woman*, appeared in 2005. It had been my first book, and now it was my eighteenth. My two children and I agreed with my friend, the novelist Cynthia Ozick: "These letters do not belong to you and your children. They belong to the world." On 12 December 2005, we donated them to the Berg Collection in the New York Public Library. Woolf scholars can now find them in the Collection among the 28 volumes of her diaries and more than 100 of her letters.

❧

In 2006, the annual Virginia Woolf Conference held in Birmingham opened my eyes to the global scope of Virginia Woof's influence. When I wrote my thesis in 1932, there was no such person as a "Virginia Woolf scholar." At the conference, however, I was accepted by a group of brilliant and enthusiastic Woolfians from all over the world. Some had even come from Australia, China, and Japan. There I learned from some of the older scholars that my study was the only one available to them during the rediscovery of Virginia Woolf by American and British feminists in the 1960s.

The conference reawakened my understanding of how much I owed to Virginia Woolf. She helped me find the courage to write as a woman, and to use words and images as my tools to fight injustice. Throughout the rest of my life, the words she spoke to me at 52 Tavistock Square were written across my heart: *We had such hope for the world*.

I wish I could tell her that, despite everything, I still have hope.

# Introduction

*by Anna Burrells, Steve Ellis, Deborah Parsons, and Kathryn Simpson*

Boundaries signal limits and extent. They contain and confine, but they also abut and adjoin. Boundaries demarcate and divide one thing from another, yet as borders they are also the site of the betwixt and between, where opposites meet, and as frontiers they point to the unknown beyond, promising exploration and discovery. Boundaries can be closed or open, and focussed inwards or outwards. Virginia Woolf was fixated by thresholds—historical, social, spatial, ontological, epistemological, and artistic—and in her writing constantly positioned herself at the site of the "in-between," as Tara Surry notes in her essay in this volume. "Now is life very solid, or very shifting?" she asked in her diary in January 1929, "I am haunted by the two contradictions" (*D3* 218). For the 16th Annual International Conference on Virginia Woolf we invited speakers to explore the idea of Woolfian boundaries—to consider not only Woolf's own transgressions and trespasses, but also to explore Woolf's work from perspectives "beyond the boundary" of her own positions and attitudes, and indeed beyond a metropolitan-centred view. The response to this invitation was impressive, as speakers crossed geographical boundaries and moved beyond established interpretative parameters in rich and fertile ways, refusing the constraints of period, generic, and methodological boundaries—as Woolf herself was persistently concerned to do—and pushing the limits and extent of our own disciplinary taxonomies. Because of the constraints of space we can only represent a fraction of the high quality papers submitted for this volume, but we hope that those included will stir new thoughts and open further perspectives and debate beyond the very literal boundaries of this Woolfian text.

One of the most fascinating perspectives on Woolf's writing and life was offered by Ruth Gruber, who wrote the first PhD thesis on Woolf in 1931/2, and shared with the conference her experience of working on her thesis and of meeting Virginia and Leonard Woolf; of crossing the threshold of their home, and, in completing her thesis, crossing another threshold and opening the door to Woolf scholarship. It was an immense privilege to hear Ruth Gruber's incredible story, some of which is included in her Foreword to this collection, a flavour of the hour-long talk that both fascinated and entertained the new and established Woolf scholars of today. Suzanne Bellamy's essay continues this work of what she calls "textual archeology" in her discussion of the first Australian MA thesis on Woolf, written by Nuri Mass in 1941/2. At the beginning of an exciting project to edit this thesis, Bellamy offers insights into another important threshold moment in Woolf scholarship, and to the prescience of this early critic, who with none of the biographical material which has proved so valuable to subsequent criticism recognised the challenges of exploring Woolf as a female and modernist writer.

Deploring absolutism, Woolf's instinct was drawn to the transitional aspect of boundaries, and to their fluctuation, their permeability, and their transgression, but at the same time she was immensely sympathetic to the human desire for definition and solidity, and despite constantly seeking to move beyond the confines of the ego, intensely aware of its fragility. "I am whirled down caverns, and flap like paper against endless corridors," thinks

Rhoda in *The Waves*, "and must press my hand against the wall to draw myself back." This ambivalence on Woolf's part is directly addressed by the thought-provoking conjunction of the essays of Elizabeth Wright and Amber Regis. Wright, for example, argues that Woolf was "keenly aware of life's dramatic dimensions and of the self as performance," and recognised in role-playing and the ability to play the part of another "a means of delving into different worlds." Regis analyses Woolf's thinking on the biographical subject in both the highly theatrical *Orlando* and her essays on biographical discourse. *Orlando*, Regis observes, is a text that "breaks down the limits that order our understandings of biographical practice and identities," so that "discreet and stable categories are disrupted, and fixed notions of gender and sexuality are fractured, dispersed, and reduced to absurdity." Woolf yet ultimately turned away from the anarchy of this kind of modernist biographical subject, Regis argues, to "the expedient re-imposition of 'Woolfian boundaries' around the self and between genres." Wendy Parkins's discussion of the performance of Nicole Kidman *as* Virginia Woolf in the film version of Michael Cunningham's *The Hours* offers an intriguing coda here. Examining the media focus on the physical aspects of Kidman's performance (her reproduction of her hand-writing as well as the famous nose), Parkins strongly critiques the twenty-first-century cultural assumptions that limit the boundaries of both Kidman and Woolf's celebrity embodiment.

The body, bodily experience, and clothing are recurrent themes in Woolf criticism, and here Susan Reid, Alyda Faber, and Randi Koppen illuminate these themes in new ways. Discussing D. H. Lawrence's and Virginia Woolf's quarrels with and yet attraction to the implicitly sexless figure of the "Angel in the House," Reid explores the challenges posed by each to conventional boundaries of sex and gender, and to the institutions of heterosexuality and motherhood. Reid's discussion focuses attention on modernist masculinities in relation to Lawrence's representation of a working-class embodiment of this powerful cultural myth in Mrs. Morel and compares this to Woolf's representation of Mrs. Ramsay. Whilst the "angels" and their protégés die, however, neither Lawrence nor Woolf solves the difficulties of "telling the truth" about bodily and sexual experience. Faber's essay draws fascinating parallels between Woolf's "shock-receiving capacity" (something Woolf recognises as central to her role as a writer) and theologian Franz Rosenzweig's understanding of revelation as a "shock of love," exploring Woolf's active desire for responsiveness to what is beautiful, unlovable, unwanted, and utterly strange within herself, others, and the world. It is Woolf's response to "the shocks of love," to the risk of making loving connections with what is unlovable in others, Faber argues, that makes Woolf so vital as person and as a writer. Koppen's essay examines Woolf's scathing critique of male sartorial display in *Three Guineas*, and considers the work of psychologist J. S. Flügel as a significant point of reference for Woolf's arguments about clothing in relation to progressive political thought, fascism, and the creation of the modern subject. Arguing that Woolf radically revises Flügel's progressive theories from a feminist perspective, Koppen makes a powerful case for Woolf's sophisticated engagement with the complexity of the signifying systems of language, bodies, and dress, and of the operation of the conscious and unconscious mind in her analysis of power.

Woolf's participation in the revival of interest in seventeenth-century writers and philosophers in the first decades of the twentieth century, and in the aligning of metaphysical aesthetics with the project of modernism promoted by critics such as T. S. Eliot, is traced in the two essays by Jim Stewart and Katie Macnamara. Identifying the 1921 tercentenary celebrations of Andrew Marvell in Hull as an important catalyst for Woolf's renewed interest in Marvell, Stewart demonstrates how Woolf incorporated Marvellian lyrics into her writing, challenging gendered assumptions of his verse as she rewrote him, investing her hybrids of his work with a feminist politics at odds with the contemporary appraisals of Marvell by Eliot. Macnamara explores Leonard and Virginia's different engagements with Montaigne, tracing in particular the influence of his concept of the essay form on Woolf's own essayistic techniques. The preservation of contradiction that Woolf finds in Montaigne's work, Macnamara argues, and her celebration of his aim to "allow opposites free play in the living essay form," is key to her resistance of definitive categories and conclusions throughout her writing. Emily Kopley's paper investigates how Woolf found new uses for old literary forms in incorporating into *Mrs Dalloway* the type of "providential" patterning scholars have identified in works like *Paradise Lost* and *Robinson Crusoe*. The crucial noon-midnight antithesis Woolf works with in the novel thereby indicates a fascination with Christian ideas which other speakers on the "Bordering Religion" panel at the conference corroborated.

A number of contributors revisit Woolf's intersection with the working classes, broadening a critical tradition that has often focused upon "The Leaning Tower" as a definitive expression of Woolf's political sentiments. Lara Feigel and Helen Southworth's papers, for example, destabilise geographical links between London as centre and Birmingham as periphery through the work of John Hampson Simpson, author of *Saturday Night at the Greyhound*. Radically reshaping narratives about Woolf and the left by exposing and elucidating the Hogarth Press's championing of working-class writing, Southworth's paper probes the publication decisions that the Press were making in the thirties with particular emphasis upon working-class writing and gender, whilst Feigel argues that Hampson's use of the socialist technique of cinematic montage influenced Woolf's own writing technique. Ben Clarke demonstrates the nexus between class and gender in his analysis of Woolf's introduction to *Life as We Have Known It*, the collection of essays by members of the Women's Co-operative Guild published by the Hogarth Press in 1931. Examining Woolf's recollection of her discomfort when attending a congress of the Guild in June 1913, and her response to the material and political concerns of the participants as that of "a benevolent spectator…irretrievably cut off from the actors," Clarke argues that even though class barriers would remain for Woolf ever-impassable, her very awareness of their economic differential nevertheless enabled her to resist the tendency to universalise any ideal of aesthetic or political sisterhood. Taken together these three papers destabilise the division of working-class experiences in Britain's industrial centres and Woolf's position within a putative Bloomsbury elite.

That the vigorously emerging field of eco-criticism is making a significant impact on Woolf studies was attested to at the conference by two panels exploring the relationship of Woolf's writing and the natural boundaries where, as Bonnie Kime Scott notes, "the cultivated garden meets the moors or the woods, or is invaded by wild 'pests,' where exotic plants and animals import echoes of the Empire, where science divides the species." The papers collected here represent the differing critical perspectives informing this debate. In Deborah Gerrard's essay trees, petals, exfoliation, and chrysalises become the touchstones of an exploration of Woolf's writing in relation to the blossoming of her spiritual identity. Gerrard unearths intriguing parallels between Edward Carpenter's philosophical challenges to late Victorian scientific materialism and Woolf's ideas about modernism's goal of privileging the spiritual, arguing not only for Carpenter as an important influence on the development of Woolf's ideas, but that his evolutionary socialism and mysticism (as well as the homosexuality that informed his thought) may have been a crucial factor in encouraging and helping to foster Woolf's development as a writer. Scott herself argues compellingly for recognising Woolf as a proto-ecofeminist, frequently traversing the boundaries of (wo)man and environment in both her fiction and non-fictional writings. "When an artist like Woolf traverses such barriers to think like a moth, take in the perceptions of a snail, or the motion of a flock of birds," Scott asserts, she counters the androcentric power paradigm of man over nature in an articulation of "solidarity across distant species." Scott's aligning of Woolf's "sympathetic" nature writing with the critique of egocentric patriarchal binary values that she suggests is fundamental to a feminist and "Woolfian" epistemology and aesthetics, sits in constructive dialogue with Christina Alt's analysis of Woolf's engagement with late nineteenth-century natural history as traced through her 1924 essay on the entomologist Eleanor Ormerod. Acknowledging that Ormerod publicly denied feminist sympathies, and that her work has come under criticism from ecofeminism for its promotion of the use of pesticides, Alt argues that what Woolf recognized and championed in her essay was the revolutionary potential of Ormerod's pioneering emphasis on the empiricism of the new entomological science against the (patriarchal) moral and religious paradigms of taxonomic natural history.

Richard Espley's paper continues the developing debate over what Scott describes as Woolf's "artistic relations to 'others' of nature" in his examination of the "otherness" of zoo animals, arguing that Woolf saw through metaphors of repression that rested upon animality. Ian Blyth takes what might seem an inconspicuous presence in Woolf's work—the common native bird the rook—and shows just how pervasive this creature is, appearing in practically every novel, as well as in Woolf's other writings. Blyth argues not only for Woolf's extreme attentiveness to the natural environment, but suggests that the rook functions "as a form of metonymy, a shorthand for rural England." Similarly concerned with the metaphoricity of animals in Woolf's writings, Jane Goldman's paper focuses upon Woolf's "signifying dog," chasing the meaning of canine references through her work in terms of discourses of repression based upon race, gender, and class.

Perhaps the most enduring of Woolf's own imposition of boundaries in literary history is her famous dating of December 1910 as the beginning of modern character and, implicitly, the modern art of fiction. Thaine Stearns's essay confronts Woolf's artistic politics in defining her literary aesthetic in terms of an Impressionist and Post-Impressionist modernism, tracing her elision of "the other modernist avant-garde" of Imagism and Vorticism from her "manifesto" essays of the late 1910s and 1920s. Woolf's exploration of the verbal/visual boundaries of her literary aesthetic, and her allegiance to the ideas of Roger Fry and the work of Vanessa Bell at the same time as she asserted the unique possibilities of her own medium, is further pursued in Tara Surry's essay on Woolf's art criticism. Woolf was always conscious of being an outsider in the matter of art, Surry notes, of standing on the metaphoric threshold of the art gallery, "doubly excluded from the 'silent kingdom of paint' as a woman and as a writer" and "trespassing" in her writing about art. It was exactly this threshold position, she argues, and Woolf's awareness of herself as spectator, that produced the dialogic relationship between art object and viewer/reader that would inform her moulding of new literary forms. Ben Harvey also takes up Woolf's interest in the space of the gallery in his study of her essay "Pictures and Portraits," turning however to her institutional critique of the cultural and ideological forces that permeate its walls and delimit "*which* objects and *which* people make it into an art gallery."

The two final essays of this volume, by Maggie Humm and Elisa Sparks, demonstrate the rewarding attention being paid in Woolf scholarship to the substantial collection of photographs within the Stephen family archives. Humm investigates how we can approach domestic photograph albums like those of the Woolfs and of Vanessa Bell through a Foucault-inspired process of "reading" that attends to the syntax, "codes and indices" of amateur photography. Humm's contribution to the emerging theory of such photography attends to the Bloomsbury albums as a form of autobiographical narrative, discussing such things as layout and chronology, as well as forms of spatial patterning within individual images. Sparks extends this focus to the role of scraps within Victorian albums, in order to think about the scraps and fragments with which Woolf metaphorically collaged her own memories of family life at Talland House in *To the Lighthouse* as an experiment in "transforming visual methodologies to writing," by which the novel becomes "a copious family album, filled with photographs, personal writing, quotations from favorite poems, and bright colored scraps commemorating famous people and events."

As well as the papers represented by the above sample, five plenary speakers addressed the conference, beginning with Victoria Glendinning who previewed her biography *Leonard Woolf: a Life* (published in September 2006), which was followed by a conversation with Paul Levy focussing on Leonard's Jewishness and Bloomsbury responses to this. The second plenary was an illustrated talk by Christopher Reed on British *Vogue* in the 1920s and Woolf's connections with the magazine, and more specifically on the *Vogue* aesthetic as a context for Woolf's *Orlando*. The third and fourth plenary speakers were Ruth Gruber and Lisa Williams respectively, who outlined a more personal response to Woolf in terms of the former's reminiscences of her and the latter's fictional letters written to Woolf. The titles of these plenary talks are given at the end of this volume in the Conference Program, and the material presented derives from works already in print or soon to be published elsewhere. Melba Cuddy-Keane drew the threads of the conference together in her concluding plenary, which also serves as the fitting conclusion to this volume, and among much else reminds us of the provisionality of Woolf's fictional endings in her commitment to the ongoing journey, which leads the editors of the present volume to wish all success to the organisers of the 17th Annual International Conference on Virginia Woolf at the Miami University of Ohio, due to take place in June 2007 as these *Selected Papers* appear. The editors would also like to thank Wayne Chapman and his team at Clemson University for their exemplary care in preparing this volume for publication, and Annabel Cole for permission to reproduce the painting by Roger Fry on the volume cover.

# Virginia Woolf
## Standard Abbreviations
(as established by *The Woolf Studies Annual*)

| | |
|---|---|
| *AHH* | *A Haunted House* |
| *AROO* | *A Room of One's Own* |
| *BP* | *Books and Portraits* |
| *BTA* | *Between the Acts* |
| *CDB* | *The Captain's Death Bed and Other Essays* |
| *CE* | *Collected Essays* (ed. Leonard Woolf, 4 vols.: *CE1, CE2, CE3, CE4*) |
| *CR1* | *The Common Reader* |
| *CR2* | *The Common Reader, Second Series* |
| *CSF* | *The Complete Shorter Fiction* (ed. Susan Dick) |
| *D* | *The Diary of Virginia Woolf* (5 vols.: *D1, D2, D3, D4, D5*) |
| *DM* | *The Death of the Moth and Other Essays* |
| *E* | *The Essays of Virginia Woolf* (ed. Andrew McNeillie, 6 vols.: *E1, E2, E3, E4, E5, E6*) |
| *F* | *Flush* |
| *FR* | *Freshwater* |
| *GR* | *Granite and Rainbow: Essays* |
| *HPGN* | *Hyde Park Gate News* (ed. Gill Lowe) |
| *JR* | *Jacob's Room* |
| *JRHD* | *Jacob's Room: The Holograph Draft* (ed. Edward L. Bishop) |
| *L* | *The Letters of Virginia Woolf* (ed. Nigel Nicolson and Joanne Trautmann, 6 vols.: *L1, L2, L3, L4, L5, L6*) |
| *M* | *The Moment and Other Essays* |
| *MEL* | *Melymbrosia* |
| *MOB* | *Moments of Being* |
| *MT* | *Monday or Tuesday* |
| *MD* | *Mrs. Dalloway* |
| *ND* | *Night and Day* |
| *O* | *Orlando* |
| *PA* | *A Passionate Apprentice* |
| *RF* | *Roger Fry* |
| *TG* | *Three Guineas* |
| *TTL* | *To the Lighthouse* |
| *TW* | *The Waves* |
| *TY* | *The Years* |
| *VO* | *The Voyage Out* |
| *WF* | *Women and Fiction: The Manuscript Versions of* A Room of One's Own (ed. S. P. Rosenbaum) |

# Textual Archeology: An Australian Study of Virginia Woolf in 1942

## by Suzanne Bellamy

This is the story of an artefact from an almost lost world, a 180,000-word MA thesis on Virginia Woolf's novels written in 1941/2, finished in the shadow of news of Woolf's death. It aroused the publishing interest of Leonard Woolf but went unpublished, as the war intervened. Its author won her MA Honours in Australia and the University Medal in English in 1942, but then put the thesis aside. Original scholarship, dashed hopes and tragedies, prescient vision, and mysterious timeliness precede its now resurfacing. The Second World War took much away from us, interrupted lives and projects, broken threads of ideas, lost chances and opportunities. In the hope of reuniting these severed parts, this paper brings together again the lives of Virginia Woolf and a young Australian student, Nuri Mass, and acts as a preliminary field survey of what will become a full length study of the Mass thesis on Woolf, an annotated version of the original and a contextual study of both the author and Woolf scholarship at the time of its writing.

Nuri Mass (1918-1993) is well known in Australia as a writer, artist, and book illustrator, publisher and peace activist. I first met her as a student in the 1970s, around the time when I was researching radio programmes on Virginia Woolf for the Australian Broadcasting Commission. She was then well known for her founding of The Writers Press, even setting up her own printing press in the late 1940s, inspired by Virginia and Leonard Woolf. She had made a career in book publishing and writing rather than in academe, had two children, was widowed early, and led a productive creative life in printing and publishing. We had long conversations, and I loved hearing and reading the stories of her almost mythic early life in the desert of Argentina, with her depressive immigrant Spanish father Pedro from Barcelona, who was a writer and gold miner, geologist and engineer, and of her Scottish mother Celeste who was a brilliant artist and considered herself psychic.

Yet lives are often mysterious and so much always remains hidden, and during all our talks over many years, Mass only once mentioned hesitantly that she had done a thesis on Virginia Woolf as a young university student in the early 1940s in Sydney. After her death in 1993, her daughter Tess collected her archive of manuscripts, letters, diaries, artwork, botanical drawings, and book illustrations, an unpublished autobiography, and all her published works, and deposited it all in the Mitchell Library in Sydney, where it has sat still uncatalogued. Buried there in a box was her pioneering study of Woolf.

Hearing of Ruth Gruber's recently re-published thesis on Woolf from 1932, I remembered Mass telling me about her thesis from 1942 (a light bulb in the brain). It seemed the time had come to find it. I thought Woolf scholars might now be interested in other early readings, so with the family's permission I went to the Mitchell Library in Sydney. There was the thesis among her papers, untouched and unread since its writing and assessment in 1942. At the time it was thought to be the first full-length academic study of Woolf on that scale, and its publication was assumed. The earlier study by Winifred Holtby was available, and of course now we know of Gruber's study. In this paper I will focus principally on some of Mass's ideas about Woolf and the circumstances of the writing of her thesis.

Already recognised as a brilliant young scholar, Mass was invited to take on a full-length study of Woolf for an MA by the Head of the English Department, Professor C. J. Waldock. Her supervisor became R. G. Howarth, a native-born Australian academic, with a BLetters from Oxford 1932, who returned to a lectureship at Sydney University in 1933. He was a modernist champion and an admirer of Woolf's writing. According to Faculty of Arts Minutes, an MA thesis would normally be expected to be 20,000 words, which Mass far exceeded by nature of the study she embarked upon with departmental encouragement. (See Minutes Books, *Southerly*, *Union Recorder*).

Everything mattered as war came, lives were under threat, intellectual life had a real edge, and student life was politically challenged by international and colonial conflicts. Mass was not a typical student coming out of an orderly school life. She had lived away from Australia in Argentina in early childhood, was home-schooled by her mother, reflecting an eccentric radical intellectual family base, youthful egotism, precocity, and passion for ideas. In fact, her initial response to the idea of writing a thesis on Woolf was reluctance:

> My flimsy exposure to Virginia Woolf's work previous to this had repelled and even angered me. I had no time for the so-called private symbolism, a strong feature among the moderns…. I saw Virginia Woolf as another literary egotist. The University's directive that I should do my Master thesis on her work *fell upon me like a sentence*!!!…. I was alone with the books themselves. No guidelines, no full scale critical analysis, only a scattering of book reviews. (*Unpublished Autobiographical Notes* 98)

Mass struggled to get her research material together, all the novels including, miraculously, *Between the Acts* which was hard to acquire, some short fiction, some articles in magazines, and Winifred Holtby's 1932 study. No reliable biographical material existed, no stories of Woolf's peers and contemporaries, no diaries and letters, no holographs, no gossip, none of the abundant nuancing material of the period since the 1970s. This was a moment in time, with the full body of fiction, and its ending point with the death just announced. Mass really did not have anything but the texts and some essays in American magazines, unlike scholars now who cannot ever go to that place of pure text again. This moment gives her work now its great new potential as original insight, layering her research method with the consequence of fugitive historical perception.

Mass was in the final stages of writing as the news of Woolf's disappearance on 28 March and likely death by drowning was announced in the *Sydney Morning Herald* on 3 April 1941. She notes the death in her thesis Preface, as "a sudden and mysterious close" (Thesis 1), and the shock of the death deeply affected her personally and her critique, especially of the later fiction. In her own words, written much later in the *Unpublished Autobiographical Notes*:

> Subjecting Virginia Woolf's philosophy and technique alike to microscopic scrutiny, I was finding each to be an integral part of the other. Three main sections emerged, precious weeks, one after the other, and in the midst of it all, Virginia herself walking out into the sea and into eternity. A darkness falling upon my

world, the spirit going out of me. Then for the first time in months a sleep so profound it was as though after weeks, I slept for 29 hours. (101-2)

A touch of youthful drama in this account nevertheless focuses the moment when the writer's life ends, the body of Woolf's work becomes finite, and the thesis is also transformed into a full and complete study. The nature of the writer's death also becomes a lens for future interpretations of text and meaning.

Reactions to the completed thesis were positive. Mass's professor and teachers expressed amazement at her study's insights. C. J. Waldock, Professor of English, described the thesis as "a remarkable piece of work—she completely understood Woolf, the first to accomplish this. In many ways this study was an advance on any criticism of VW that had up to that time been published, and I hope still that it may appear in print" (Reference and Letters). Correspondence had begun between Mass and Leonard Woolf in August 1941 and led to the possibility of the Hogarth Press publishing some version of the final work (Woolf, Letters). There was also an expectation that an academic career would unfold for Mass.

"It was the high point of my life," Mass says (*Unpublished Autobiographical Notes* 102). Waldock had written to her "Eventually you will become the first lady professor of English in the history of the University…" (quoted in *Unpublished Autobiographical Notes* 103). None of this happened, and indeed it was another twenty-five years until the appointment of Dame Leonie Kramer to that position, when I was a student in the same department. Life for Nuri Mass took a different path, including responsibilities for a family which she supported, a kind of a breakdown after finishing the thesis, and certainly a massive loss of confidence. She put academia on hold for the duration of the war, and took a trainee editorship with a publishing company, Angus and Robertson in Sydney.

Reading the thesis, *Virginia Woolf the Novelist*, in 2006, a vigorous and original critical energy is immediately apparent. It is structured in three sections. 1. Woolf's Philosophy (dealing with her ideas and influences), 2. Woolf's Art: Prose and a Poet's Vision (mainly focussing on her method), and 3. The Novels (focussing on continuous and gradual development from one work to the next). There is little repetition over these broad distinctions. It has depth and broad sweep, and allows for a conversation about the unity of the whole life's work on its own terms. Principally Mass sees Woolf as a "writer of fiction" (Thesis 1), and so does not include *Three Guineas* or *A Room of One's Own* in her main texts, regarded more as polemics at that time. By focussing on the novels in unfolding continuity, she fashions a portrait of the writer which is centrally imbedded in the texts. It takes on in fact the texture of a kind of imbedded biography. Mass sees Woolf as a hopeful writer (with the exception of *Between the Acts*), restoring something to literature after "the trials of disillusionment since the war" (Thesis 89). Even though this is written in 1941/2, it is clear that Mass understands Woolf's war as World War 1, and that people saw the Great War as a trauma still affecting life well into the 1930s. She presents Woolf as a very different kind of modernist, not like the male modernist writers. She compares her favourably against Lawrence and Joyce (Thesis 212), and establishes her originality from them, invoking and supporting the idea of a gendered modernism. More research can later establish some of the wider reading by Mass which informed these positions.

In *The Voyage Out*, she sees Woolf making clear her position, "feminist, atheist, rebel, a declamation" (Thesis 226). Mass claims, "It gives the voice to the rage of a new generation" and is "a vigorous breaking free from old shackles and conventions" (Thesis 215). Although not including *Three Guineas* in the scope of her thesis at all, Mass identifies Woolf's general critique of Church, Psychology, Conformity, Uniformity, and Tyranny, all explored in the Philosophy section (Thesis 3: 117). She clearly sees Woolf as ideas-driven. Mass argues that in *Orlando* Woolf engages the idea of one energy through time, and follows with *The Waves* as the parts within the one, thus establishing the idea of the creative vision wave unfolding from text to text seamlessly. Mass explores *The Waves* as a spiritual growth cycle (Thesis 420) in a reading which appears to show the informed ideas coming through her own family experiences, such as her mother's philosophical involvement with Unitarian, Christian Science, Theosophical, and Transcendentalist ideas, certainly an area for future study.

The concentration on the development of the novels as ideas and forms in a sequence helps Mass to pick up the framework of the whole body of work, the developmental shifts as a kind of spiritual creative journey. Mass calls Woolf a "visionary escapist" (Thesis 202). *Between the Acts*, as the last novel in the life, becomes for Mass the dystopic other, the break in the process, although valiant and still brilliant. However Mass reads *Between the Acts*, the last novel and the last text to come to her just as she is completing her thesis, with the shock of her knowledge of the suicide. She sees the novel as a paradox, with signs of "a certain world weariness" (Thesis 484), "a bitterness and venom like Swift," "it's a sorrowful book, bitter, with weariness and doubt, a great book nonetheless, a microscopic and expansive vision, restating the conviction that human life is renewed" (Thesis 483). Mass finds the women characters in all the later works, especially the older women, as having "a gift for exaggeration, with exuberance and variety," like Mrs Swithin (Thesis 202). These are women represented by a woman, and as in Dorothy Richardson's writing, she recognises it is something really new in English literature. She answers the literary criticisms about weakness of character in Woolf and issues of class with the defence that Woolf was not creating conventional characters at all. These are not stories with characters so much as an inner landscape or composition like music being composed from within. She sees Woolf creating a language of her own mind, that which she sees, the multiplicity of the senses and the selves, a very modern psyche fractured and yet disciplined. In Mass's view, Woolf's work purpose is not to include all social classes any more than if she were composing music or a painting.

The young Mass has no way to know or wonder what life is like in Sussex during the war, nor really any depth of knowledge about the rise of Fascism, and she judges the politics in *Between the Acts* as its core failure. She says, "The volley of abuse and protest poured forth from the megaphone in [Woolf's] last novel is the most offensive of her outbursts, but it is an exception" (Thesis 216). Mass was writing during a time of deeply pressured and reconfigured patriotism, when a rage at defeatism and ideas about the separation of art and politics were prevalent. Possibly this leads to a misreading of satire and humour in the work, and too close a reading of Miss La Trobe as Woolf herself. Mass sees despair where more recent critics do not, and thus she misreads some of the humour and satire.

In a letter to her mentor, W. G. Cousins of publishers Angus and Robertson, she writes: "The thesis would have been impaired by a lack of first-hand acquaintance with BTA, lucky to get a copy. I needed someone else's opinion of it, once I had written 11,000 words about it…" She had asked Cousins for help, and he sends her articles. Mass responds,

The book contained a number of complexities, a review from November and a notice of the book coming in Dec 1941, very helpful. I like the reproduction of the portrait by Vanessa Bell. She is her sister, you know, and has a style almost as much her own in painting as Virginia has in writing. Altogether a most interesting family. (Letter to W. G. Cousins, 16 November 1941)

At my first excited reading of the thesis the most striking material involved Mass's exploration of Woolf's writing method as a form of synaesthesia and abstraction, of visual language: "Like in dreams, things are either fast or very slow, sound, light, shadow have tangible form, this is the territory of the mind not the body" (Thesis 157). Mass defines her use of the term synaesthesia as "the mingling of the senses," a modern technique from psychology, expressing impressions from one sense in terms of another, the subtlest forms of perception (Thesis 158). For Mass, the visual sense is brought through to words and the visible is used to express abstract ideas: the characters in the novels are trying to give pictorial form to abstractions, some secret language which we feel but never speak, and act as a screen filled with potential powers. Mass argued that Woolf can write the full whole of her vision, use words to their limit, make words stretch and encompass a whole sense of all things being connected, through perception, dream, synaesthesia, psychology, and filmic structure. Words, objects, things take on symbolic meanings which are not fixed, but which jump across to other meanings; it is not metaphor, but "the thing itself," a concept remarkable when coming from a student reader who has not read "A Sketch of the Past." Mass finds a parallel universe language, pictographic form, where words are connective not separating. As a philosopher Woolf dealt with high abstractions, says Mass (Thesis 52, 87, 159). The thesis is then in part a spiritual analysis of a hybrid kind of modernism, modernist abstraction, new visual language, with symbolism, theosophy, a severe break with realism through the experimental, using compression and visual reduction. The thesis brilliantly reads and places the early experimental stories ("Kew Gardens," "Monday or Tuesday") as the pivot which creates the new way of seeing and writing (Thesis 118, 497).

In Mass's *Unpublished Autobiographical Notes* "Passing Through," she writes:

After Virginia Woolf's death, and when my thesis was nearing completion, I wrote to her husband Leonard Woolf, whose publishing house, The Hogarth Press, had been responsible for presenting her books to the world. I explained what I was doing. In his reply he expressed great interest in the thesis, and asked if I would let him know the outcome of it. In due course I did. His answering letter contained warm congratulations and an interesting suggestion. Owing to critical wartime shortages, the publication of such a massive work would be impossible. However if its length could be about halved, the Hogarth Press might be interested in handling it. To my deep and everlasting shame, I never as much as answered that letter.... I remember the completeness of my identification with Virginia Woolf, followed by an exorcism—using perhaps too strong a word, but a graphic one. And together with this, I remember the feeling that never, as long as I lived, would I be able to look at that thesis again, let alone rework it. Now week after week I kept failing to communicate all this to businessman and realist Leonard Woolf—until it was too late. (120)

In amongst her papers I did indeed find two original letters from Leonard Woolf bearing out what Mass had said. The first was dated 8 August 1941 (from Tavistock Square, just four months after Virginia Woolf's death) and the second dated 3 July 1942 (postmarked from Monk's House). Leonard advised her among other matters, in the first, on finding *Monday or Tuesday*, then out of print, and in the second letter he says that paper shortages mean she would need to cut the thesis down to 80,000 or 90,000 words. She had also asked him apparently if she could herself have publishing rights to any essays as yet unpublished (as she planned and did start her own press) and he says that he has plans to bring out various more volumes himself. The second letter is clearly in a negotiating mode, but there it all ends. Remarkably, Leonard Woolf actually entered into a controversial argument with Mass's supervisor R. G. Howarth, in the pages of the Sydney literary magazine *Southerly*. Leonard writes a piece called "A Note on Virginia Woolf's *Night and Day*" in December 1942, effectively a retraction of a claim made by Howarth in April 1942 in an essay called "Dayspring of Virginia Woolf." Howarth had argued that *Night and Day* is an earlier work than *The Voyage Out* and suggests that because Woolf was ill after *The Voyage Out* she must have revived the earlier manuscript as her next work. Leonard very firmly and politely says "its an ingenious argument but just not factual." He quotes from Virginia Woolf's unpublished diary entry of 27 March 1919, about her finishing the manuscript, and says that she saw the book as part of a process of mastering her craft, a deliberate exercise in a traditional form. He further comments on her illness, her mental breakdown in 1913, her being able to work again by 1916, but dealing with "acute neurasthenia, which she suffered all her life making any prolonged strain or fatigue dangerous." Leonard's range of guardianship of the legacy of Virginia Woolf stands out here, even unto the other side of the world, which would also suggest some link between this colonial English Department and the London scene yet to be researched.

Mass herself wrote an essay for *Southerly* in the September issue of the same year, 1942, on *Between the Acts*, called "Virginia Woolf's Last Novel," expanding upon part of her thesis. At the time of her death a view of her work was being newly constructed, from immature work to late dystopic visions, a complete package with virtually no access to biography. However the moment of interest passed, Woolf ceased to be taught, teachers like Howarth failed to be promoted, and modernist texts fell from favour. Howarth finally left and went to Cape Town, South Africa, and Woolf disappeared from the teaching canon. The only teaching of Woolf in any undergraduate courses was *Mrs. Dalloway* in 1942, then *To The Lighthouse* in 1947 and 1948, then no more. The late 1930s and early 1940s seem to have been a brief time for a breakaway interest in modernism at the University of Sydney, soon engulfed by the older and more nationalistic bush tradition of literature.

The research of Nuri Mass on Virginia Woolf found no traction in its emergent form for a complex of reasons. In its resurfacing and eventual publishing in some edited annotated form in another century, there is the possibility of its finding a new set of meanings. Let this then stand as a preliminary report in the archeology of a curious new Woolfian artefact.

**Copyright Permission**

I have been granted exclusive rights from the copyright holders, the Horwitz family, to quote from the Nuri Mass papers, and to prepare, edit, and research the MA thesis on Virginia Woolf, and related unpublished autobiographical materials deposited in the Mitchell Library, Sydney, Australia.

## Works Cited

Cousins, W. G. Letters from W. G. Cousins to Nuri Mass (1937-1955). Angus and Robertson Publishers, Sydney. Folder ML MSS 3269/459.
Gruber, Ruth. *Virginia Woolf: The Will To Create as a Woman*. New York: Carroll and Graf, 2005 (thesis originally published in Leipzig, 1935).
Holtby, Winifred. *Virginia Woolf*. London: Wishart, 1932.
Howarth, R. G. "Dayspring of Virginia Woolf." *Southerly*. Sydney, April 1942: 18-21.
Mass, Nuri. Material deposited in the Nuri Mass Papers, Mitchell Library, Sydney. 10 boxes. ML289/94
——. *Virginia Woolf the Novelist*. MA Thesis, University of Sydney. University Medal, 1942. Archives of Nuri Mass, Mitchell Library, Sydney.
——. *Unpublished Autobiographical Notes* (1988-1992). Bound as "Passing Through." Box 2B ML 289/94 (the manuscript was edited and substantially rewritten from an earlier version called "I've Had My Magic" into two volumes of typescript).
——. Letters to/from W. G. Cousins 1937-1955, Angus and Robertson's Publishers File, Vol.459. Pp.301-407. Mitchell Library. ML MSS 3269/459.
——. "Virginia Woolf: Between the Acts." *Southerly*. Sydney, September 1942: 34-35.
——. "Virginia Woolf's Last Novel." *Union Recorder*. University of Sydney Union, Sydney, 9 July 1942: 101-02
Minutes Books, Faculty of Arts, University of Sydney, late 1930s and 1940s. Fisher Library, University of Sydney Archives. Group G.3, Series 1, Item 4.
*Sydney Morning Herald*, News Report 3 April 1941. AAP source quoting the *Times* (London).
*Union Recorder*. Issues through late 1930s and early 1940s. Fisher Library Archives, University of Sydney.
University Calendars. Calendars for late 1930s and 1940s. Fisher Library Archives, University of Sydney (text/teaching references to Virginia Woolf).
Waldock, C. J. Reference and Letters from Professor C. J. Waldock to Nuri Mass, 17 January 1946. ML 289/94 Box 1.
Woolf, Leonard. Letters from Leonard Woolf to Nuri Mass, 8 August 1941, 3 July 1942. ML 289/94 Box 1.
——. "A Note on Virginia Woolf's *Night and Day*." *Southerly*. Sydney, December 1942: 10-11.

# "From All This Diversity...Not a Riot of Confusion but a Richer Unity": The Limits of Self-Representation in Virginia Woolf's *Orlando: A Biography*

## by Amber K. Regis

When *Orlando* was first published in 1928, many bookshops placed it upon their biography shelves: "But it is a novel, says Miss Ritchie"—the Hogarth Press travelling salesperson—"But it is called biography on the title page, they say" (*D3* 198). In her diary Woolf speculated that this ironic shelving would carry an economic cost, a reduction in *Orlando*'s sales figures. She remarked that it was "a high price to pay for the fun of calling it a biography" (*D3* 198). However, *Orlando*'s sales were brisk, and the book proved to be Woolf's most commercially successful work to date. In this paper, I will examine a further significant effect of *Orlando*'s mischievous subtitle, exploring the aesthetic cost of invoking a biographical subject.

Pamela Caughie has argued that Woolf's fiction "explores the ways characters come into being" (63). However, the eponymous Orlando "come[s] into being" through a discourse of biography, albeit infused with parody and satire, and the conventions of biography are traditionally linked to a limited subjectivity. In his *Aspects of the Novel*, published the year before *Orlando*, E. M. Forster drew the important distinction between historical subject and fictional character, between "Homo Sapiens and Homo Fictus" (63). For Forster, the historical subject can only be known approximately, whereas the novelist is free to delineate character completely, to reveal "the hidden life at its source" and produce subjectivities outside the limits of history (56). In contrast to these free and knowable characters of fiction, the subject produced by biographical discourse derives from limited understandings and fixed parameters, emerging from a completed and closed past. Therefore, with what result did Woolf substitute the "subject" of biography for the "character" of her fiction?

Writing to Vita Sackville-West in 1927, Woolf discussed her ideas behind the book, and announced her intention to "revolutionise" the genre "in a night" (*L3* 429). *Orlando* disrupts our expectations: it breaks down the limits that order our understandings of biographical practice and identities, discreet and stable categories are disrupted, and fixed notions of gender and sexuality are fractured, dispersed, and reduced to absurdity. However, this revolution produces a dilemma within the text and results in the expedient re-imposition of "Woolfian boundaries" around the self and between genres. Woolf employed an image of reversed movement to characterise her writing in *Orlando*, describing a wish to "untwine and twist again some very odd, incongruous strands" in Vita (*L3* 429). Woolf untwines the biographical subject and thus places its representation in jeopardy. Therefore, she must twist it back up again. It is this dilemma that constitutes the aesthetic cost of calling *Orlando* a biography and for substituting a subject for character. It is this dilemma that marks the limit of self-representation in *Orlando*.

### The Old and "New" Biography

*Orlando*'s six chapters emulate the development and conventions of traditional biography, and a major aspect of this satire is the critique of incomplete and distorted representations of the self. *Orlando* exposes the narrator-biographer's inability to keep hold of the subject, and the inability of traditional biography to represent subjectivity in all its various and diverse forms. "Tantalising fragments" (*O* 122) that remain from Orlando's time as an ambassador in Turkey produce a subject riddled with holes. As a Victorian woman writer, Orlando keeps "slipping out" of the narrator-biographer's "grasp" (255). She does not fit the model of a genre dominated by the lives of men, and her difference is marked by a lack of external action, her "pretence of writing and thinking" (256). *Orlando* ridicules this one-sided dependence upon evidence and activities external to the subject, exposing the elision of personality and subjective interiority.

However, as the damp mists of the nineteenth century rise and disperse, the narrative of *Orlando* undergoes a significant change, entering what James Naremore has called the "extreme of modernity" (210). The narrator-biographer's parodic metanarratives become less prominent and a new form of biographical discourse emerges, a form that approximates more closely to the "lyric vein" (*D3* 131) characteristic of Woolf's other experimental novels. This shift in *Orlando*'s register is the product of a new narrative drive to represent subjectivity through a "new" biography. Connections between *Orlando* and Woolf's 1927 essay of this name are widely recognised, with the former often identified as the novelistic playing out of the essay's theoretical argument.[1] In "The New Biography," Woolf argues that the new biographer, no longer a passive chronicler, is a creative artist, and she celebrates the generic indeterminacy that would characterise her writing in *Orlando*: the combined truths of fact and fiction, the "queer amalgamation of dream and reality" (*CE4* 235). Woolf argues that this creative biographical discourse would express "the pith and essence of…character" and the "light of personality" in all its diversity (*CE4* 232, 229).

"The New Biography" is rarely read as a demonstration of Woolf's theoretical ambivalence and her ambiguous equivocation, yet this essay is at the root of *Orlando*'s dilemma of representation and is the source of the untwined subject being twisted again. Woolf's essay retains a demand for biographical "integrity," warning that its loss would result in disaster: an "incautious movement" in the combining of fact and fiction would blow the book "sky high" (*CE4* 229, 233). The new biographer must combine the incompatible, yet must do so with consistency and balance, with the stability implicit in Woolf's metaphor of "perpetual marriage" (*CE4* 235). The use of fiction should not be taken "too far," or introduced with "incongruity" (*CE4* 234). Such warnings lie behind and cast their shadow over Woolf's argument, qualifying her utopian vision of playful genres and ceaseless diversity.

The textual practice and subjectivity produced by *Orlando*'s modernity is in breach of this demand for sustained integrity. As the "new" biography and its subject *dis*-integrate, *Orlando*/Orlando comes to a point of narrative and representational crisis. Therefore, the narrator-biographer must re-impose order and restore integrity; the narrator-biographer must prevent the book being blown sky high.

### "Entirely Disassembled": Orlando and the "New" Biography in Crisis

Narrative and subject reach this point of crisis as *Orlando*/Orlando arrives at "the present moment" (*O* 284). The narrator-biographer is faced with a subject that is still alive; a subject that does *not* derive from a fixed and completed past and who remains outside fixed limits of identity. Travelling out of London in her motorcar, Orlando undergoes a total dissolution of self:

> Nothing could be seen whole or read from start to finish...the body and mind were like scraps of torn paper tumbling from a sack and, indeed, the process of motoring fast out of London so much resembles the chopping up small of identity which precedes unconsciousness and perhaps death itself that it is an open question in what sense Orlando can be said to have existed at the present moment. (293)

Orlando is transformed into "a person entirely disassembled" (293) and a coherent biographical subject disappears from the text. This "chopping up small of identity" frustrates comprehension. Like the rushing views that surround her, Orlando cannot be seen and, significantly, cannot be *read* "from start to finish." She defies the expectations of her biographer and reader, with the former conceding that we are now in the uncertain "region of 'perhaps' and 'appears'" (295). Orlando is marked by an absence equated with unconsciousness and death, with her lack of existence in biographical discourse. She is revealed to be fluid and multiple, characterised by flux: Orlando is "changing her selves as quickly as she drove," and this "great variety of selves" engage in a noisy and chaotic internal colloquy (295, 294). Orlando has become a *dis*-integrated subjectivity, and the discourse of modernity is shown to replicate the problems of the old biography; the subject is lost and exceeds the scope of biographical representation.

Ira Bruce Nadel has argued that *Orlando* represents Woolf's "solution" to the problem of biographical representation, a test of the genre's limits and a display of its "flexibility" (141). For Nadel, Orlando's multiple subjectivity is productive of a "loosening of biography" (144). However, this loose biographical narrative cannot be sustained. An unlimited and changing subjectivity is necessarily ineffable and thus the narrative of *Orlando* is placed in threat of extinction. The reader and narrator-biographer join Orlando on a wild goose chase, the search for a coherent and readable self. "Words like nets" are flung after the wild goose, but these "shrivel" and snatch only a meagre glimpse of the subject; words cannot catch a multiple subjectivity (299). To ensure the continuance of biographical discourse, this loose and untwined subject must be tightened and twisted again. *Orlando*'s solution to the problem of biographical representation is compromised. Thus I argue, in contrast to Nadel, that Woolf exposes the *in*flexibility of the genre.

"Woolfian boundaries" are re-imposed upon Orlando's subjectivity to enable the reconstitution of a viable and coherent biographical subject. The rushing green views of rural countryside compress the tumbling scraps of Orlando's chopped-up and fragmented identity, and this containment provides a "relief," the "illusion of holding things within itself" (293). "Orlando?" (293) she calls to herself, wishing to invoke a stable identity. The narrator-biographer follows Orlando's search for this "true self": an "uppermost" and "conscious self" that "wishes to be nothing but one self" (296, 295-96). This is the "Captain" who wields power to command and keep order; the "Key" that is able to lock up and fix identity; the self that "amalgamates and controls" (296).

As this Captain and Key take possession of Orlando, a significant change takes place:

The whole of her darkened and settled, as when some foil whose addition makes the round and solidity of a surface is added to it, and the shallow becomes deep and the near distant; and all is contained as water is contained by the sides of a well. So she was now darkened, stilled, and become, with the addition of this Orlando, what is called, rightly or wrongly, a single self, a real self. And she fell silent. (299)

Orlando is re-inscribed and reconstituted into the possibility of biographical discourse. Her water-like fluidity is contained and her ebb and flow is limited; her multiple subjectivities are commanded, locked up, amalgamated, and controlled. The final published version of *Orlando* also employs the word "compact" (296) to describe this newly reconstituted subject. However, Woolf's holograph manuscript reveals her uncertain use of this expression and, where it occurs in the draft, it is crossed out and an alternative is inscribed above: "medly [sic]" (267). The holograph draft does not, however, produce an endless and multiple subjectivity: the eponymous heroine only fragments into a duality, the "tangible" and "other" Orlando (267). With this duality being exceeded in the final version, so too is the potential for harmony and control implied by the musical terminology. As Orlando's subjectivity fragments into chaotic multiplicity, Woolf reinstates her first term with all its implication of constriction, limitation, and solidity. At the beginning of the novel, Orlando is marked by verve, vitality, and luminescence. Sasha describes him as a "million candled Christmas tree…hung with yellow globes; incandescent," glowing with "radiance, from a lamp lit within" (52). However, as this later Orlando enters her family estate—enters the solidity of its walls and its history—she is reconstituted as a fixed, stable, and readable self. Her vitality is stilled, her light is darkened, and her internal colloquy is silenced; the result, Woolf's draft notes reveal, of Orlando's new "unity," her being now "entire: contented" (277).

The reconstitution of the subject in *Orlando* was the aesthetic cost of calling the text a biography, and thus biographical discourse is revealed to provide a restrictive *fiction* of coherent and limited subjectivity. The effect of the "green screens" (293) upon Orlando is an illusion, a visual metaphor for the trick of narrative. *Orlando*'s narrator-biographer describes human subjectivity as "a perfect rag-bag of odds and ends…lightly stitched together by a single thread" of memory (75). This thread runs "in and out, up and down, hither and thither," a chaos of "odd, disconnected fragments" (75, 76). However, a biographical discourse will seek to organise this chaos, to order, direct, and fix the thread of subjectivity. The martial and authoritative image of a Captain or Key self reveals the inherent coercion of narrative's fixing of identity, a forced subjective order. Inscribed through narrative, Orlando is compared to the containment of water in a well, an uncertain and artificial containment with the threat of flood and dissolution still latent. Despite the provisional nature of this watery image, such boundaries and limits are shown to be desirable and necessary. Makiko Minow-Pinkney has argued that Orlando's newly "totalised self" is dependent upon secure and rigid distinctions (149). The Captain or Key self is repulsed by the image and threat of transgression. Orlando is shocked by exposed flesh, a finger without a nail, and her violent reaction is due to the "confusion of what should have been separated": the "vulnerable inside" that should have been "covered by the fingernail (the tough…outside)" (Minow-Pinkney 150). A discourse of biography restricts the threat of such transgression, maintains distinctions, and holds the illusion of a totalised self together.

For a biographical subject to be read and understood, it must be fixed through language. A fundamental aspect of *Orlando*'s subversion of biographical convention was the depiction of a living subject; a subject that is incomplete and open-ended, and who thus does not exclude the threat of change, multiplicity, and non-comprehension. Where Woolf's critical writings on biography are filled with funereal and deathly images, highlighting the tendency of biographical conventions to "kill" the life of its subject, the ever-continuing life of Orlando is in danger of turning this on its head and killing biography through the exhaustion of discourse. Thus *Orlando*'s narrative must end with a final moment of fixity. The aggressive march of time is marked throughout the text, with the chiming clocks of the present moment eliciting a visceral and physical response from Orlando, as if "she had been violently struck on the head" (284). *Orlando*'s closing sentence strikes the fatal blow, with the final rejection of the ambiguous term "the present moment" and the enumeration of an exact time and date: "midnight, Thursday, the eleventh of October, Nineteen hundred and Twenty Eight" (284, 314). Woolf had planned to finish the novel with an enigmatic ellipsis, a false conclusion as open-ended as her living subject, and this is how the holograph version of the text concludes. Following this ellipsis, the holograph contains the final note: "The End" (287). This note does not appear in the final version; it is replaced with the date and thus suggests their interchangeable meanings. Although we do not see Orlando die, this fixed narrative closure completes the textual body of the biography, functioning as a surrogate and necessary "death" of the subject, re-inscribed into history.

## "WOOLFIAN BOUNDARIES"

*Orlando*'s "new" biographical discourse, then, withdraws from a radical model of multiple and fluid inter-subjectivity. In his reading of *Orlando* as "solution," Nadel argues that Woolf introduces a "fragmented sense of experience" into a modernist biography that "concentrates on the making rather than the content of the life" (141, 145). However, the formation of internal subjective experience and the blurred boundaries that merge rather than separate individuals are features celebrated by the liberating fiction and characters of Woolf's next work, *The Waves* (1931); features outside the scope of *Orlando*'s biographical discourse marked by the demand for integrity.[2] In 1939, Woolf returned to the theme of biography in her critical writing, crystallising the important distinction between characters of fiction and the subject of biography: the "invented character lives in a free world," dependent on nothing but the truth of the artist's vision; where the "novelist is free; the biographer is tied" (*CE4* 225, 221).

This later essay, "The Art of Biography," is often conflated with Woolf's earlier work on the "new" biography due to a shared critique of deathly Victorian biographical practice. However, "The Art of Biography" was written alongside Woolf's most formal biographical work, *Roger Fry* (1940), and in the shadow of her experiences writing *Orlando* and *Flush* (1933). Returning to the truths of fact and fiction in *Flush*, Woolf had enjoyed the freedom of a biographical subject displaced from the human world, a freedom tempered by the more formal substance provided by the Brownings' correspondence. In writing her life of Fry, Woolf had submitted to family wishes and to the demands of fact; demands that pulled against her instincts as a novelist: "How can one cut loose from facts, when there they are, contradicting my theories?" (*D5* 138). Therefore, this later essay offers a very different vision of biography, a revised and more finely nuanced understanding of a "new" biographical practice.

The experience and experiment of writing *Orlando* marks a culmination and turning point in Woolf's critical thinking on biography. Woolf's later essay tempers the optimism of "The New Biography," and reacts against the vision of a malleable biographical subject and an equally malleable genre. "The Art of Biography" opens by questioning a fundamental precept of Woolf's "new" biography. Is biography, in fact, an art? Exploring the *rules* of biography and what the genre *cannot* do, Woolf offers a new conclusion: the biographer is not an artist but a "craftsman," and if biography is treated as an art, the art "fails" (*CE4* 227, 222). Writers must make a choice between the "worlds" (*CE4* 226) of fact and fiction, and they must remain within the limits of their chosen discourse. Foregrounding the call for biographical integrity that had remained latent within "The New Biography," Woolf closes down the potential for generic experimentation and for the diverse and heterogeneous representation of the subject. No longer joined in perpetual marriage, Woolf tells us that the "life" of biography is very different from "the life of poetry and fiction" and, although the biographer should be ready to "admit contradictory versions of the same face," the integrity of the subject must be maintained: Woolf argues that "from all this diversity it will bring out, not a riot of confusion, but a richer unity" (*CE4* 227, 226). In contrast to the violent image of revolution that lay behind the project of *Orlando*, Woolf now cast off such anarchy in favour of generic and subjective unity. The biographical subject was to be fixed, surrounded, and safely contained by the biographer's "outline" (*CE4* 227), a limiting function of narrative.

However, in continuing to look to a future form of biography, Woolf does not exclude the potential for creativity, generic and subjective. Returning to the argument put forward in "How Should One Read A Book?" Woolf reconstructs the reader as a biographer's "fellow-worker and accomplice" (*CR2* 259). The biographer's craft must be used to select and produce the "fertile fact; the fact that suggests and engenders" (*CE4* 228), to create an outline filled in by the reader's active imagination. Ultimately a "new" biography, an untwisted representation of the biographical subject, was not to be achieved within the genre of biography itself, but through a creative exchange marking the process of *reading* biography.

## Notes

1. For example, Kathryn Miles argues that "The New Biography" is the "original theoretical rubric" behind *Orlando* (212).
2. For example, see Bernard's final dramatic soliloquy in *The Waves*: "Yet I cannot find any obstacle separating us. There is no division between me and them" (222).

## Works Cited

Caughie, Pamela L. *Virginia Woolf and Postmodernism: Literature in Quest and Question of Itself*. Urbana: University of Illinois Press, 1991.
Forster, E. M. *Aspects of the Novel*. 1927. Ed. Oliver Stallybrass. London: Penguin, 1990.
Marcus, Laura. *Auto/biographical Discourses: Theory, Criticism, Practice*. Manchester: Manchester UP, 1994.
Miles, Kathryn. "'That perpetual marriage of granite and rainbow': Searching for 'The New Biography' in Virginia Woolf's *Orlando*." *Virginia Woolf and Communities: Selected Papers from the Eighth Annual Conference on Virginia Woolf*. Ed. Jeanette McVicker and Laura Davis. New York: Pace UP, 1999. 212-18.
Minow-Pinkney, Makikow. *Virginia Woolf and The Problem of the Subject*. Brighton: Harvester, 1987.

Nadel, Ira Bruce. *Biography: Fiction, Fact and Form*. New York: St. Martin's Press, 1984.
Naremore, James. *The World Without a Self: Virginia Woolf and the Novel*. New Haven: Yale UP, 1973.
Woolf, Virginia. "The Art of Biography." 1939. *Collected Essays*. Vol. 4. New York: Harcourt, Brace & World, 1967. 221-28.
——. *The Diary Of Virginia Woolf*. Ed. Anne Olivier Bell with Andrew McNeillie. Vol. 3. London: Hogarth, 1980.
——. *The Diary Of Virginia Woolf*. Ed. Anne Olivier Bell with Andrew McNeillie. Vol. 5. San Diego: Harvest, 1985.
——. "How Should One Read a Book?" 1926. *The Common Reader, Second Series*. Ed. Andrew McNeillie. London: Vintage, 2003. 258-71.
——. *The Letters Of Virginia Woolf*. Ed. Nigel Nicolson and Joanne Trautmann. Vol. 3. London: Hogarth, 1977.
——. "The New Biography." 1927. *Collected Essays*. Vol. 4. New York: Harcourt, Brace & World, 1967. 229-35.
——. *Orlando: A Biography*. 1928. Ed. Rachel Bowlby. Oxford: Oxford UP, 1998.
——. *Orlando: The Original Holograph Draft*. Ed. Stuart Nelson Clarke. London: S N Clarke, 1993.
——. *The Waves*. 1931. Ed. Kate Flint. London: Penguin, 1992.

# Brown-ness, Trees, Rose Petals, and Chrysalises: The Influence of Edward Carpenter's Mystical Evolutionary Socialism on the Writing of Virginia Woolf, with Particular Reference to *The Years*

## by Deborah Gerrard

We may imagine Mrs. Brown in the middle of Oxford Street. 'Buses and cabs are running in different directions, carts and drays are rattling on all sides of her. This is her environment, and she has to adapt herself to it. She has to learn the laws of the vehicles and their movements, to stand on this side or that, to run here and stop there, conceivably to jump into one…and so get carried to her destination as comfortably as may be. A long course of this sort of thing "adapts" Mrs. Brown considerably…. But Mrs. Brown has a destination…. The question is, "What is the destination of Man?" (Carpenter, *Civilisation* 138-39)

The above passage is neither a Woolf pastiche nor a lost draft of "Mr. Bennett and Mrs. Brown"; in fact it was written by Edward Carpenter over thirty years earlier in an essay entitled "A Science of the Future." In that essay and its antecedent, "Modern Science: A Criticism," Edward Carpenter had addressed issues very similar to those addressed by Woolf in her more famous essay and in very similar terms. Taking as his target not the Georgian novelist but the late-Victorian scientific materialist, Carpenter had argued that the goal of human progress should be not material but spiritual, and that the scientist of the future should, therefore, study not man's body but his soul. Attacking not literary but scientific methods, Carpenter had argued (using a rather familiar image) that under the current regime "we see only the skirts of her [Truth's] garments" (*Civilisation* 96). What was needed, he continued, was "a…psychologic Truth—an understanding of what man is" that would only be arrived at by "the deepening back of consciousness itself" (*Civilisation* 129, 137).

The parallels between Carpenter's paired essays and Woolf's "Mr. Bennett and Mrs. Brown" are only one example of an influence that pervades the whole of Woolf's work, casting light on its mysticism and on its social vision. Reading Woolf through Carpenter helps to illuminate such mysterious moments as the ancient woman singing by the Tube in *Mrs. Dalloway*; the collocation of moth-hunt and falling tree in *Jacob's Room* and "Reading"; and the haunting image of "many mothers and before them many mothers" rising out of and sinking back into the sea in the first draft of *The Waves* (7). And yet Woolf never mentions Carpenter's name in relation to her writing. What, one wonders, could be the reason behind such a significant erasure? One explanation would seem to lie in the rationalism and philosophic materialism that had been so defining a characteristic of Woolf's parents and that was also the predominant outlook within Bloomsbury itself. A romantic socialist and a mystic, Carpenter analysed late-Victorian and Edwardian society from a visionary perspective that drew on such anti-rational sources as Shelley, Whitman, Schopenhauer, Theosophy, and Hindu mysticism. His world-view could not have been more at odds either with Woolf's upbringing or with her immediate intellectual context. And yet we know that Woolf, too, read Shelley, Whitman, and works on Eastern religion and was fascinated by anti-rational ideas regarding the nature of thought, being, and reincarnation, the origins of which remain obscure.

The sheer preponderance of Carpenterian echoes in Woolf's writing suggests that he was her foremost—if concealed—guide to the mystical. His influence also helps explain the humanist optimism that Woolf maintained in the face of the prevalent pessimism and elitism of her own circle, for his mysticism was part and parcel of an evolutionary socialism based not on economics but on faith in the capacities of the human heart. Finally, it is possible that Carpenter may have played an even more crucial role in giving Woolf the courage to find her own voice as a writer, surrounded as she was by Bloomsbury men who were often oppressively confident that they had reason on their side. In such a masculinist context and in the light of her own psychological history, Carpenter's belief in, firstly, the evolutionary superiority of women's powers of intuition and, secondly, the creative potential of mental illness, may have acted as a much-needed talisman for Woolf in some of her darkest moments.

For reasons of space, this paper concentrates on exploring how a reading of *The Years* through Carpenter allows us to link a series of key motifs and images within the text and so reach a fuller understanding of how these work. Also for reasons of space, I will leave the dialogic nature of the text out of consideration, stopping only to acknowledge that the life-affirming, mystical intuitions that Carpenter appeared to validate for Woolf, are held in tension with—and at times overwhelmed by—a bleakly Darwinian view of human existence. Before embarking on *The Years,* I would like to add two further observations regarding the nature of Carpenter's appeal for Woolf. A key factor in that appeal was his light-hearted and provisional approach. In making his forays into the mystical, Carpenter always has a weather-eye for the absurd and—as that arch-rationalist Desmond MacCarthy admitted—he "never intimidates the doubting who wish they were not skeptical" (173). An equally important factor was the space Carpenter allows within the Cosmic for individuality, human agency, and, above all, creativity. He neither disallows the belief "that it is right to develop your powers to the utmost," nor "solves all personal energy, all irregularity, into one suave stream," characteristics that troubled Woolf in several other mystics (*E1* 173).[1]

Given what might be regarded as the illicit nature of Woolf's interest in Carpenter, it is hardly surprising that we know nothing about when or how she first encountered his work. An important clue, however, is provided by the brown book which the semi-autobiographical Sara Pargiter reads in bed whilst listening to dance music from a neighbouring garden, in the 1907 episode of *The Years*. This episode was derived from personal experience—in writing it, Woolf reworked her own 1903 diary entry entitled "A Dance in Queen's Gate"—and although in the diary entry there is no mention of the young Virginia Stephen reading, we know that this was a period in which she was reading not only intensively, but with a new independence from the guidance of her dying father.[2] These circumstances suggest that whatever the brown book was, Woolf came across it in her early twenties, around the time of her father's death. The subject of the brown book, according to Sara, is the idealist notion that "the world's nothing but thought" (113). Although this statement is recognizably Berkeleyan, I would like to suggest that the young Sara is reading not Berkeley himself but Carpenter's *The Art of Creation*, in which the latter quotes Berkeley in support of his own rather different idealist argument.[3]

The evidence for my argument is circumstantial. After reading from the brown book, Sara attempts to enact philosophical idealism imaginatively by thinking herself into becoming a tree. Again the choice of a tree immediately makes one think of Ronald Knox's well-known limerick about Berkeley and the tree in the quad (seen by God when no one is there), but we can find a closer analogue in *The Art of Creation*, where Carpenter uses the tree to help the reader imagine *how* the universe is created by thought, arguing that "a dominant Idea informs the life of the Tree; persisting it *forms* the tree" (29). In addition, Berkeley—as it turns out—was not particularly interested in trees, whereas for Carpenter in *The Art of Creation* the tree image becomes a unifying figure illustrating a message that is predominantly evolutionary socialist as opposed to theological. Drawing on a range of mystical influences, including Schopenhauer, Whitman, and Theosophy, Carpenter uses the tree as a figure for a world branching out from but ultimately rooted in a Universal Will. A Carpenterian reading of Sara's imaginary tree thus provides a mystical socialist answer to Maggie's related question: "Are we one, or are we separate?" (113). Carpenter's answer, namely that we are both, is echoed later in the novel in North's image of the bubble and the stream (329-30).

A recognition of Carpenter's textual presence in the 1907 episode of *The Years* can deepen our understanding of how that episode functions as the turning-point or hinge of the novel, but first more needs to be said about Carpenter's mystical evolutionary socialism.[4] As a homosexual, a socialist, and a mystic, Carpenter's interest in Berkeleyan idealism was driven by his concern with personal and social growth. The notion that all the individual elements of Creation emanate from a Universal Self provided him with a philosophical argument in favour of breaking down a whole range of barriers—including those of class and gender. In describing the inhibiting presence of such barriers within late-Victorian society, Carpenter frequently used images of brick walls and being buried alive. For example, in his epic poem *Towards Democracy*, he imagines the allegorical figure of Democracy buried "deep underfoot": "The clods press suffocating closer and closer—grit and filth accumulate in the eyes and mouth, I can neither see nor speak" (18). The use of such imagery connects the brown book with Sara's other reading matter in the 1907 episode, the *Antigone*. And it is here that the hinge of the novel is located. Stretched out under the single white sheet of her bed, Sara imagines two stark alternatives not only for herself but also for English society as a whole: being enclosed and suffocated to death—like Antigone—by the brick walls of a coercive materialist culture, or thinking and feeling oneself—like Carpenter's thought-tree—into new, organic forms of psychological and social wholeness. It is the second of these spiritual choices that the Georgians—in Woolf's "novel of fact"—attempt , with agonizing slowness, to work towards (*D4* 129).

Carpenter's mystical presence in *The Years* does not end there. It presides over the Georgian struggle towards a more spiritually honest, organic society through the character of Nicholas Pomjalovsky, otherwise known as Brown. The colour of the book Sara was reading—you will recall—was brown, but Nicholas's brown-ness also links him to Carpenter's Mrs. Brown in "The Science of the Future" as does Eleanor's first meeting with him, in which he tells her that he and Renny have been "considering the psychology of great men...*by the light of modern science*" (*Civilisation* 226, emphasis added). As Mrs. Brown's male counterpart, Brown is the pre-eminent advocate of the spiritual or psychological enquiry Carpenter had called for in his essay. Like Carpenter, he is also homosexual.

In Woolf's novel, Brown, like the historical Edward Carpenter, takes the role of a mystical evolutionary socialist guide, although his theories are more tentative and inconclusive than Carpenter's, reflecting Woolf's own post-war pessimism. In *Civilisation: Its Cause and Cure*, Carpenter had diagnosed and suggested a cure for the diseased state of late-Victorian society; similarly, it is to the "medical" and "priestly" Brown that the victims of Victorianism in *The Years* turn for help in curing their crippled lives (234). Brown's diagnosis that contemporary lives are "screwed up into one hard little, tight little—knot" echoes the second stage of the three-stage evolutionary socialist scheme put forward by Carpenter (238). In this second stage, modern Man abandons the communal harmony of primitive society for the narrow egotism of competitive materialism and his life is described as "strangled tied and bound" (sic) (*Democracy* 27). In addition, Brown's prescription that "the soul…wishes to expand…to form new combinations" (238) closely echoes Carpenter's prediction that (in the third evolutionary stage) the human soul will expand in ever-widening circles and the creative mind "continually mak[e] new combinations" (*Art* 106).

Most significantly, behind Brown's anti-Fascism—and perhaps even behind *Three Guineas* itself—can be discerned the anti-statist political philosophy that was Carpenter's response not to fascism but to Victorian homophobia. Brown's question—"If we do not know ourselves, how then can we make religions, laws that…'fit'?" (227)—implies Antigone's intuitive "unwritten" law, defined by Woolf in *Three Guineas* as "the private laws that should regulate certain instincts, passions, mental and physical desires" (203), but both are further linked to Carpenter's goal of a non-governmental society in which the heart's internal authority takes precedence over external law.[5] In addition, Carpenter's prediction that Man will evolve beyond hero-worship—or the worship of "idols"—is reflected in Brown's refusal to accept the role of Teacher or Master and in Rose's confirming laughter, that seems to chime "no idols, no idols, no idols" (*Art* 152; *TY* 341).

Finally, Brown himself functions as an exemplar of Carpenter's third and final evolutionary stage in which the soul expands to such a degree that it becomes one with the Universal even while retaining its own individuality. Within this cosmic consciousness, Carpenter argues, there is self-reliance but "no more self-consciousness" and in Woolf's novel, Brown's complete lack of self-consciousness is repeatedly emphasized (*Civilisation* 70). A capacity to see life from a cosmic perspective is also suggested by Brown's otherwise rather shockingly detached description of the air-raid in the 1917 episode as "only children letting off fireworks in the back garden" (236). Furthermore, the mysterious operation of Brown's "spontaneous subterranean benevolence" (337) on the other characters in the novel would seem to illustrate the non-coercive, ripple-like process whereby, according to Carpenter, "a new sentiment of life" "passes *by some indirect influence* from one to another" (*Ideal* 72, emphasis added). Thus Eleanor's contact with Brown "seemed to have released something in her; she felt not only a new space of time, but new powers, something unknown within her," and under Brown's presiding influence at the final party scene, this "new sentiment of life" spreads mystically to the younger generation of North and Peggy (239).

Two striking pieces of imagery from *The Years*—that of the flowering bud and that of the winged insect emerging from its chrysalis—confirm the centrality of Carpenter's inter-textual presence within the novel, given his frequent use of very similar imagery to illustrate his theory of psychological and social evolution or "exfoliation." According to this theory, both personal and social transformation are driven by internal desire; new growth comes from within.⁶ Initially, inherited external forms such as laws and customs serve to protect that new growth, but, in a radical move, Carpenter argues that such external forms eventually become constricting and must be cast off or "exfoliated." In the terms of Carpenter's floral metaphor: "The outermost petals...form a husk, which for a time protects the young bud. But it also confines it. A struggle ensues, a strangulation, and then the husk gives way." Within Carpenter's cosmic time-span, this process is seen as an endless creative cycle: "And now the petals uncurl and free themselves like living things to the light. But the process is not finished.... The flower, the petals, now drop off withered and useless.... And the circle begins again"(*Ideal* 58-59).

As early as 1919, in "Reading"—an autobiographical essay that has obvious links with Sara's bed-time reading in *The Years*—Woolf too, had used the image of the blossoming bud as a figure for psychological transformation, comparing her own experience of psychological awakening as a young woman to that of "some bud [which] feels a sudden release in the night and is found in the morning with all its petals shaken free" (*E3* 153). At the end of *The Years,* as a new day dawns and the younger generation begins to imagine the possibility of a world free from the constraints of Victorian materialism and hypocrisy, the characters experience a communal moment of release, again pictured in similar terms. Flowers and flower petals "fall and fall and over all": someone showers Rose with petals; Brown paddles his hands in fallen petals as he contemplates a toast to the spiritual evolution of the human race; Maggie arranges petals in a bowl of water and tosses a flower at Sara to wake her (341). Finally, Eleanor is presented with a "bunch of many coloured flowers," as she watches a young man and a young woman emerging from a shared cab (349). Coming at the end of a series of floral allusions to Carpenter's theory of exfoliation, this final image of androgyny recalls one of Carpenter's chief evolutionary goals, namely the emergence of an intermediate sex combining male and female characteristics and possessing exceptional powers of creativity.⁷ As Sandra Gilbert has noted (217), Carpenter had been an important source for *A Room of One's Own*, Woolf's earlier meditation on "the art of creation" (*AROO* 99), in which the idea of imaginative androgyny is presented using a very similar figure—a young man and a young woman getting *into* a taxi.

When Woolf draws on Carpenter's second trope of exfoliation in the memorable image of Sara curled up "like a chrysalis wrapped round in the sharp white folds of the sheet" as she drifts off to sleep at the end of the 1907 episode, the image tells a more personal story (117). For Carpenter himself, inside his concealing "Brown" book, has been written into Sara Pargiter's chrysalis stage—or rather that of the young Virginia Stephen—as the catalyst that will enable her to transform herself into a butterfly or some kind of winged insect, dancing not her mother's but her own dance. A key to Carpenter's role in Woolf's psychological and creative development can be found in scattered allusions—throughout Woolf's writing and in particular in her bildungsroman, *The Voyage Out*, and the diaries of the 1920s and early 30s—to a little known appendix on *The Art of Creation*, "The May-Fly: A Study in Transformation." The latter is a parable of human exfoliation in which certain physical and mental illnesses in humans are equated with the pupal stage in the life-cycle not only of the may-fly but of other Woolfian insects such as butterflies, bees, gnats, dragon-flies, and the privet-hawk-moth. Just as, in may-flies and related species, the "quiescent" chrysalis stage prepares for the emergence of "the perfect insect," so, too, in humans, Carpenter argues, "weeks and months of depression and lethargy...or even of accompanying physical illness and incapacity" are often the prelude to an "outbreak of fresh life," involving a "veer[ing] round" of "the whole nature" and "a considerable and rapid mental advance": "discomfort and uneasiness," enforced physical inaction, and detachment from the outside world are the necessary accompaniments of worthwhile transformation (*Art* 107, 248-52). Carpenter's mystical evolutionism thus turns such illnesses from "signals of failure" into "steps *forward* in the line of evolution," celebrating the fluidity of the human mind (*Art* 251). It is not difficult to imagine the appeal of such a conception to Woolf as a writer battling against mental and physical illness.

Turning to Woolf's own writing, the fate of her semi-autobiographical heroine, Rachel Vinrace, in her first novel, *The Voyage Out*, may be read as a *failed* version of the central miracle of "The May-Fly." Just as Carpenter's may-fly begins life as "a brownish...creature" (238), so the face of Woolf's heroine at the opening of *The Voyage Out* lacks "colour and definite outline" (13). However, though the may-fly emerges from its "lethargic subaqueous existence" as a chrysalis at the bottom of the stream to become "a little fairy with four pearly lace-like wings" dancing in the sunshine (237-38), at this stage in Woolf's writing career Rachel cannot achieve the freedom of creative flight, remaining "curled up at the bottom of the sea" unable to escape her illness (322).[8] In her diary, Woolf similarly described her own "glooms" as "a plunge into deep waters" and referred to "that odd amphibious life of headache" (*D3* 38, 112). Yet, as early as 1921, she began to see the "feminine" mental and physical instability associated with her bouts of illness as a *productive* form of fluidity, "full of interest," and preparatory to leaps forward in her creative life (*D3* 112).[9] Significantly, in a diary entry for 16 February 1930, she imagines this process as a pupal stage: "It [my mind] refuses to go on registering impressions. It shuts itself up. It becomes chrysalis. I lie quite torpid.... Then suddenly something springs... & this is I believe the moth shaking its wings in me" (*D3* 287). Alternatively, in "On Being Ill" (1926), the *deliverer* of this creative lethargy—the "hero" Chloral—is itself pictured as an ethereal insect "with the moth's eyes and the feathered feet" (*E4* 319). Finally, and most revealingly, the ultimate meaning of Carpenter's "May-Fly" as a parable of immortality—of the human spirit's ability to "slip[] her [bodily] shroud"—contributed to the most mystical of Woolf's books, *The Waves* (1931), for which, of course, she had originally intended the title *The Moths* (*Art* 254).

## Notes

1. For a useful summary of Woolf's acerbic comments on a variety of mystics see Kane (328-31).
2. See Gordon (82-83) and Lee (171).
3. Carpenter quotes from Berkeley's *Principles*: "all the choir of heaven and furniture of the earth...have no subsistence without mind" (*Art* 39n1; Berkeley 55).
4. See Woolf's observation that the scene of "Elvira [Sara] in bed" is "the turn of the book" which "needs a great shove to swing it round on its hinges" (*D4*: 149).
5. For Carpenter's anti-statist views, see Cachin.
6. For an account of the influence of both Lamarck and Whitman on Carpenter's theory of exfoliation, see Gershenowitz.
7. See Carpenter's *The Intermediate Sex*.
8. In *Melymbrosia*, Rachel expresses the view that "love and flying" are what matter in life (192). Rachel can also be identified with the moth trapped beneath the hotel sky-light in *The Voyage Out* (322).
9. See *D2*, 8 August 1921, 126; also *D3*, 28 September 1926, 112; *D3*, 16 September 1929, 254 and "On Being Ill" (*E4* 317-29).

## Works Cited

Berkeley, George. *Principles of Human Knowledge and Three Dialogues between Hylas and Philonous*. Ed. Roger Woolhouse. London: Penguin, 1988.
Cachin, Marie-Françoise. "'Non-governmental Society': Edward Carpenter's Position in the British Socialist Movement." *Edward Carpenter and Late Victorian Radicalism*. Ed. Tony Brown. London: Cass, 1990. 58-73.
Carpenter, Edward. *The Art of Creation*. Enlarged ed. London: Allen, 1907.
———. *Civilisation: Its Cause and Cure*. Complete ed. London: Allen & Unwin, 1921.
———. *England's Ideal*. 4$^{th}$ ed. London: Sonnenschein, 1902.
———. *The Intermediate Sex*. London: Allen & Unwin, 1908.
———. *Towards Democracy*. Complete ed. London: Sonnenschein, 1911.
Gershenowitz, Harry. "Two Lamarckians: Walt Whitman and Edward Carpenter." *Walt Whitman Review* 2.1 (1984): 35-39.
Gilbert, Sandra M. "Costumes of the Mind: Transvestism as Metaphor in Modern Literature." *Writings and Sexual Difference*. Ed. Elizabeth Abel. Brighton: Harvester, 1982. 193-219.
Gordon, Lyndall. *Virginia Woolf: A Writer's Life*. Oxford: Oxford UP, 1986.
Kane, Julie. "Varieties of Mystical Experience in the Writings of Virginia Woolf." *Twentieth Century Literature* 41 (1995): 328-49.
Lee, Hermione. *Virginia Woolf*. London: Chatto, 1996.
MacCarthy, Desmond. "Edward Carpenter: Minor Prophet." *Listener* 7 September 1944: 270-71.
Woolf, Virginia. *The Diary of Virginia Woolf*. Ed. Anne Olivier Bell with Andrew McNeillie. 5 vols. London: Hogarth, 1977-1984.
———. *The Essays of Virginia Woolf*. Ed. Andrew McNeillie. 4 vols. to date. London: Hogarth, 1986-1994.
———. *Melymbrosia*. Ed. and introd. Louise DeSalvo. San Fransisco: Cleis, 2002.
———. *A Room of One's Own*. London: Grafton, 1977.
———. *Three Guineas*. Introd. Hermione Lee. London: Hogarth, 1986.
———. *The Voyage Out*. Ed. and introd. Jane Wheare. London: Penguin, 1992.
———. *The Waves: The Two Holograph Drafts*. Ed. J. W. Graham. London: Hogarth, 1976.
———. *The Years*. London: Penguin, 1968.

# Mapping Woolf's Montaignian Modernism

## by Katie Macnamara

> It is more of a job to interpret the interpretations than to interpret the things, and there are more books about books than any other subject: we do nothing but write glosses about each other. The world is swarming with commentaries; of authors there is a great scarcity. (Montaigne, "Of Experience" [III.13; 818])

In his 1989 book *Cosmopolis: The Hidden Agenda of Modernity*, the British philosopher, rhetorician, and historian of science Stephen Toulmin begins to speculate about what the last four centuries might have been like had the *Essais* of Michel de Montaigne and not the writings of René Descartes been taken as the foundational texts of modern European thought. Having been deeply moved by the intellectual and political movements of the 60s and 70s, Toulmin writes that "In choosing as the goal of Modernity an intellectual and practical agenda" that centered on "the pursuit of mathematical exactitude and logical rigor, intellectual certainty and moral purity" inspired by seventeenth-century Cartesian thought, modern Europe turned away from the tolerant skepticism of sixteenth-century humanists like Montaigne. In doing so, he claims, Europe "set itself on the cultural and political road that has led to its most striking technical successes and deepest human failures" (x).

Like Frankfurt Marxists Theodor Adorno and Max Horkheimer writing nearly forty years earlier as well as countless thinkers in the post-war West, Toulmin finds himself disappointed by Enlightenment's unfulfilled promises, and his turn away from Descartes specifically toward Montaigne is not unlike Adorno's own in "The Essay as Form" (1958).[1] Yet while Toulmin focuses primarily on what he calls the "reasonable" (as opposed to rational), tolerant, and skeptical *content* of Montaigne's essays, Adorno is more interested in how the *form* of the genre Montaigne invented is determined by its content. This difference in perspectives on Montaigne's work—one centered on content, acknowledging only minimally its influence on form; the other positing that form arises organically and necessarily from content itself—has something significant in common with Leonard and Virginia Woolf's contrasting attitudes toward the Renaissance Frenchman, his thought, and his writing style. While Leonard and Virginia certainly found common ground in an allegiance to Montaigne that had developed before either Adorno or Toulmin had made mention of him, they each valued and incorporated his work into theirs for their own unique reasons. And we can even see in their contrasting approaches traces of an ongoing debate in the fields of philosophy and literary criticism that continues today.

Philosophers from successive generations (born not twenty years apart), Toulmin and Adorno both agree that their own discipline can learn a great deal from art and literary criticism; and both agree that philosophic writing must position itself in opposition to several basic Cartesian principles.[2] For Toulmin, Descartes wrongly seeks a universal foundation for various forms of knowledge within the transcendent realm of mathematics, and his first book *The Uses of Argument*, published in the same year as Adorno's "Essay as Form," represents Toulmin's opening gesture toward Anti-Cartesianism with its insistence that arguments in different disciplines must be governed by "field-dependent" criteria rather than any universal logic.

Adorno, however, is more radical and is much more concerned that the form of his writing draw philosophy away from any pretension to science and closer to art; the essay naturally proceeds, Adorno writes in his unmistakable dialectically aphoristic prose, "methodically, unmethodically" (101). Thus, Adorno has no use for such Toulminian structural terms as "claim," "data," "warrant," "backing," or "rebuttal," for in the essay "concepts do not build a continuum of operations, thought does not advance in a single direction." Rather, Adorno continues, "the aspects of the argument interweave as in a carpet.... The thinker does not think, but rather transforms himself into an arena of intellectual experience without simplifying it" (101). The apparently more autonomous subject of Toulminian argumentation, a subject committed to the "control of nature and material production" (98) thus dissolves for Adorno into an open space in which ideas appear to bounce off one another with radical freedom.

This emphasis on free play, for Adorno, is closely related to his understanding of rhetoric, which, like Toulmin, he sees as something that the "scientific mentality," privileged since Descartes, has long sought to "do away with" (108). But unlike Toulmin, Adorno associates rhetoric more with presentation than with persuasion. Adorno also goes further than the young Toulmin in his explicit rejection of the Cartesian philosophic model, declaring that the essay, which passively "*shys* [sic] away from the violence dogma" (98) also "*gently defies* the [Cartesian] ideals of *clara et distincta perceptio* and of absolute certainty" (102).[3] At the same time, he writes, the essay even more aggressively registers a "*protest* against the four rules that Descartes' *Discourse on Method* sets up at the beginning of Western science and its theory" (102; non-Latin emphasis added).[4]

Though their styles are very different, Montaigne, Adorno, and Virginia Woolf all write in a mode that wavers between submission, assertion, passivity, and activity, even presentation and persuasion. We might even begin to think of the essay itself as a "passive-aggressive" form—one, however, detached from the negative associations contemporary psychology has conferred upon its associated tendencies. Rather than symptomatic of illness, we might see this mode of writing as part of a deliberate strategy for opposing authoritarian entities, avoiding dogmatism, resisting (in Adorno's language) "identity thinking."[5]

In fact, it seems quite appropriate—especially when we think of Woolf's and Adorno's writing (and inevitably, by association with the latter, Walter Benjamin's)—that passive-aggressive "disorder" was first introduced in a United States war department bulletin in 1945 by psychologists dealing with "reluctant and uncooperative soldiers" who only followed orders with "smoldering resentment and chronic, but veiled hostility." Their behavior was characterized by "a mixture of passive resistance and grumbling compliance" that clinical psychologist Michael Stone observes, "has probably been an aspect of human nature for millennia" (360). Even the associations of passive-aggressive behavior with procrastination and inaction link it to the essay—memorably described in Johnson's dictionary as a "loose sally of the mind" and more recently as a form "branded as idleness" (Adorno 93) by more rigid "enlightened" minds, bent on categorizations, not unlike the term "passive-aggressive disorder" itself. My own use of the term represents something of a loose and idle misuse that recognizes the tension and uncertainty inherent in the concept rather than irrefutable truth.

Toulmin's 1989 invocation of Montaigne, if not his more methodical writing style in *Cosmopolis,* would certainly have resonated with a writer like Virginia Woolf, for whom Montaigne was a major cultural touchstone, though she never lived to see the decade of the 1960s that proved so influential for the English philosopher. Toulmin himself was born in London in the year Woolf published *Jacob's Room.*[6] Technically, with luck and good health, she *might* have witnessed with wonder at least the initial years of that notorious decade of cultural and intellectual upheaval, born as she was in 1882. And it's hard not to wonder what she might have said about it (indeed, countless Woolf scholars have been doing that for years). But it is easy to forget that her husband Leonard—two years her senior—actually *did* manage to survive well into the 60s, and to keep writing to boot.

Not unlike Toulmin, Leonard—who was also Cambridge-educated—was something of a social philosopher who saw fit to invoke Montaigne later in life in an attempt, it seems, to heal the wounds of history. Nearly thirty years after his wife's suicide Leonard opens the final installment of his five-part autobiography in a chapter titled "Virginia's Death" with a discussion that leads to the French inventor of the essay form. In fact, Leonard had even chosen to title that 1969 volume with a paraphrase from the *Essais* that he and his wife had both used in various manifestations to describe one of Montaigne's most important lessons for them: *The Journey Not the Arrival Matters.*

We might wonder what would prompt Leonard to use a Montaignian message to name and to begin the end of his autobiography in 1969. Perhaps, nearing ninety, he identified even more closely with the Frenchman in his library, in retreat from the world. Indeed, the 67-year-old Toulmin might have felt this way as well when he penned *Cosmopolis,* or again in 2001 when he, at 79, reiterated his campaigning on behalf of Montaigne as philosopher in *Return to Reason* (of course, we must remember that given the shorter life spans common in the sixteenth century, Montaigne considered himself elderly and deserving of peaceful "retirement" by his late forties). But Leonard might also have been thinking of the reverence he shared with his late wife for this Renaissance writer, whose home they had visited in 1931, right before Europe began the second phase of its rapid decline. Toulmin himself even waxes (Virginia) Woolfian—as best he can—when he recounts a visit to the great essayist's tower later in life in the penultimate chapter of *Return to Reason.*

Another compelling explanation for Montaigne's presence in this opening chapter of this closing book has to do with the Frenchman's position for the atheist Leonard as a sort of secular savior figure, indeed, a prophet who, if duly heeded, might have saved Europe and perhaps even Virginia from the demise Leonard describes so despairingly in these opening pages.

Leonard's begins his chapter titled "Virginia's Death" from a decidedly un-Montaignian impersonal and historical distance by dating the outbreak of the "second of the great world wars" and giving a rough psychological map of England at the time (9-10). Virginia is first mentioned more than five pages into his narrative when Leonard tells how her brother Adrian, horrified by the prospect of the new conflict, had offered poison to his sister and her husband so that they might commit suicide if brutal war should come again (15).

Leonard speaks rather drearily and again impersonally of the profound effect the years 1933-45 had upon the communal psychology of his world, "the world," he writes shifting unsubtly into the first person "in which *I have had to* spend my life" (17, emphasis added). It his here, almost ten pages into the nearly ninety-page chapter, that he hearkens Montaigne's essay "Of Cruelty" in an attempt to make sense of these terrible effects. But it is not so much the quotation itself—relating Montaigne's skittishness about seeing even chickens, pigs, and hares being killed—as what Montaigne stands for that is of interest to Leonard. Having had his say nearly four hundred years before Leonard pens this final fragment of his memoir, Montaigne was, Leonard believes, the "first person in the world to express this intense, personal horror of cruelty. He was, too, the first completely modern man…a man of the Renaissance, that movement…which created a new modern civilization" that "was destroyed in 1914" (18). The non-believer Leonard idealizes—we might even say he secularly canonizes—Montaigne as a saint of the very civilized modernity he is mourning. In fact, writing in a review more than forty years earlier Leonard, perhaps seeing his own image in Montaigne's self-portrait—as writers like his wife Virginia and André Gide had observed the Frenchman's *Essais* often compel people to do—had referred to the ostensibly Catholic agnostic as one who disbelieved in God ("Montaigne" 778). Virginia Woolf, by contrast, seems to be more careful about preserving Montaigne's skepticism as well as her own agnosticism. At the very end of her 1924 essay on the Frenchman, she assumes his voice asking "is the beauty of this world enough, or is there, elsewhere, some explanation of the mystery? To this what answer can there be? There is none. There is only one more question: 'Que scais-je?'" (*CR1* 68).

In the earlier 1927 review of a new Montaigne translation, Leonard, still rattled by the First World War, would begin to speak of two Montaignes. The traditional Montaigne, he writes, "is the man and writer whom thousands have recognized and loved; perhaps the most loveable, wisest, sanest, and wittiest Frenchman who ever wrote a book; the man who asks the question: 'Que sçay-je?' and wrote a masterpiece in *not* answering it." This first Montaigne, continues Leonard, echoing his own wife's description of the Frenchman three years earlier, is the one we can still "see and hear, sitting in his library …with a half-smile on his lips…engaged in…conversation."[7] But inspired by recent work on Montaigne that had clearly gained a political charge in the aftermath of the First World War—just as our own work today may be charged by the war in Iraq—Leonard speaks of a second Montaigne who writes with a "definite and persistent" purpose—a man who "lived in a time of horrible chaos and cruelty, and barbarism due to the struggles of religious sects [fighting]…in the name of absolute truth." In such an atmosphere, Leonard reminds us, Montaigne rejected these absolute truths, and managed to be nothing less than one of the most "humane, rational, and civilized men that [had] ever lived." With great "persistence and subtlety," this second Montaigne, according to Leonard, "used his Essays to attack the religious beliefs in France that were making life intolerable." And since it was impossible to attack them directly—indeed, Montaigne protected himself by professing Catholicism—he "adopted a method of attrition pursued through perpetual irony, innuendo, and asides" (778).

It is interesting to note that in studies of Leonard's wife's work over the last forty years, two Woolfs, we all know, tended to emerge as well. On the one hand, there was the apolitical one who *shied away* from the public activism of her husband, relied too much on charm and the lessons of her "tea-table training" to be an effective feminist writer, and escaped into a myth of androgyny that Elaine Showalter famously asserts betrayed the claims of difference so important to the feminist project (263-97). On the other hand, there emerged the Woolf of *protest*, the revolutionary feminist and angry author of *A Room of One's Own* and *Three Guineas*, the "guerilla fighter in a Victorian skirt," trembling as she "prepared her attacks, her raids on the enemy" in Jane Marcus's words (1).

But Virginia, I believe, who wrote her own essay on Montaigne nearly three years before Leonard's 1927 review, did not see two Montaignes just as she did not see two Virginia Woolfs. And by employing the essay—that passive-aggressive form—she did not have to choose. Like Montaigne, like Adorno, she avoided subsuming works, ideas, concepts into rigid categories. The author of the two *Common Reader* volumes of 1925 and 1932 was the same yet always changing writer of *A Room of One's Own* and *Three Guineas*. If anything, both Montaigne and Woolf see themselves as one *and* many. A number of critics have pointed out the unity of Woolf's plan for and execution of the *Common Reader* books.[8] And Montaigne himself, while admitting to constant revision, producing ever-expanding editions, still declares that his book is "always one," though only an "ill-fitted patchwork" (736), a metaphor echoed in Woolf's description more than three hundred years later of the common reader, chasing after "ramshackle fabric," "snatching…scrap[s] of old furniture" (*CR1* 1). And the book, he insists, is consubstantial with himself. Montaigne explains in several places that he avoids "fixing" his essays to reflect a new position he might take on a subject because, he admits, he might change his mind again. So to preserve the accuracy of his self-portrait, ironically, he preserves these contradictions. Virginia, too, preserves such contradiction, making liberal use of the word "but" and celebrating Montaigne's eternal "perhaps" (*CR1* 63) to allow opposites free play in the living essay form. Like Adorno, Woolf and Montaigne recognize that, as Maurice Merleau-Ponty puts it in an essay on the Renaissance Frenchman, "contradiction is truth" (47).

But Adorno, unlike Woolf, it seems to me, fails to acknowledge the degree to which the Montaignian essay he so prizes *does,* in fact, arise even in Montaigne's time, from a notion of self akin to the fractured and floundering one both he and Woolf describe as a distinctly modern one. Following Horkheimer, he seems to fall prey to the idea that, as Juliet Dusinberre puts it, Montaigne's essays are "relics of a period which uncompromisingly fostered a belief that a human self could be constructed and communicated" (45). But to hold such a view, she warns us, is to "[conflate] modern views of [bourgeois] humanism with a sixteenth-century version" and to misrepresent "Montaigne's view of the human subject" (45).

By keeping this in mind, we can better make sense of Woolf's repeated insistence on the connections between what we have come to call the early modern period—catching on rather belatedly to Woolf's declaration of Montaigne as the "first of the moderns" ("Decay" 25)—and the modernist one. The term "early modern," used to describe a period still known more universally as the Renaissance, was first coined, Leah S. Marcus explains, by a group of French historians in the 1940s. But it wasn't really taken up by literary scholars until the 1980s and 90s—around the time when Toulmin expressed his epiphany about Montaigne's importance to modernity. Marcus continues:

> To look at the Renaissance through a lens called early modern is to see the concerns of modernism and postmodernism in embryo—alienation, a disjunction from origins, profound skepticism about the possibility for objectivity (in literary studies or anywhere else), an emphasis on textual indeterminacy as apposed to textual closure and stability, and an interest

in intertextuality instead of filiation. (43)

While Adorno does not find as much that is useful to the twentieth-century subject in Montaigne himself as he does in the form he invented, Woolf—in a rather Adornian way, in fact—sees the two as inseparable.

Nicola Luckhurst points to Woolf's reliance in letters and diaries on a sort of "talismanic" paraphrase of Montaigne's—"Its [sic] life that matters"—that goes hand in hand with Leonard's "the journey not the arrival matters." For Virginia, however, this mantra is taken more deeply to heart than it is for Leonard as an aesthetic and essayistic credo. She repeats this paraphrase more publicly in her *Common Reader* essay about Montaigne to conclude the same paragraph in which she writes that "the journey is everything," and further warns that "in the name of health and sanity" we must "not dwell on the end of the journey" (*CR1* 65-66). In an equally Montaignian essay that comes a bit earlier in the *Common Reader*—"On Not Knowing Greek"[9]—she writes similarly again that "what matters is not so much the end as our manner of reaching it" (*CR1* 32). To Virginia, this phrase represents more than just a cliché life philosophy as it does, for the most part, for Leonard. For like Adorno, Virginia sees her "philosophy" as inextricably bound up with her writing style. Leonard, closer to the Cambridge mindset Toulmin would eventually *try* to reject—a mindset governed by order and still deeply influenced by Bertrand Russell's neo-Cartesianism—was less able than his wife to surrender his subjectivity to the object at hand to be treated. His more methodical writing style—with the exception of occasional digressions—ultimately exposed the tensions between his own writing practice and the philosophy for which he reached.

While our brief glance at literary modernism's invocation of early modern Montaigne may bring us no conclusion, that is precisely the reason why, I am suggesting, though Montaigne is not usually studied in philosophy (or literature) courses as Toulmin points out, is not read by ladies and gentlemen of leisure as he once was, and is rarely recognized as a major influence on the mighty Shakespeare, he is not, as Juliet Dusinberre fears, so near to becoming, "for most specialists and *all* the reading public a dead duck" (43).

But then again: "Que sçais-je?"

### Notes

1. In the latter text, Montaigne is directly cited only minimally and accessed mainly through Adorno's references to the work of Georg Lukács. Despite an affinity between Montaigne's and Adorno's conceptions of the essay, the later German philosopher's lesser emphasis on the Renaissance Frenchman is to some extent influenced, I believe, by Max Horkheimer's "Montaigne and the Function of Skepticism" (193). Horkheimer's emphasis on the changing role of skepticism over time leads him to overlook, I believe, the very similarities between post-war and early modern Europe that Toulmin, by contrast, emphasizes too much.
2. I turn to philosophers here because as Geoffrey Hartman points out, in *Criticism in the Wilderness* (1980), figures like Derrida, Benjamin, and Adorno—non-"'creative writers' in the accepted sense of the phrase"(190)—were among the most prominent theorists and practitioners of the essay form in the twentieth century. All three, according to Hartman, produce a kind of philosophical criticism which "has a scope that, though not autotelic, seems to stand in a complex and even crossover relation to both art and philosophy" (191). Philosophy also serves as a hospitable disciplinary ground over which to draw links between Leonard and Virginia's varied and contrasting writings.
3. In the original "*Der Essay als Form*," these lines read "*Er schreckt zurück vor dem Gewaltsame des Dogmas*" (17) and "*De Essay fordert das Ideal der clara et distincta perception und der zweifelsfreien Gewißheit sanft heraus*" (22).

4. Adorno's entire sentence in the original reads: "*Insgesamt wäre er zu interpretieren als Einspruch gegen die vier Regeln, die Descartes' Discours de la méthode am Anfang der neueren abendländischen Wissenschaft und ihrer Theorie aufrichtet*" (22).
5. David Held helpfully explains that identity thinking "aims at the subsumption of all particular objects under general definitions and/or a unitary system of concepts. The tendency in contemporary social institutions to 'total' organization is, Adorno claimed, the historical counterpart to this mode of thinking; the particular is subsumed under the general concept as the individual is subsumed under 'the plan'" (202).
6. 1922 is also the year, Michael North reminds us, that T. S Eliot's *The Waste Land* made its debut, James Joyce's *Ulysses* appeared, and the translation of *Tractatus-Logico-Philosophicus* by Ludwig Wittgenstein (who was to be one of Toulmin's professors at Cambridge in the 1940s) inaugurated philosophy's "linguistic turn" in the English-speaking world (31).
7. Virginia had written: "It is impossible to extract a straight answer from that subtle, half smiling, half melancholy man, with heavy-lidded eyes and a dreamy, quizzical expression" (*CR1* 61). Nicola Luckhurst smartly points to the way in which Virginia subtly incorporates her own self portrait in her essay on Montaigne's art of self-portraiture. And Luckhurst supports this argument by juxtaposing actual portraits of a half-smiling Woolf and a half-smiling Montaigne within the body of her article (42). She also reads Leonard's echo of Virginia in the 1927 review as an indication of how their writings on Montaigne constitute "an intimate and ongoing conversation" (43) with each other and with the Frenchman himself.
8. The most thorough case is probably presented by Georgia Johnston.
9. It is this essay that Melba Cuddy-Keane brilliantly uses to discuss what she has described as Woolf's "turn & turn about method" (138)—or, we might say, her unmethodical method.

## Works Cited

Adorno, Theodor W. "The Essay as Form." *The Adorno Reader*. Ed. Brian O'Connor. Oxford: Blackwell, 2000. 91-111.

———. "Der Essay als Form." *Noten zur Literatur I*. Frankfurt am Main: Suhrkamp, 1974. 9-33.

Adorno, Theodor W. and Max Horkheimer. *Dialectic of Enlightenment: Philosophical Fragments*. Ed. Gunzelin Schmid Noerr. Trans. Edmund Jephcott. Stanford: Stanford UP, 2002.

Allen, Judith. "Those Soul Mates: Virginia Woolf and Michel de Montaigne." *Virginia Woolf: Themes and Variations: Selected Papers from the Second Annual Conference on Virginia Woolf*. Ed. Vara Neverow-Turk and Mark Hussey. New York: Pace UP, 1993. 190-99.

Cuddy-Keane, Melba. *Virginia Woolf, the Intellectual, and the Public Sphere*. Cambridge: Cambridge UP, 2003.

Dusinberre, Juliet. *Virginia Woolf's Renaissance*. London: Macmillan, 1997.

Hartman, Geoffrey H. *Criticism in the Wilderness: The Study of Literature Today*. New Haven: Yale UP, 1980.

Held, David. *Introduction to Critical Theory: Horkheimer to Habermas*. Berkeley: University of California Press, 1980.

Horkheimer, Max. "Montaigne and the Function of Skepticism." *Between Philosophy and Social Science: Selected Early Writings*. Trans. G. Frederick Hunter, Matthew S. Kramer and John Torpey. Cambridge, Massachusetts: MIT Press, 1993. 265-311.

Johnson, Samuel. A Dictionary of the English Language, 1755.

Johnston, Georgia. "The Whole Achievement in Virginia Woolf's *The Common Reader*." *Essays on the Essay: Redefining the Genre*. Ed. Alexander J. Butrym. Athens, GA: University of Georgia Press, 1989. 148-58.

Luckhurst, Nicola. "To quote my quotation from Montaigne." *Virginia Woolf: Reading the Renaissance*. Ed. Sally Greene. Athens: Ohio UP, 1999. 41-64.

Marcus, Jane, ed. "Thinking Back Through Our Mothers." *New Feminist Essays on Virginia Woolf*. Lincoln: University of Nebraska Press, 1981. 1-30.

Marcus, Leah S. "Renaissance/Early Modern Studies." *Redrawing the Boundaries: The Transformation of English and American Literary Studies*. Ed. Stephen Greenblatt and Giles Gunn. New York: The Modern Language Association of America, 1992. 41-63.

Merleau-Ponty, Maurice. "Reading Montaigne." *Modern Critical Views: Michel de Montaigne*. Ed. Harold Bloom. New York: Chelsea House, 1987. 47-60.

Montaigne, Michel. *The Complete Essays of Montaigne*. Trans. Donald M. Frame. Stanford: Stanford UP, 1958.

North, Michael. *Reading 1922: A Return to the Scene of the Modern*. New York: Oxford UP, 1999.

Showalter, Elaine. *A Literature of Their Own: British Women Novelists form Brontë to Lessing*. Princeton: Princeton UP, 1977.

Stone, Michael H., M.D. *Abnormalities of Personality: Within and Beyond the Realm of Treatment.* New York: W. W. Norton, 1993.
Toulmin, Stephen. *Cosmopolis: The Hidden Agenda of Modernity.* Chicago: University of Chicago Press, 1992.
——. *Return to Reason.* Cambridge: Harvard UP, 2001.
——. *The Uses of Argument.* Cambridge: Cambridge UP, 1958.
Woolf, Leonard. *The Journey Not the Arrival Matters: An Autobiography of the Years 1939-1969.* New York: Harcourt, Brace & World, 1969.
——. "Montaigne." *Nation and Athenaeum.* 17 September 1927: 778.
Woolf, Virginia. *The Common Reader, First Series.* Ed. Andrew McNeillie. New York: Harcourt Brace, 1984.
——. "The Decay of Essay-Writing." *The Essays of Virginia Woolf, Volume I: 1904-1912.* Ed. Andrew McNeillie. New York: Harcourt Brace Jovanovich, 1986. 24-27.

# Woolf and Andrew Marvell: The Gendering of Modernism

## by Jim Stewart

According to Alice Fox, Marvell's lyrics were "a permanent part of [Virginia] Woolf's mind" (69); and he was, along with Herrick and Shakespeare, among "the poets to whom she most frequently turned" (72). Thus, "Woolf always used Marvell in a functional way" in her fiction; and he was often "alluded to casually in [Woolf's] diary and letters" (73). To illustrate Woolf's practice, Fox refers to the 1925 diary, to *Orlando* (1928), to *The Years* (1937); and gives, in all, four paragraphs of her study to Marvell (73-74). However, the space given him reflects neither his importance to Woolf as a resource, nor the uses she found for Marvell within the gender politics of modernism itself. This is not a negative criticism: Fox's exploration of Woolf's responses to Renaissance literature is more wide ranging than that kind of focus would have allowed.

While Juliet Dusinberre also discusses a range of Renaissance writers who mattered to Woolf (such as Montaigne and Donne, or Pepys and Bunyan), she does not take up Fox's limited exploration of Woolf's allusions to Marvell; and indeed, her book simply does not refer to him. Sally Greene (despite that Marvellian surname) did not receive from the various contributors to her edited collection of essays any discussions of Woolf's relation to Marvellian lyric. Her contributors treated such writers as Elizabeth I, Donne, and Milton, and forms like the sonnet, but did not touch upon Marvell. Most recently, Jane de Gay has chosen to pass Marvell by in her attempt to locate Woolf's writing practices within what T. S. Eliot famously called "tradition." De Gay discusses Milton, Sir Thomas Browne (of whom more later), and Shakespeare. But in the course of exploring what *The Waves* owes to Dante, she has a moment of blindness. Quoting Jinny's words, "The iron gates have rolled back.... Time's fangs have ceased their devouring" (*TW* 190), de Gay calls this "an allusion to the gates of Dante's *Inferno*" (177), as does Gillian Beer in her Oxford World's Classics edition (*TW* 257 n 190). Perhaps so. But surely Jinny, who is sexually active throughout *The Waves*, also refers to Marvell's "To his Coy Mistress," with its equally keen, hortatory "Rather at once our Time devour," and its persona's longing to "roll all our strength… / Thorough the Iron gates of Life" (Marvell 27). Those "fangs" may also distantly echo the idea of Time's "slow-chapt pow'r" in that poem. Yet while the points of allusion to Marvell appear specific and clustered, it seems he is not on de Gay's mind, nor on Beer's.

In Greene's collection, however, David McWhirter's essay "Woolf, Eliot, and the Elizabethans: The Politics of Modernist Nostalgia," does draw some useful contrasts between Eliot's and Woolf's notions of the Renaissance literary past. McWhirter notes that Woolf's political agenda "differed substantially from Eliot's conservative aims" (250). Whereas Eliot aspired to an ideal, quasi-theocratic metanarrative, Woolf herself wanted "exuberant, expansive, and unruly possibility, [and] a disorderly fecundity" (251); and this was to comprise, in turn, "heterogeneity and generic instability" (260). One wonders, then, what uses Woolf would find for a male writer quite so guarded, lapidary, and secretive as Marvell; and how such uses would further the distinctive aims which McWhirter identifies.

At the end of March 1921, the City of Hull held a tercentenary celebration honouring Andrew Marvell. Augustine Birrell and others gave various addresses; and these, along with critical pieces contributed by, for example, T. S. Eliot and Edmund Gosse, appeared in 1922, edited by William Bagguley the city librarian, under the title *Andrew Marvell 1621-1678: Tercentenary Tributes*. In his introduction to this 1922 volume, Bagguley briefly cited a toast proposed by James Downs to Hull's distinguished visitors, which had confirmed that:

> Andrew Marvell's high position in English letters stands more firmly established today in the minds of English-speaking people than possibly at any time during the 250 years that have elapsed since he died, and to Mr. [Augustine] Birrell's great [1905] study of Marvell may be traced the increasing estimation of his writings. (Bagguley 18-19)

Birrell's "great study" was part literary biography and part verse anthology; and it belonged to the "English Men of Letters" series, to which Woolf's father had himself contributed five volumes. In this study, Birrell traces the process whereby Marvell had risen to his present height. Critically, this had begun with Lamb's *Essays of Elia* and a selection by Hazlitt (Birrell 61, 230). There were also verse anthologies, such as Palgrave's *Golden Treasury* and Thomas Humphry Ward's *The English Poets* (230). There were editions of the poetry: Thomson's of 1776; Grosart's of 1872; and Aitken's of 1892, reprinted in 1905 (Birrell 229, 7-8, 47). The thirty-sixth volume of *The Dictionary of National Biography* (which had Woolf's father as a founding editor) contained an entry on Marvell, as Birrell appreciatively acknowledged (210). Owing to this build-up of critical and editorial attention, Birrell concluded, "Marvell's fame as a true poet has of recent years become widespread, and is now…well established" (230).

Hence in his Tercentenary Address at Hull in March 1921, Birrell did not need to exaggerate when referring to those verses by Marvell "that we all know and love," and which had "endeared him to our memories" (Bagguley 57). In his own 1905 study, he had himself given a generous sampling of verse—extracts from "Upon Appleton House" (Birrell 36-45, 227-28); much of "The Garden" (45-46, 228); and all of "To his Coy Mistress" (46-47). In the 2 April 1921 issue of the *New Statesman*, Desmond MacCarthy could assume his readership's familiarity with Marvell's "To his Coy Mistress," which received his praise in an "Affable Hawk" column opposite Woolf's own review of a Congreve play (757). Eliot, in his essay "Andrew Marvell" of March 1921 for the *Times Literary Supplement*, which Bagguley reprinted in *Tercentenary Tributes* the following year, endorsed the general sentiment that "Marvell has stood high for some years" (Eliot 161). Signs of Marvell's high standing would continue to accumulate throughout the 1920s. H. J. C. Grierson included some of Marvell's poems in his 1921 anthology *Metaphysical Lyrics and Poems of the Seventeenth Century*, which Eliot reviewed that same year (Eliot, *Selected Prose* 59-67). H. M. Margoliouth's two-volume edition of the poems and letters was anticipated, in Bagguley's introduction to the *Tercentenary Tributes*, as "a new and complete edition of Marvell's Works" (Bagguley 3-4). It eventually appeared in 1927, and the Woolfs owned a copy.

Why then do we find Woolf telling her diary for 29 April 1921: "I mean to read Marvell" (*D2* 114)? It was not as though she hadn't read Marvell before. Two years prior to her diary entry, we find another one, for 7 October 1919, recording her already "old sense of the race of time 'Time's winged chariot hurrying near,'" in a straight quotation from "To his Coy Mistress" (*D1* 304). Her 1921 diary entry is therefore a statement of new intent; and it may not be fanciful to detect a certain emphasis in its verbs: "I *mean* to *read* Marvell." Undoubtedly the tercentenary celebrations had something to do with this new interest and resolve. But at the same time, Woolf can hardly have been insensitive to how "To his Coy Mistress" valorises male at the expense of female anxiety, or to the poem's vaunted sexual egalitarianism, reflected in the plural pronouns of the last strophe with its urgent project of coupling. She would have been similarly aware of how "The Garden," another celebrated lyric, explicitly connects male pastoral ease and mentation with the absence of women. And she was certainly conscious of Eliot's emergent authority both as literary critic and canon-shaper. We should not be surprised to find, then, that there is a critical and political edge to this renewed desire to "read Marvell."

Marvellian lyric is in fact a strong presence in *Mrs. Dalloway* (1925), in *To the Lighthouse* (1927), and in *The Waves* (1931), besides in those novels already mentioned. What is more, Woolf's pleasured but sceptical handling of this body of verse differs from the kind of gushing appreciation Vita Sackville-West offered in her 1929 monograph, *Andrew Marvell*, which was the first volume of the series "The Poets on the Poets." But for the purposes of this essay, attention will be confined to four important moments in *To the Lighthouse*. These are: Mr. Ramsay's notorious demand for his exhausted wife's sympathy; Mrs. Ramsay's hosting of her dinner party; Lily's failure of sympathy in the garden with Mr. Ramsay ten years after; and part of the long postponed boat trip to the lighthouse. Before considering what Woolf does in the first of those passages, we might refresh our memories of the relevant lines from Marvell:

> Here at the Fountains sliding foot,
> Or at some Fruit-trees mossy root,
> Casting the Bodies Vest aside,
> My Soul into the boughs does glide:
> There like a Bird it sits, and sings
>         "The Garden" VII (Marvell 49)
> Now let us sport us while we may;
> And now, like am'rous birds of prey,
> Rather at once our Time devour
>         "To his Coy Mistress" 37-39 (27)

The salient words from "The Garden" combine a fountain, a fruit tree, boughs, and the benign presence of a bird. The lines from "To his Coy Mistress," on the other hand, project the coupling of two predatory birds as equals. Mrs. Ramsay is described in precisely the terms from "The Garden." She produces a "delicious fecundity, this fountain and spray of life" (*TTL* 34), such that "James...felt her rise in a rosy-flowered fruit tree laid with leaves and dancing boughs" (35). But in calling notice to Mr. Ramsay's intrusive "beak of brass" (34), and in referring to that beak's form as a "scimitar" (35), Woolf invokes the shape of beak characteristic of Marvell's "birds of prey." The male raptor of "To his Coy Mistress" has in that case flown out of his own poem and into "The Garden." When Mr. Ramsay's curved and hooked beak "plunged and smote" (35) in among his wife's "delicious fecundity," it was incongruously that he did so, for it is hard to see what a flowering fruit tree has to offer a hunting predator. By associating Mrs. Ramsay with Marvell's fountain and fruit tree, Woolf in effect reclaims from his poem the notion of a pastoral space which had been notoriously monosexual and exclusive of women. But by having Mr. Ramsay land in and enforce that space from a far different lyric of male sexual angst, Woolf emphasises the patriarchal determination to deny women any practical scope for a replenishing solitude that doesn't refer to men. So her endorsement of Marvellian lyric is qualified (even while admired on aesthetic grounds for its beauty and precision) by a refusal of its masculinism. This amounts to a rather drastic rewriting of Marvell. It is at the same time a tacit denial of Eliot's pleasure in Marvell's "tough reasonableness beneath the slight lyric grace" (Eliot, *Selected Prose* 162), which Woolf clearly found more tough than reasonable, the grace more lyrical than spiritual.

This brings us to the second moment from the novel, namely Mrs. Ramsay's dinner party. In this scene, Mrs. Ramsay suffers the usual panics that go with being a hostess. But at her moment of triumph, when she realises that the event has been a success, she experiences her own and her guests' presence as if they were all "minnows balancing themselves, [with] the sudden silent trout…all lit up hanging," while she herself also "hung suspended" (*TTL* 99). Similarly, "The stupid Fishes hang, as plain / As *Flies* in *Chrystal* overt'ane," in Marvell's "Upon Appleton House" (Marvell 80). The pleasurable stasis achieved in the dinner party, which is a comic victory for Mrs. Ramsay, resembles the pleased stupefaction young Maria Fairfax created in Nature by her progress through her father's gardens in Marvell's country house poem.

The novel's third and fourth incidents reuse some very well known lines from Marvell, along with some less familiar ones. From stanza VI of "The Garden" we have: "Annihilating all that's made / To a green Thought in a green Shade" (Marvell 49). And in stanza LXXXIV of "Upon Appleton House," we read how "such an horror calm and dumb, / *Admiring Nature* does benum" (Marvell 79). It's worth repeating here that "The Garden" celebrates the *male* mind's peace to withdraw into its peculiar happiness, and that this peace depends, unapologetically, on the absence of women from the garden of the title. A phrase in those lines just quoted from "Upon Appleton House" also appeared in the avant-texte of *The Waste Land*: "I was / Frightened beyond fear, horrified past horror, calm" (Eliot, *Waste Land* 59, 67). It was one of a number of appropriations, symptomatic of Eliot's wish to subject Marvellian lyric as part of the literary "tradition" to his own "individual talent."

But by way of contrast to that pleased exclusion of women from "The Garden," Mr. Ramsay desperately seeks peace mediated by female sympathy from Lily Briscoe *in* the garden. He puts Lily in a painful position, for she feels hopelessly unable to help him. The dilemma is accidentally resolved by her praising his boots, but even so, it's important to note what she goes through, and in what terms: "A woman, she had provoked this horror.… It was immensely to her discredit, sexually, to stand there dumb…she looked up expecting to get…complete annihilation" (*TTL* 146). Lily's pain at Mr. Ramsay's hands entails just the opposite of the comic stasis created by Maria Fairfax, and by Mrs. Ramsay. His demand for the assuaging of his need in the garden is an effective obliteration of womanhood, in its insistence that womanhood be constructed around male need. It's a graver version of William Bankes's bathetic feeling about the hole in Minta Doyle's stocking, which had "meant to him the annihilation of womanhood" (164). And it's different again from Lily's feeling, in private, that her impotent grief for Mrs. Ramsay was as much as to "step off her strip of board into the waters of annihilation" (172).

It will be obvious from the above passages, that Woolf is rather over-using this word "annihilation." Her most frequent Renaissance encounter with it would not have been in Marvell, but in Sir Thomas Browne, whose *Urn Burial*, *The Garden of Cyrus*, and *Religio Medici* she had surveyed in her article "Sir Thomas Browne" for the *Times Literary Supplement* of 28 June 1923 (*D2* 245 and n.). Browne had used the word twice in the *Religio* (Browne 117, 124), and once in the *Urn Burial* (314)—in all cases in a narrowly religious sense. Woolf may also have encountered it twice in Browne's *Christian Morals* (Browne 425, 472), and five times in the *Pseudodoxia Epidemica* (Browne 196; Browne 1981 13, 43, 59, 588), almost all of those usages religious or metaphysical. In Marvell's verse however (no matter how that corpus is defined), "Annihilating" is a *hapax legomenon* or word used just the once. It appears only in "The Garden" where, as the poem's argument shows, women are conspicuously among the "all that's made" which, for the retreating male mind's greater "happiness," undergoes "Annihilating" (Marvell 49). Woolf's returning again and again to this word is redolent of Browne; but her exploration of its meanings in the context of gender has that more specifically counter-Marvellian inflection.

"The Garden" and "Upon Appleton House" lines cited above, are used again by Woolf in the boat scene en route to the lighthouse, as Cam fantasises. Underwater, she muses, "in the green light a change came over one's entire mind and one's body shone half transparent enveloped in a green cloak" (*TTL* 174). This mind-body duality, and also the idea of the body as vestment, comes from Marvell's "Garden," stanzas VI and VII, as do the prismatics (Marvell 49). So too, Cam's "fountain of joy…this sudden and unthinking fountain of joy" (180), reclaims from that poem a central symbol of male exclusivity. This is the moment when the breeze drops and the boat is becalmed. Mr. Ramsay, of course, as we had been told earlier, "hated hanging about" (155), unlike Marvell's charmed "Fishes." And Cam's mind also becomes "numbed" "as they hung about in that horrid calm" (174), in a lifting, from "Upon Appleton House," of words and phrases more or less as straight as Eliot's own borrowing in the avant-texte of *The Waste Land*. But for Cam, this is a moment for realising her truest feelings about her father, which it turns out are not wholly malign, and which are connected to her capacity for privacy, and for dreaming. Marvell's original terms had been part of a gallant hyperbole, in which his tutee Maria was over praised. And indeed, Mr. Ramsay's either giving or withholding praise is an issue on his daughter's mind during this boat trip (196). James, equally fraught, and anxious to understand his feeling about his father, moves back through early memories, to find "Everything tended to set itself in a garden" (176). There is no primal time present to memory in which James's father did not figure, and so his presence and influence have to be dealt with.

These allusions—in the passage from "The Window" where Mr. Ramsay demands and gets his wife's human assurances; from the dinner-party episode; from Lily's tortured encounter with the bereaved Mr. Ramsay ten years on in the garden in Skye; and from Cam's inner experiences in the boat en route to the lighthouse—serve to show that Woolf was not inclined to leave Marvell's lyricism alone. "I mean to read Marvell," the statement of intent from Spring 1921, meant what it said.

More could be said about Marvell's presence in this novel, though this is a question of having world enough and time. The almost unnaturally rank and notionally crossbreeding flowers and produce of the garden during the ten year hiatus of "Time Passes" (*TTL* 131-32) deserve notice, as does the entry of George Bast as mower with his scythe

(133-34); and so does the amputation done by a reaping machine in "The Window" (10). For those motifs remember the group of erotic lyrics known as the "Mower" poems. "The Mower against Gardens," for instance, with its forced horticulture's "Forbidden mixtures" (Marvell 41), is clearly ironized in "Time Passes." In "Damon the Mower," the "whistling Sythe" inflicts reflexive damage as "By his own Sythe, the Mower [is] mown" (44). Woolf also seems to have had in mind the mowers who worked the meadows around Appleton House. There again, we meet those scythes, with their "Edge all bloody" from the death of birds that had been nesting in the grass (71).

But maybe enough has been said to demonstrate that Woolf's use of Marvell was far from casual, or merely incidental. She had, on the contrary, a need to appropriate and rewrite him. This was owing in part to the momentum towards canonisation that, as we saw earlier, had been under way for some time, and behind which Eliot was throwing his significant critical weight.

As I have suggested, Woolf's uses of Marvellian lyric could be disruptive. McWhirter's description of her allusive praxis as often "unruly" or "disorderly," and as the enactment of fertile "instability," seems justified by what she did with Marvell (251, 260). For as we have seen, she can lift images from widely different poems and create new hybrids, so as to make explicit the gendered assumptions of those verses. She is sceptical of the "tough reasonableness" Eliot credits to Marvell, which was, as she saw it, sometimes bought at women's expense. His lyricism was easy to love, but perhaps it was too immediately attractive and gratifying. There could be generous experience of his poetic charm. But in Woolf's case this was not uncritical. It was accompanied by a strong sense of his imaginative limits, especially in the stances his poetic voice assumed towards women. Her writing-large of those assumptions, and her atomising and reassigning of his imagery, signal a deeper rebellion against *facile* assimilation of Marvell into any ideal artistic order, Eliot's included; and amounts to a contesting, through figure, and by proxy, of Eliot's critical authority.

**Works cited**

Bagguley, W. H., ed. *Andrew Marvell 1621-1678: Tercentenary Tributes*. Oxford: Oxford UP, 1922.
Birrell, Augustine. *Andrew Marvell*. London: Macmillan, 1905.
Browne, Sir Thomas. *The Major Works*. Ed. C. A. Patrides. Harmondsworth: Penguin, 1977.
———. *Sir Thomas Browne's* Pseudodoxia Epidemica. Ed. Robin Robbins. Vol. 1. Oxford: Clarendon, 1981.
de Gay, Jane. *Virginia Woolf's Novels and the Literary Past*. Edinburgh: Edinburgh UP, 2006.
Dusinberre, Juliet. *Virginia Woolf's Renaissance*. London: Macmillan, 1997.
Eliot, T. S. *Selected Prose of T. S. Eliot*. Ed. Frank Kermode. London: Faber, 1975.
———. *The Waste Land: A Facsimile and Transcript of the Original Drafts Including the Annotations of Ezra Pound*. Ed. Valerie Eliot. London: Faber, 1971.
Fox, Alice. *Virginia Woolf and the Literature of the English Renaissance*. Oxford: Clarendon, 1990.
Greene, Sally. *Virginia Woolf: Reading the Renaissance*. Athens, OH: Ohio UP, 1999.
MacCarthy, Desmond. "Affable Hawk". *New Statesman* 2 April 1921: 757.
McWhirter, David. "Woolf, Eliot, and the Elizabethans: The Politics of Modernist Nostalgia." *Virginia Woolf: Reading the Renaissance*. Ed. Greene. 245-66.
Marvell, Andrew. *The Poems & Letters of Andrew Marvell. In Two Volumes*. Vol. 1. Ed. H. M. Margoliouth. Oxford: Clarendon, 1927.
Sackville-West, Vita. *Andrew Marvell*. London: Faber, 1929.
Woolf, Virginia. *Mrs. Dalloway*. Introd. Elaine Showalter. London: Penguin, 1992.
———. *The Diary of Virginia Woolf*. Ed. Anne Olivier Bell with Andrew McNeillie. Vols 1 and 2. Harmondsworth: Penguin, 1979, 1981.
———. *To the Lighthouse*. Ed. Susan Dick. Oxford: Shakespeare Head, 1992.
———. *The Waves*. Ed. Gillian Beer. Oxford: Oxford UP, 1998.

# "But The Barrier Is Impassable": Virginia Woolf and Class

## by Ben Clarke

In June 1913, Virginia Woolf attended a Women's Co-operative Guild conference in Newcastle, and in 1931, when the Hogarth Press issued a collection of autobiographical essays by members of the Guild entitled *Life as We Have Known It*, she contributed a substantial introductory letter. As Anna Davin observes, her "connection with the Guild is surprising enough to need comment" given that she "had little interest (or faith) in organized politics." It originated not only in her political commitments but in her personal relationships, and specifically "her marriage to Leonard Woolf, an active Fabian, and her friendship with Margaret Llewelyn Davies" (Davin viii). Davies was secretary to the Guild from 1889 to 1921 and a dedicated advocate of a movement she believed represented the "beginning of a great revolution" (Davies xi) that would "see the Community in control, instead of the Capitalists" (xii). She was a forceful figure and reaction to her varied. As Hermione Lee notes, although Leonard Woolf described her in his autobiography as "an exhilarating Joan of Arc figure," Quentin Bell characterised her "as a battle-axe and a bore." For Woolf herself, Lee argues, Davies was one of "those vigorous political women who made her feel insignificant, sceptical and lightweight" (Lee 328). Davies represented direct activism, and, in particular, a working-class activism rooted in the organized politics of the labour movement.

Woolf's introductory letter to *Life as We Have Known It* is addressed to Davies and engages with working-class women, their writing, and their concerns from the explicit perspective of one "shut up in the confines of the middle classes" (xxx). It is, as Rachel Bowlby states, "partly a retrospective analysis of the embarrassment for a 'lady' in attending a working women's conference and finding herself unable to feel at one with the demands for material improvements which were the main preoccupation of the participants." This discomfort forms the basis of an analysis of class that emphasises material and social divisions and in so doing "troubles any wish to imagine Woolf having a straightforwardly immediate feeling of sisterhood, whether political or literary, with other women, whatever their backgrounds" (Bowlby xxvii). Woolf's letter moreover provides a position from which to question and indeed undermine what Alison Light describes as the widespread "tendency to universalise women's experience," something frequently enabled, she argues, by a "blindness to the categories of class" (xi-xii). Its contradictions expose class divisions between early twentieth-century feminists, divisions to which there was, as Woolf recognised, no simple solution, despite her hope that in the future women would meet "casually and congenially as fellow-beings with the same wishes and ends in view" ("Introductory Letter" xxix).

Like all texts, *Life as We Have Known It* can be read within a variety of historical, political, and literary contexts. It bears, for example, an obvious relation to books such as Maud Pember Reeves's *Round About a Pound a Week* (1913) and Margery Spring Rice's *Working-Class Wives* (1939), which reported on the condition of working-class women in the first half of the twentieth century. However, it differs from such texts, and, as Davin argues "has exceptional value," insofar as it provides "accounts by 'us' rather than 'them'" and deals "not just with the generalities of working class life, but with the specific experience of women, as they chose to tell them" (vii). The emphasis upon women's representation of their own lives is, of course, appropriate to a political organisation that encouraged its members to participate in "public life" (Davies xiv). It means the text is also a distinctive contribution to a broader extension of authorship in the 1930s, a decade which saw the publication of an increasing number of working-class autobiographies, many, as George Woodcock observed, "bound in the limp orange covers of the Left Book Club" (125). This development, was, of course, enabled by a political and intellectual environment shaped by events such as the First World War, the Russian Revolution, the Wall Street Crash, the Depression, and the rise of Fascism. In "The Leaning Tower," a paper delivered to the Workers' Education Association in May 1940, Woolf argued that in "1930 it was impossible—if you were young, sensitive, imaginative—not to be interested in politics," and one product of a literary culture in which many young writers and publishers "read Marx" and "became communists" and "anti-fascists" (*CE2* 172) was an increasing interest in working-class life. This led to an increase in texts both about and by the working class, though inevitably the former predominated. In his preface to *Seven Shifts*, Jack Common noted:

> My friends include members of the literary bourgeoisie and lads from the unprinted proletariat. Both parties talk well, and you'd probably enjoy a crack with them as much as I do. But here's the pity. The bourgeois ones get published right and left—especially left; the others are mute as far as print goes, though exceedingly vocal in public-houses. Now I've often felt it would be good to swop them round for a change. (vii-viii)

*Life as We Have Known It* is an example of precisely such a shift, of the publication of the previously "unprinted," those who "do not belong to the writing classes" (vii). As a collection of essays by women, the text is all the more remarkable, as many of the working-class writers published by editors who "read Marx" and "became communists" were men drawn from "traditional" industries such as mining, shipbuilding, and steel production, men who conformed to the dominant image of the proletariat. In this context, descriptions of, for example, domestic labour, domestic service and midwifery, of women who "had gone into factories when they were fourteen" (Woolf, "Introductory Letter" xxxiii) extended and developed images of working-class life, exposing both tensions and solidarity.

Woolf insisted that she was "keenly roused" (xxxii) by the prospect of reading the papers Davies had collected. Nonetheless, she argued that it

> cannot be denied that the chapters here put together do not make a book—that as literature they have many limitations. The writing, a literary critic might say, lacks detachment and imaginative breadth, even as the women themselves lacked variety and play of feature. Here are no reflections, he might object, no view of life as a whole, and no attempt to enter into the lives of other people. Poetry and fiction seem far beyond their horizon. Indeed, we are reminded of those obscure writers before the birth of Shakespeare who never travelled beyond the borders of their own parishes, who read no language but their own, and wrote with difficulty, finding few words and those awkwardly. (xxxix)

This is not to say the essays did not possess "some qualities even as literature that the literate and instructed might envy" (xxxix-xxxx). Nonetheless, the "pages are only fragments," containing traces of voices beginning to "emerge from silence into half articulate speech" (xxxxi). The women are defined by their lack of sophistication, by their limitations, their constraints. This determines even the valuable quality of their writing, which "judging from a phrase caught here and there, from a laugh, or a gesture seen in passing, is precisely the quality that Shakespeare would have enjoyed" had he wished to escape the "brilliant salons of educated people" (xxix). They are, in short, mechanicals, "half articulate" speakers of prose, unable to produce poetry. The description of their writing matches that of the women themselves. They not only lack "variety and play of feature," but are "indigenous and rooted to one spot," to the extent that their "very names were like the stones of the fields—common, grey, worn, obscure, docked of all splendours of association and romance" (xxiv). It is not explained why names such as "Mrs. Thomas, or Mrs Langrish, or Miss Bolt of Hebden Bridge" (xxiii) are inherently more "common" or "grey" or less romantic than, for example, Fry, Bell, Stephen or, for that matter, Woolf. Nonetheless, the description defines these working-class authors in terms of their limitations, and in opposition to "educated people" whose writing would be favoured by the "literary critic."

In part these passages are simply the work of a professional author emphasising the boundaries of her trade. In addition, however, they construct a materialist model of class and writing. Woolf argues that she is divided, even in imagination, from the working-class women who attended the Newcastle congress because "the imagination is largely the child of the flesh" and

> one's body had never stood at the wash-tub; one's hands had never wrung and scrubbed and chopped up whatever the meat may be that makes a miner's supper.... One sat in an armchair or read a book. One saw landscapes and seascapes, perhaps Greece or Italy, where Mrs. Giles or Mrs. Edwards must have seen slag heaps and rows upon rows of slate-roofed houses. (xxiii)

The self-conscious vagueness about the meat itself emphasises the social division between observer and observed. In contrast to an unnamed Lancashire Guildswoman and Poor Law Guardian, who recorded that most "of my lectures and addresses have been thought out when my hands have been busy in household duties—in the wash-tub, when baking (and by the way I have never bought a week's baking during my married life of over twenty-one years), or doing out my rooms" (133-34), Woolf, as she herself acknowledged, was removed from such domestic labour. Indeed, in "Mr Bennett and Mrs Brown" she traced the changes in "human character" in the early twentieth century through the "homely illustration" of the "character of one's cook" (70). Nonetheless, she was conscious of the ways in which her domestic arrangements separated her from those who did not have cooks, who balanced their writing with "household duties." Moreover, as "writing is a complex art, much infected by life" (xxix), her introductory letter traces the impact working-class households had on the texts produced within them. The members of the Guild, Woolf observed, had produced their essays "in kitchens, at odds and ends of leisure, in the midst of distractions and obstacles" (xxxxi). Exhaustion caused by work, and a lack of time, space, and privacy were obvious problems for working-class writers, male or female. As Andy Croft argues, the demands of work in particular restricted working-class authors, as for "miners like Heslop and Brierley, plasterers like Hilton and Halward, the physical exhaustion of long shifts made sustained writing very difficult," and "John Sommerfield, James Hanley and George Garrett, all seamen" were only able to write because of "long and regular periods of unemployment" (99). Indeed, one of the authors of *Seven Shifts* excused his essay to Common by observing that "I am a labourer and have to labour to live, it leaves me no time or energy for this game" (Common x). Even when potential authors did find time, the conditions in which they wrote often presented them with further difficulties. Another potential contributor who failed to complete a manuscript, for example, explained to Common that "I got 3,000 words done, Jack, but it can't be helped, you know the way we live in this bloody tenement, while I was out the baby got hold of the sheets and messed 'em up, so you'll have to count me out" (ix). Cyril Connolly's famous "enemy of good art," the "pram in the hall" (127), presented the greatest difficulty to those who lacked access to studies, nurseries, and nannies.

In *A Room of One's Own*, Woolf had explored the ways in which poverty, domestic work, and a lack of privacy had prevented women from writing. The problem, she insisted, was that

> Intellectual freedom depends upon material things. Poetry depends upon intellectual freedom. And women have always been poor, not for two hundred years merely, but from the beginning of time.... Women, then, have not had a dog's chance of writing poetry. (106)

The solution was "five hundred a year for each of us and rooms of our own" (112). As George Orwell later observed, the "first necessity" for a writer "just as indispensable to him as are tools to a carpenter, is a comfortable, well-warmed room where he can be sure of not being interrupted; and, although this does not sound much, if one works out what it means in terms of domestic arrangements, it implies fairly large earnings" (236). This necessity was available to few working-class writers, and fewer still, if any, had the "five hundred a year" Woolf advised the students of Girton to earn "by your wits" (*AROO* 66). The inter-war period saw a widespread reduction in working-class incomes caused by unemployment and the resultant pressure on wages. In 1927, two years before *A Room of One's Own* was published, 1,194,000 insured workers were unemployed, and by the end of 1930, when *Life as We Have Known It* was issued, this figure had reached 2,500,000 (Laybourn 9). The emphasis on insured workers, as Richard Croucher observes, itself excluded a number of important groups, not least "married women" for whom "there was no financial benefit in signing on but who would have welcomed work" (14). For many of those in work, any reductions in money wages were offset by deflation. However, the 1930s in particular saw an increasing "gap between those in and out of work" (108) and by 1937 "the average workless man or woman received in benefit only half the money value of a normal wage" (McKibbin 117). The Depression had a particular impact on areas dominated by "traditional" industries, with 18.2 per cent of coal workers out of work by 1929, rising to 41.2 per cent by 1932 (Laybourn 8). This had an immediate effect on a number of the contributors to Davies's collection. Mrs. F. H. Smith, for example, whose husband, a collier, was out of work, and who had to keep her family "out of £1 12s and to pay 7/10 rent out of that" (69), observed that it "is heartbreaking to see the unemployed miners at the Labour Exchange—boys, young men in their prime and old men, idle owing to the pits being shut down" (72). Woolf, contemplating the "beef with its attendant greens and potatoes" at Girton, a meal which for her evoked "women with string bags on Monday morning," was perfectly correct in her observation that "coal-miners doubtless were sitting down to less" (*AROO* 19).

These conditions, Woolf argued, prevented the members of the Women's Co-operative Guild from becoming sufficiently "detached and easy and cosmopolitan" ("Introductory Letter" xxiv) to write prose that would satisfy the discerning "literary critic." Indeed, in "The Leaning Tower," she argued that they prevented the development of any significant working-class writing to the extent that if one were to take away "all that the working class has given to English literature...that literature would scarcely suffer; take away all that the educated class has given, and English literature would scarcely exist" (*CE2* 168). The comments brought a response from, among others, the miner and writer B. L. Coombes, who argued "if one accepts the statement by Virginia Woolf as it is written it means that no one who works at manual labour can ever hope to be a writer. She may not have thought of it that way but the result must be so (Jones and Williams 65). As Bill Jones and Chris Williams observe, Coombes acknowledges Woolf's arguments and himself emphasises the ways in which material conditions constrain working-class writers. Nonetheless, although he "adopts the broad parameters of Woolf's analysis" he insists that the "value of working-class writing" lies in its origin in varieties of experience not available to the writers with "an expensive education" (Jones and Williams 64). Indeed, he argues it is a distinct form of literature, albeit an evolving one inevitably constructed using inherited structures and techniques. The tension is founded, in part at least, however, upon Woolf's concept of art as "detached" and "cosmopolitan." In *A Room of One's Own*, for example, she observes that although Charlotte Brontë "had more genius in her than Jane Austen," this was undermined by her "indignation," with the result that *Jane Eyre* became "deformed and twisted," as she "will write in a rage where she should write calmly." Without material security, Brontë could not attain the "detachment" that would have prevented or at least limited such "rage," and Woolf speculates about what might have happened had she "possessed say three hundred a year—but the foolish woman sold the copyright of her novels outright for fifteen hundred pounds" (*AROO* 70). For working-class women such as Mrs. F. H. Smith, living on one pound twelve shillings a week, it was obviously impossible to attain "intellectual breadth" on such terms. The "good gifts" of "wit and detachment, learning and poetry," are consequently things "we" give to "them," the preserve of those "who have never answered bells or minded machines" (Woolf, "Introductory Letter" xxx). The culture of the "writing classes" existed and had an established form. It could be extended to "Mrs. Thomas, or Mrs. Langrish, or Miss Bolt" through education and material prosperity, but was not modified by an "adventurer in literature" (Jones and Williams 65) such as Coombes, whose work, far from being "detached," explicitly dealt with economic and political conditions in the South Wales coalfields.

In her description of the Women's Co-operative Guild congress she attended in 1913, Woolf noted:

> All these questions—perhaps this was at the bottom of it—which matter so intensely to the people here, questions of sanitation and education and wages, this

demand for an extra shilling, for another year at school, for eight hours instead of nine behind a counter or in a mill, leave me, in my own blood and bones, untouched. If every reform they demand was granted this very instant it would not touch one hair of my comfortable capitalistic head. Hence my interest is merely altruistic. It is thin spread and moon coloured. There is no life blood or urgency about it. However hard I clap my hands or stamp my feet there is a hollowness in the sound which betrays me. I am a benevolent spectator. I am irretrievably cut off from the actors. ("Introductory Letter" xx-xxi)

Economic divisions produced class boundaries that seemed "impassable" (xxx), divisions of experience, perception, and values. Woolf's analysis of these divisions and their implications is, perhaps inevitably, marked by contradictions and tensions. It is an interpretation of class by one "shut up in the confines of the middle classes," an effort to both understand a series of texts by working-class women and to locate "wit and detachment" in a particular class experience. It attempts to sympathise with the aspirations of those who want "baths and ovens and education and seventeen shillings instead of sixteen, and freedom and air" (xxiv) and at the same time to legitimise the statement that it is "much better to be a lady; ladies desire Mozart and Einstein—that is, they desire things that are ends, not things that are means" (xxviii). However, as Bowlby argues, the "stumblings of this essay…are often much more interesting than the moments in other essays on literature where Woolf falls smoothly back on to the props of conventional wisdom about artistic value" (xxviii). The text exposes some of the key problems of political engagement, revealing the multiple lines upon which commitment is defined and produced, the complex ways in which the politics of class and gender intersect and modify one another. It is, as Hermione Lee writes, an "honest, uneasy essay, there is a genuine interest in the details of the women's lives, an inability to understand them fully, and a hope for a time—a New World still not in existence in 1930—when middle-class women would not meet working-class women as 'mistresses or customers,' and when 'perhaps friendship and sympathy would supervene'" (361).

## Works Cited

Bowlby, Rachel. Introduction. *A Woman's Essays*. By Virginia Woolf. Ed. Rachel Bowlby. Harmondsworth: Penguin, 1992. Ix-xxxiii.
Common, Jack. Preface. *Seven Shifts*. 1938. Ed. Jack Common. Wakefield: EP Publishing, 1978. Vii-xi.
Connolly, Cyril. *Enemies of Promise*. 1938. Harmondsworth: Penguin, 1961.
Croft, Andy. *Red Letter Days: British Fiction in the 1930s*. London: Lawrence and Wishart, 1990.
Croucher, Richard. *We Refuse to Starve in Silence: A History of the National Unemployed Workers' Movement*. London: Lawrence and Wishart, 1987.
Davies, Margaret Llewelyn, ed. *Life as We Have Known It: by Co-operative Working Women*. 1931. London: Virago, 1977.
Davin, Anna. Introduction. Davies, *Life as We Have Known It*. Vii-ix.
Jones, Bill and Chris Williams. *B. L. Coombes*. Cardiff: University of Wales Press, 1999.
[Lancashire Guildswoman]. "Pioneer Poor Law Guardians." Davies, *Life as We Have Known It*. 131-35.
Laybourn, Keith. *Britain on the Breadline: A Social and Political History of Britain 1918-1939*. 1990. Stroud: Sutton, 1998.
Lee, Hermione. *Virginia Woolf*. 1996. London: Vintage, 1997.
Light, Alison. *Forever England: Femininity, Literature and Conservatism Between the Wars*. London: Routledge, 1991.
McKibbin, Ross. *Classes and Cultures: England 1918-1951*. 1998. Oxford: Oxford UP, 2000.

Orwell, George. "The Cost of Letters." *The Collected Essays, Journalism and Letters*. Ed. Sonia Orwell and Ian Angus. Vol. 4. Harmondsworth: Penguin, 1970. 236-38.
Smith, F. H. "In a Mining Village." Davies, *Life as We Have Known It*. 67-72.
Woodcock, George. *The Crystal Spirit: A Study of George Orwell*. London: Jonathan Cape, 1967.
Woolf, Virginia. "Introductory Letter to Margaret Llewelyn Davies." Davies, *Life as We Have Known It*. Xvii-xxxxi.
——. "The Leaning Tower." *Collected Essays*. Vol. 2. London: Hogarth, 1966. 162-81.
——. "Mr Bennett and Mrs Brown." Bowlby. *A Woman's Essays*. 69-87.
——. *A Room of One's Own*. Harmondsworth: Penguin, 2000.

# "OUTSIDE THE MAGIC (AND TYRANNICAL) TRIANGLE OF LONDON-OXFORD-CAMBRIDGE": JOHN HAMPSON, THE WOOLFS, AND THE HOGARTH PRESS

## by Helen Southworth

In honor of the choice of location for this year's conference, my paper explores the relationship between the Woolfs, their Hogarth Press, and the work of Birmingham-born writer John Hampson Simpson (1901-1955).[1] Hampson, the name under which he wrote, published two novels with the Hogarth Press, the highly successful *Saturday Night at the Greyhound* (which was among the top ten bestsellers at the press) in February 1931 and a second novel entitled *O Providence* in 1932. A short story, "The Long Shadow," was included in the Hogarth Press volume of prose and poetry entitled *New Country* edited by Michael Roberts in 1933. Two subsequent novels were rejected by the Woolfs, as had been Hampson's first submission in 1928—a homosexual novel called *Go Seek a Stranger*.

This paper pursues Hogarth Press historian J. H. Willis's assertion that Hampson's *Saturday Night at the Greyhound* offered the Woolfs "an uncharted literary landscape" and situates Hampson's work in terms of the Woolfs' agenda at the press (189). Hampson's twenty-five-year-long relationship with the Woolfs tells an interesting story about the kind of author and the kind of material published by the Hogarth Press and about the Woolfs' attention to the political climate at a moment when the press, in operation since 1917, had already become as close as it got to being a commercial operation. To this end I will look at two things—first the significance of the Woolfs' decision to publish *Saturday Night at the Greyhound* and *O Providence* and second their decision not to publish *Go Seek a Stranger*. While the latter has never been published it does exist in manuscript.

Hampson has shown up in a couple of recent publications: two letters in Sybil Oldfield's collection of condolence letters (90, 153-55) and another in Beth Daugherty's collection of letters from readers to Woolf in which Hampson expresses his admiration for *The Waves* (94). What becomes clear in all three of these letters and others exchanged with the Woolfs is the respect and affection Hampson felt for both Virginia and Leonard Woolf and vice versa. Even after the Woolfs stopped publishing his work, Hampson maintained ties with them, dedicating his 1936 novel, *Family Curse*, "to Leonard Woolf, with gratitude." By the time of Virginia Woolf's death in 1941 Hampson had a wide circle of literary friends, many of whom he had acquired via the Woolfs and via the Press: among them South African based Hogarth Press writer William Plomer, E. M. Forster, Hogarth Press employee, poet and publisher John Lehmann, from whose autobiographical work *In My Own Time* the title quote of this paper is taken, and even Birmingham based author Walter Allen who says he first contacted Hampson through the Hogarth Press (*As I Walked* 58).[2] After Virginia Woolf's death Hampson maintained contact with Leonard; he also wrote a radio play tribute about Virginia Woolf called "A Room of One's Own" for the Midlands Home Service (May 1946), an article about food and wine in her work for *Wine and Food* magazine (1944) and included a reference to Woolf's Oxbridge lunch and dinner scenes in *A Room of One's Own* in his *The English at Table* (part of the *Britain in Pictures* series, 1944, 45-46).

Who was John Hampson? Hampson wasn't exactly the working-class writer that the Woolfs and others billed him as. Hampson's forefathers were managers of the Theatre Royal in Birmingham and his father prospered in the brewery business. After the family fell on hard times, Hampson went out to work "in a wild and wide variety of jobs," "shops, hotels, warehouses, clubs, dance-halls and munitions factories," and did a short stint in prison for stealing books, apparently *Gray's Anatomy* was his text of choice! (*Under Thirty* 207).

In 1925 Hampson found work as caregiver for a man with Down's syndrome, called Ronald Wilson, whose mother and father, the managing director of a large firm of wholesale grocers, were what Walter Allen describes as "wealthy Nonconformists" (*As I Walked* 59). While in their employ, Hampson found the intellectual and financial freedom to continue writing novels, short stories, and documentaries for the BBC.

Hampson was homosexual. However he did marry, spurred on by W. H. Auden and by an ardent anti-fascism, a German actress called Therese Giehse. Giehse, like her friend Erika Mann (whom Auden had married), was in flight from Nazi Germany and in need of a British passport. In *As I Walked Down New Grub Street*, Allen offers an amusing account of the wedding and ensuing afternoon and evening of honeymoon at a pub then a restaurant and finally at the Futurist Cinema (described in more detail in Lara Feigel's essay in this volume). The proceedings were choreographed by Auden and paid for, Allen says Auden announced "philosophically" to the group, by Erika Mann's father, Thomas Mann (55-58). Although this was a marriage of convenience and the couple lived apart, Allen suggests (and surviving letters confirm) that Hampson and Giehse became good friends (58), and Mercer Simpson that the marriage was in fact consummated (23).

*Figure 1. John Hampson by Howard Coster, 1935. National Portrait Gallery, London.*

With the publication of his novels first at the Hogarth Press and then at Heinemann, Hampson became a minor celebrity. He was photographed by celebrity photographer Howard Coster and appeared in a *Daily Mail* cartoon alongside Radclyffe Hall and Una Troubridge at a Heinemann publicity party, although he swore he had not actually spoken to either one of them there! (Allen, *As I Walked* 60). Even if he lacked working-class credentials himself, Hampson became an important figure in terms of providing a bridge between writers from the Midlands, among them Walter Brierley, Walter Allen, Leslie Halward, and the so-called Birmingham Group, and the London literary establishment.[3] Hampson submitted Brierley's novel *Means-Test Man* (Methuen 1935) to the Hogarth Press in 1934, although unsuccessfully (Croft 179). During the same period, approximately 1928-1932, Birmingham based poet Louis MacNeice also suffered a series of rejections at the hands of the press, in his case mainly due to the antipathy of Hogarth Poetry Series patron Dorothy Wellesley, despite support from Leonard Woolf, T. S. Eliot, and John Lehmann (Willis 260-61).[4]

Hampson's first Hogarth Press novel, which was originally written as a play, takes place over a single afternoon and evening in a pub called the Greyhound in a Derbyshire mining village. Ivy and Fred Flack have left the pub business in Birmingham for the same in rural Derbyshire in order to escape bad influences on Fred, and Ivy has persuaded her responsible younger brother Tom to come along and help them out. Tom, the protagonist of the work, is a standard character in Hampson's novels: the younger brother "in permanent estrangement from society [usually] homosexual"—an astute observer of the tragedy of the human condition, although he's incapable of changing it (Allen *Tradition* 226). Thus Tom looks on somewhat helplessly as his brother-in-law Fred drinks during working hours, liberally distributes free beer to customers and cheats on his wife with the barmaid Clara. Over the course of the evening at the Greyhound we meet not only the pub's staff and pub's customers, but also the local squire's son and an upper-class young woman friend called Ruth Dorme who stop at the pub for food and become enmeshed in the lives of the villagers. By the end of the evening and the end of the novel, the Flacks have lost their license having been caught (turned in by a spiteful Clara) for serving drinks out of hours.

*Saturday Night at the Greyhound* offers a careful portrait of the working classes, the miners, the shepherds, and the women who frequent the pub. While Christopher Hilliard has recently suggested that the novel is "no ode to the people's alehouse" and that Hampson is not sympathetic towards the pub's customers (122), Tom clearly admires the villagers despite their hardness:

> They were difficult to understand, these people; their hard exterior hostility was something he had never met before. The gaunt countryside was reflected in their grim faces. Suffering and poverty made them hard and callous in their speech, though drink betrayed them as sentimental…. In spite of all, [Tom] admired them; their persistent struggle to gain the means of their existence was great in its way. (70)

This semi-autobiographical novel is also a carefully drawn psychological portrait of the interrelationships among the two central families in the novel. Tom is fiercely protective of his sister Ivy, for whom he functions in many ways as a surrogate spouse. However there is a suffocating quality to family which does not really provide a refuge from the claustrophobic, sinister atmosphere of the pub.

Stylistically, the writing is stark, a good match in this case to its subject matter. Walter

Allen has described Hampson's American-inspired, pared down style as "appear[ing] at first harsh, even crude" (*Tradition* 226) and William Plomer has characterized this first novel as "very English" in flavor, sober and direct, marked by a "deep and unsentimental tenderness" (xi). Trekkie Ritchie, later Trekkie Parsons, designed the cover for *Saturday Night at the Greyhound* and the Woolfs highlighted the regional quality of the work in their marketing of it as "a story of village life [showing] Hampson's powers of story telling and character drawing." The book was praised for its simplicity, dramatic realism, and truth.

Hampson's novel worked well with the Woolfs' mandate at the press which was to launch new authors and to publish work that would not find a home with a mainstream publishing house (*Saturday Night at the Greyhound* had been rejected by Jonathan Cape in

*Figure 2. Trekkie Ritchie, dust jacket for* **Saturday Night at the Greyhound,** *1931*

1929). The Hogarth Press was in a position to take risks in 1931 with close to their highest ever yearly profit in 1930, a success repeated in 1931 before profits declined in 1932 (Willis Appendix B). Certainly the support of Hogarth Press author William Plomer and also the presence at the press between 1931 and 1932 of John Lehmann, recently called "the most successful supporter of working-class writing" in the 1930s, would have been factors in the Woolfs' decision to continue working with Hampson, as well as perhaps a factor in their discontinuing their relationship with him (Hilliard 130).[5]

Another factor in the Woolfs' support of Hampson at a time when they were becoming increasingly professionalized might have been that other publishing houses were actively seeking working-class fiction at the time.[6] Virginia Woolf made much of Hampson's putative working-class status, celebrating him as "Our Cardiff waiter" in a letter to Clive Bell (*L4* 292) and describing him as "ravaged, exhausted, has been a bootboy, a waiter, also in prison" in a letter to Lady Ottoline Morrell (*L4* 347). Several concurrent Hogarth Press titles suggest an interest in the working class, the most obvious Margaret Llewelyn Davies's *Life as We Have Known It: by Co-operative Working Women* for which Virginia Woolf wrote an "Introductory Letter" in which she lamented her status as merely a "benevolent spectator" of working-class women's lives (xxi). Possibly publishing Hampson's novels provided Woolf with an opportunity to do more than merely look on.

Hampson followed the success of *Saturday Night* with what appears to be at first sight a quite different work of fiction. An autobiographical novel, the early chapters of *O Providence* are reminiscent of D. H. Lawrence's short story "Rocking Horse Winner" (1926). While Hampson's protagonist, the delicate, quaint, youngest child of the Stonetun family, Justin, begins his life in luxury at Five Ways, a collapse in his father's business investments forces the family into poverty. Thus, later scenes take place against a background of poverty and hardship.

Again Hampson pays careful attention to the working classes in this story of a Midlands childhood.[7] While Justin's mother at first despises both the new place and people to which her change of fortune has reduced her, Justin, here perhaps echoing Hampson's own tastes, finds that poverty brings him closer to his family and that his imagination has much more to work with in a bustling town than in the stifling nursery (108).

Family relationships are central to this second Hogarth Press novel as they were to Hampson's first. But *O Providence* is a more difficult novel than *Saturday Night at the Greyhound* and the fact that the Woolfs recommended it be published after *Saturday Night*, even though the two were submitted simultaneously, suggests that they realized they were taking a risk. As in the earlier novel there is a threatening, cruel undercurrent to the work, but in *O Providence* it exists in a broader and deeper fashion. The extreme alienation experienced by the young protagonist on top of the hostile and stifling quality of home and family adds a level of discomfiture to the reading of this novel that was not there in *Saturday Night*. Hampson includes challenging scenes such as the molestation of Justin and a precocious young girl by a drunk in an unfamiliar park. The novel is clear about Justin's homosexuality, Justin's youth, as Mercer Simpson has suggested, making it possible to include this (28).

Again the style is spare and angular, the novel built on "short unconnected sentences," to the degree that William Plomer warns Hampson in a letter that despite his own distaste for "the sort of 'fine writing' & pretentiousness which abounds in these days," he finds Hampson's work not "quite 'literary' enough," and that the "staccato" style of this second longer novel renders it almost "too unadorned." This second longer novel, as Mercer Simpson suggests, is "uneven" and "formless," in comparison with its tighter and more energetically paced predecessor (17).

Surrealist John Armstrong designed the cover for *O Providence*. The book was marketed as a follow up to the "remarkabl[y] success[ful]" *Saturday Night*. While initial sales were good, this second novel failed to perform as successfully, perhaps a factor in the Woolfs' decision not to continue publishing Hampson. Other reasons might have been Lehmann's break with the Woolfs in 1932 and a shift in emphasis at the press onto leftist politics, as well, of course, as the Woolfs' perception that the work was inferior in quality to Hampson's earlier novels.

Perhaps one of the most intriguing aspects of the Hampson-Woolf relationship is the work that never made it into print, that is the unpublished explicitly homosexual work *Go Seek a Stranger*, a work universally judged his best, by among others Virginia Woolf. Hampson submitted this novel to the Hogarth Press in 1928, before *Saturday Night at the Greyhound* and *O Providence*. What remains of the manuscript is somewhat fragmented—Hampson's nephews Mercer Simpson, author of a thesis on Hampson, and Roger Hubank, Hampson's literary executor, believe that Hampson destroyed certain parts of it himself on the advice of Belfast writer Forrest Reid (an early mentor for Hampson) and also that John's sister Mona McEvoy (the model for Ivy of *Saturday Night at the Greyhound*), in an effort to protect her brother, took a pair of scissors to the more explicit passages such as the seduction scene of the protagonist Alec by his school master.

As Hubank has suggested, *Go Seek a Stranger* is a kind of twentieth-century picaresque novel which follows Alec away from home after he is dismissed from his job as essentially "unsuitable for work" after reporting an attack made on him by two co-workers (personal communication). This failure to fit in is a theme that runs across the length of the work which sees Alec move first to Nottingham to find work in a hotel kitchen, then on a brief but idyllic holiday with lover Bill, then to Liverpool, after Bill leaves for France, then to London. Only in London does Alec finally find the liberty to live as a gay man in the company of Richard—with whom he is planning a trip to France as our version of the novel closes.

Very much like Forster's *Maurice*—"Begun 1913. Finished 1914. Dedicated to a Happier Year," published posthumously in 1971—Hampson's *Go Seek a Stranger* offers a highly candid and sympathetic portrait of the dilemma of the homosexual man in the 1920s and 1930s. As in *Saturday Night at the Greyhound* and *O Providence*, the world of work plays an important role in this first novel. Unlike the earlier novels, *Go Seek a Stranger* is stylistically complex.

It is clear that the Woolfs would have published *Go Seek a Stranger*, as suggested by Leonard Woolf's kind rejection letter to Hampson, dated 13 October 1928 (the letter is dated just two days after the date on which Virginia Woolf's *Orlando* concludes: "at the twelfth stroke of midnight, Thursday, the eleventh of October, Nineteen Hundred and Twenty Eight" (*O* 329)). This coincidence is relevant in the sense that *Orlando* is a novel often considered to have been lucky to have escaped the censors.[8] Leonard Woolf tells Hampson that "[the work] has interested us greatly and has such merits that we should have liked to publish." "Unfortunately [he concludes] we do not think that this would be possible under present circumstances." Forster confirms the Woolfs' support of the work in a letter to Forrest Reid in 1931 where he writes: "I should think [Hampson's] unpublished book, where he can be always himself, must be splendid.... The Woolfs read it and praised it highly to me a couple of years ago: he actually submitted it to them for publication—they were very sorry they couldn't take it" (*Selected Letters* 103).

The Woolfs' experience with Joyce's *Ulysses*, for which they were unable to find a printer willing to risk prosecution on obscenity charges, and their involvement with Radclyffe Hall's *The Well of Loneliness* trial at the very moment in 1928 when Hampson's manuscript landed on their desks likely discouraged them from publishing *Go Seek a Stranger*. Although vocal in their condemnation of censorship in their capacity as writers—Virginia Woolf wrote a short piece with Forster entitled "The New Censorship" in the *Nation and Athenaeum* in 1928 in which they argue that the writer cannot write good literature until his/her mind is free—in their capacity as publishers they were not in a position to risk the legal proceedings that publication might entail. In this sense the decision not to publish *Go Seek a Stranger* represents a missed opportunity, although not the first, for the Hogarth Press. Norah James's novel *Sleeveless Errand* (1929) was also rejected by the Woolfs. It was subsequently banned when published by Scholartis in England and appeared with Jack Kahane's Obelisk Press in Paris in 1929 (Marshik 119).

Although a great admirer of John Hampson, Birmingham writer Walter Allen, in a comment which captures the tensions that existed between Birmingham and London, suggests Hampson's involvement with the Woolfs was somewhat detrimental to his work. Allen suggests that the excellent reception of his first novel at the Hogarth Press "led [Hampson] to equate Bloomsbury with the world and to overrate the nature of literary success" (*As I Walked* 62). However, the shape of Hampson's relationship with Leonard and Virginia Woolf and the Hogarth Press was not that unusual. It was not uncommon for the Woolfs to publish one or two works by a particular author only to see him/her move on for one reason or another to a different publisher. Furthermore the Woolfs did not abandon Hampson. Thus, as late as June of 1939, Virginia Woolf, having read, it seems, the reader's report for Hampson's *Care of "The Grand,"* responds to questions about the use of slang ("bog" instead "W-C," "bugger" rather than "bitch"). She closes her last letter to Hampson looking forward to a moment when writers will be free from taboos in language and with a proposal that beautifully anticipates this conference: "This pen is such that I cant write more, but we hope to see you again in London, or in Birmingham. Yours sincerely, Virginia Woolf" (*L6*: 339).

## Notes

1. Thanks especially to Roger Hubank and Joy Kirk and to Mercer Simpson for their support and generous hospitality, also to Verity Andrews at Reading University Special Collections, Dr. Patricia McGuire at King's College Library, Cambridge, Andrew Gray at Durham University, Laila Miletic-Vejzovic at Washington State University, Matthew Bailey at the National Portrait Gallery, Peter Alexander and David Lodge. Unpublished correspondence is reproduced with the permission of The Society of Authors as agent for the Provost and Scholars of King's College Cambridge, Duff Hart-Davis and Durham University Library, and Roger Hubank. The cover of Hampson's *Saturday Night at the Greyhound* is reproduced by permission of The Random House Group Ltd. and Washington State University. Thanks also to Emma, Simon, and Leo Hall.
2. Other close friends include Louis MacNeice, W. H. Auden, both with Birmingham connections, Robert Graves, Graham Greene, and Murray Constantine (Katharine Burdekin), author of *Swastika Night*.
3. The term Birmingham Group was first coined by American journalist and editor of *New Stories* Edward O'Brien, to include Hampson, Walter Allen, Leslie Halward, and Peter Chamberlain. Walter Brierley and Hedley Carter were from Derbyshire and also attended meetings of the group, although irregularly.
4. MacNeice was one of several writers who responded to Virginia Woolf's essay "The Leaning Tower" (under the title "The Tower that Once") in John Lehmann's Hogarth Press *Folios of New Writing* Spring 1941. Woolf's essay had appeared in the same journal in Autumn 1940.
5. It is unclear who if anyone suggested the Hogarth Press to Hampson.
6. In his documentary "Birmingham Writers in the Thirties" (Central TV, 1982), David Lodge argues that England developed a social conscience in the 1930s and therefore there formed a ready-made audience for working-class writers.
7. Forster felt that it was "the fiction of the Midlands, as opposed to southern or suburban life…brilliantly done" that constituted the real value of the work (Letter to John Hampson).
8. Thanks to Leslie Hankins for noting this.

## Works Cited

Allen, Walter. *As I Walked Down Grub Street*. London: Heinemann, 1981.
——. *Tradition and Dream: The English and American Novel from the Twenties to Our Time*. London: Dent, 1964
Croft, Andy. *Red Letter Days: British Fiction in the 1930s*. London: Lawrence and Wishart, 1990.
Daugherty, Beth, ed. *Woolf Studies Annual 12*. New York: Pace UP, 2006.
Davies, Margaret Llewelyn, ed. *Life as We Have Known It: by Co-operative Working Women*. 1931. London: Virago, 1977.
Forster, E. M. Letter to John Hampson. 29 July 1933. E. M. Forster Papers. King's College Library, King's College Cambridge.
——. *Maurice*. New York: W. W.Norton, 1971.
——. *Selected Letters of E. M. Forster*. Ed. Mary Lago and P. N. Furbank. Cambridge, Mass.: Harvard UP, 1983-5.
——, and Virginia Woolf. "The New Censorship." Letter to the Editor, *Nation and Athenaeum*. 43, 8 September 1928: 726.
Hampson, John. *The English at Table*. London: Collins, 1944.
——. *Go Seek a Stranger*. Unpublished ms. John Hampson Papers. Property of Roger Hubank, Loughborough, U.K.
——. *O Providence*. London: Hogarth, 1932.
——. *Saturday Night at the Greyhound*. 1931. London: Hogarth, 1986.
Hilliard, Christopher. *To Exercise Our Talents: The Democratization of Writing in Britain*. Cambridge: Harvard UP, 2006.
Lehmann, John. *In My Own Time: Memoirs of a Literary Life*. Boston: Little, Brown, 1969.
Marshik, Celia. *British Modernism and Censorship*. Cambridge: Cambridge UP, 2006.
Oldfield, Sybil, ed. *Afterwords: Letters on the Death of Virginia Woolf*. New Brunswick: Rutgers UP, 2005.
Plomer, William. "Introduction." *Saturday Night at the Greyhound*. London: Eyre and Spottiswoode, 1950. Vii-xi.
——. Letter to John Hampson. 8 January 1931. Plomer Collection. Durham University Library, Durham U.K.
Simpson, Mercer F. Hampson. "The Novels of John Hampson." MA Thesis, University of Wales, September 1975 (Reading University Hogarth Press Collection).
*Under Thirty: An Anthology*. Ed. Michael Harrison. London: Rich and Cowan, 1939.
Willis, J. H. *Leonard and Virginia Woolf as Publishers: The Hogarth Press 1917-1941*. Charlottesville: University Press of Virginia, 1992.
Woolf, Leonard. Letter to John Hampson. 13 October 1928. John Hampson Papers. Property of Roger Hubank, Loughborough, U.K.
Woolf, Virginia. *The Letters of Virginia Woolf*. Ed. Nigel Nicolson and Joanne Trautmann. 6 vols. London: Hogarth, 1975-1980.
——. *Orlando*. San Diego: Harcourt Brace Jovanovich, 1956.

# Buggery and Montage:
## Birmingham and Bloomsbury in the 1930s

### by Lara Feigel

In 1931 the Hogarth Press published *Saturday Night at the Greyhound* by John Hampson Simpson, a working-class writer from Birmingham. Virginia Woolf's initial reaction to Hampson was somewhat sceptical: 'We have discovered a good novelist, homosexual, a waiter, I think, in Cardiff; but he wont help—his rags will further diminish our hoard' (*L4* 221). Despite his dubious provenance, Hampson turned out to be very profitable and *Saturday Night* quickly sold ten thousand copies. Hampson was fêted by the younger generation of Bloomsbury intelligentsia, hungry for contact with the working classes, and soon Birmingham would be the unlikely twin-town of Bloomsbury, as young upper and working-class writers passed freely between the ivory towers and grubby brickworks factories. In this paper I shall explore the connections between London and the Midlands, first by looking at the friendships developing between the two groups of writers and then by looking at a particular technique, cinematic montage, that I see as bonding these writers artistically. I shall suggest that, far from diminishing Woolf's hoard, Hampson was responsible for enriching not only the Press's purse but also Woolf's own artistic vocabulary as she moved towards cinematically inspired montage in her politically engaged 1930s writing.

John Hampson himself formed the hub of the wheel linking working-class Birmingham with chattering-class Bloomsbury. He was a key figure in the Birmingham Writers' Group that developed in the mid-thirties and formed the nexus for literary Birmingham. Hampson's working-class credentials are in fact slightly dubious. He was born into the affluent home of middle-class, double-barrelled parents. Leslie Halward, a more convincingly working-class member of the Birmingham Group chastised Hampson for his apparently working-class short story, "Man About the House," in 1935 saying: "only middle and upper-class parents *explain* to their children why they are thrashing them" (cited by Simpson 22). Nonetheless, Hampson's parents fell rapidly into penury and Hampson went on to live in poverty and prison as a kitchen-hand, billiard marker, and book thief, before beginning his literary career and becoming a key player in the Birmingham Writers' Group.

The Birmingham Group itself was brought into being, rather surprisingly, by the American critic Edward O'Brien, who was editing the best short stories of 1935 and noticed that many of the strongest stories of working-class life had been written in Birmingham. In an introduction to Halward's *To Tea on Sunday* O'Brien announced the existence of "a new group of writers emerging in the Midlands, chiefly in and near Birmingham" and listed them as Hampson, Halward, Walter Allen, Walter Brierley, and Peter Chamberlain (cited by Croft 162). The only three writers actually in touch at this point were Hampson, Brierley, and Allen. Walter Brierley had started writing during a period of unemployment as a miner, and Hampson had contacted him after reading his article in the *Listener* detailing the trials of being a working-class writer. It was Hampson who suggested the idea for the novel that would become *Means-Test Man*, Brierley's most successful work, with Walter Allen providing the title. Hampson and Allen met and became great friends whilst Allen, the best educated of the group, was studying English at Birmingham University.

The group widened when Leslie Halward, reading O'Brien's piece, decided to get in touch with Chamberlain and Hampson. He noted:

> Chamberlain's reply was very vague, intimating that it would not be a bad idea if we had tea together somewhere, some time. Hampson's was much more to the point. It began: "Do you know a pub off Corporation Street…?"…and stated that at seven o' clock on the following Thursday evening he and Allen would be there. (Halward 247)

Chamberlain's aloofness was characteristic. Allen described him as "very much the public school man" who "knew London at least as well as he did Birmingham and…had his own circle there" (68). Halward's first impressions of Hampson were not favourable: he found him "a frail little gentleman…toying with a glass that had a drop of whiskey in the bottom" (247). However, he quickly hit it off with both Hampson and Allen and the Thursday evening meetings became a regular fixture.

By this point, John Hampson had been established as part of Bloomsbury with the publication of *Saturday Night at the Greyhound*. Allen wrote that the novel "had brought John into contact with Virginia and Leonard Woolf, both of whom he idolised, and had brought him the friendship of Forster, whom he adored" and that his chest of drawers at this time displayed photographs of Hampson with Virginia Woolf and Forster (62). Allen himself also forged strong links with the younger generation of Bloomsbury through his studies at Birmingham University, in particular with Louis MacNeice. MacNeice had come to Birmingham as a Classics tutor in 1930 and Allen wrote: "I realised later that probably the most important thing that had happened to me [at university] was that I met Louis MacNeice" (45). The poet wrote in his own autobiography that in 1936 "literary London was just beginning to recognise something called the Birmingham School of novelists" stating that "they wrote about the People with a knowledge available to very few Londoners" that he found "very refreshing" (*Strings* 154).

MacNeice's attitude to Birmingham itself is best documented by his 1933 poem, "Birmingham," in which he describes life in the suburbs where the masses "endeavour to find God and score one over the neighbour / By climbing tentatively upward on jerry-built beauty and sweated labour" (*Collected Poems* 17). In *Autumn Journal* he rather disparagingly describes his time at the university:

> I came to live in this hazy city
> To work in a building caked with grime
> Teaching the classics to Midland students…
> And to hear the prison-like lecture room resound
> To Homer in a Dudley accent. (115)

Allen said that whilst being taught by MacNeice he "gazed at him as at a rare wild animal caged in a redbrick university and quite out of place there" (45). He catches MacNeice's own early feelings about Birmingham, although for MacNeice the wildness is Birmingham's and not his own. In his autobiography MacNeice describes the reactions of his friends to his appointment: "'But my dear,' they said. 'You will not be able to live in Birmingham!' Birmingham was darkest Africa" (*Strings* 128). He describes the university itself as "a mass, a mess of grimy neo-Gothic" that "could have passed for a typical block of insurance offices" (130). The students came in for a similarly unfavourable reaction: "they were all so unresponsive, so undernourished, I just could not be bothered" (131).

It was after his marriage broke up that MacNeice began to appreciate Birmingham and to make friends with students like Walter Allen. He wrote that he surprised himself with the discovery that "the students were human" and found that they were refreshingly free from the obsession with politics prevalent amongst students at Oxbridge (154). He and Allen became friends in 1934 and Allen documents the friendship in his autobiography. He describes dinners in Louis's flat after the end of his marriage, always accompanied by Betsy, the handsome Borzoi bitch who Allen cites as "one of the hazards of visiting Louis": "she had the habit of poking her long snout into the private parts of his guests, behaviour which seemed to amuse him rather than not. I had the feeling that he saw one's reaction to Betsy as a test one passed or did not pass" (46). Their friendship continued after MacNeice and Allen had both made the transition from Birmingham to Bloomsbury, and perhaps reached its peak the day after Chamberlain came back from Munich, waving his ineffectual piece of paper:

> MacNeice telephoned me to say that, since there'd be war by Monday and petrol, even if obtainable at all, would be rationed, he'd just sold his car for £14. Would I join him for lunch at the Café Royal? I think both of us assumed it was the last good meal we'd have and we did ourselves proud. Then, floating on brandy and cigar-perfumes, we took a taxi to the Tottenham Court Road, where a cinema was showing one of our favourite Westerns. (114)

With MacNeice, of course, came Auden, and both Hampson and Allen got to know Auden fairly well, with Allen acting in the first staged reading of *The Ascent of F6* at Birmingham University. Auden himself was from Birmingham, and Allen included him in a BBC Midland Region series he wrote on Midlands authors, the others being Henry Green, C. Day Lewis, and Hampson. Allen met Auden whilst writing the programme and saw him sporadically over the next few years. Although Auden claimed that: "Clearer than Scafell Pike, my heart has stamped on / The view from Birmingham to Wolverhampton" (88), Allen said that he did not think Auden actually regarded himself as a true Birmingham man. Hampson's own friendship with Auden was cemented by his bizarre wedding. Auden himself by this point had married Thomas Mann's daughter, Erika, in order to save her from Nazi Germany. He prevailed on Hampson to marry Erika's friend, Therese. Hampson asked Allen what he thought of the suggestion and Allen writes:

> I said all the conventional things; I advised caution; later, he might discover he wasn't a homosexual, fall in love with a woman and want to marry in the real sense…. He listened to me and said: "Wystan says, what are buggers for?" I knew I was defeated. Put in that form, Auden's appeal, I realised, was irresistible. (56)

The ceremony itself is described by Allen, who vied for years with MacNeice over the literary rights to the wedding. Present were Allen, MacNeice, Auden, Reggie Smith, and the happy couple. Auden played the part of the MC in the "prep school or scoutmaster vein" (56). He bought tickets, produced the ring, and, arriving at the station, in a "voice that had become high-pitched, demanded a taxi of astonished porters" (56). A taxi was found and they were dispatched with all haste to Solihull registry office which turned out to be only a hundred yards away. During the service, Auden answered every question, barely giving bride or groom a chance to speak and plying the clerk with questions throughout: "Would you say this is a *popular* registry office? What do you find the favourite month for weddings in Solihull?" (57). After the service Auden took them all to the nearest pub, ordered brandies and demanded whether there was a piano:

> "Yes sir," the barmaid answered "but you can't play it." This made Wystan very indignant. "Who is to stop me?" he wanted to know. The girl answered: "It's Mr ... He's dead. He's in there." She pointed to the billiard room. Led by Auden, we rose and went into the billiard room. There was a coffin on the billiard table. (57-58)

Hampson and Therese had a brief honeymoon at the cinema in Birmingham and did in fact consummate the marriage. Hampson's sister stated that "John said there should no mistake about her being a British subject" (cited in Croft 23). And thus Hampson achieved his status as a fully paid up member of Bloomsbury, willing to love in triangles and live in squares and fulfil his true role as an intellectual bugger.

It seems appropriate that the honeymoon of the marriage between Birmingham and Bloomsbury should have taken place in a cinema. And that MacNeice and Allen's trip to the Western should have provided a cinematic end to a decade of peace. Appropriate in more ways than one, because cinema was not only the dominant medium of the thirties; cinematic technique, and particularly montage, was the dominant technique for thirties politically engaged writing, and can be seen as one of the strongest factors linking the literature produced in Birmingham and Bloomsbury.

Allen wrote that in Birmingham "it was in the Film Society more than anywhere else that young artists came together" and he himself was an active member, and later became more involved in cinema as a reader for MGM (42). Hampson made documentaries for the BBC during the war and Auden's involvement with John Grierson's GPO films is well-known, as is MacNeice's work at the BBC.

In Birmingham, montage was the order of the day. At this point, I should define montage, which is essentially the cutting and pasting of shots, and say that I am referring principally to Eisensteinian shock montage, which tends to involve the juxtaposition of discordant extremes. Eisenstein saw montage as inextricably linked with radical leftist politics. He defined cinema as "first and foremost, montage" and said that through montage, cinema becomes a "tractor ploughing over the audience's psyche in a particular class context" (Taylor 82, 56).

In Hampson's letter advising Brierley on the novel that would become *Means-Test Man* he suggests a montage between work and unemployment: "Make capital of each and every difference between the state of the man in employment and the man workless. The idea of contrast is, I feel, important" (cited in Croft 178). *Saturday Night at the*

*Greyhound* itself uses cross-class montage to juxtapose the young squire, and his friend Ruth, with the working-class local people who run and patronize the Greyhound Pub. Hampson montages their perspectives on each other, so that Ruth is mocked for idealising the working class: "these people really lived" (95) and, at the same time, the working-class Mrs Tapin is mocked for immediately coming to the wrong conclusion about Ruth and assuming that she is a prostitute: "if Master Roy wanted fancy women he had better seek elsewhere" (121).

Walter Allen makes his commitment to cinematic technique explicit in his recollection of writing *Blind Man's Ditch*:

> It was a time when a lot of people were experimenting with novels written from several points of view…the influence of cinema was tremendous, I think, on the 'montage' novel…what I usually used to do was to try and get on the page the image as a film-director might present it. That was what I was after, and what I think everybody was after. (cited in Croft 256)

*Blind Man's Ditch* is built of a montage of quickly changing scenes, from different points-of-view, which juxtapose the life and thoughts of the upper-class and lower-class characters, and show the (usually false) perspective of each on the other. Allen praised *Living*, a novel set in Birmingham by another Midlands writer, Henry Green, specifically for its filmic qualities: "the story is told mainly in very short episodes rather in the manner of a film, the author cutting from character to character, from scene to contrasted scene" (134) and Green himself provides another interesting link between Birmingham and Bloomsbury, although he is beyond the scope of this paper.

Meanwhile in London, Auden was pioneering what MacNeice described as a telegrammatic technique, "an up-to-date technique to express an up-to-date mood" (Heuser 1). And MacNeice's own *Autumn Journal* is filled with montage, with the section on Birmingham providing a classic cross-class montage of Birmingham life. He juxtaposes himself and his friends—"We slept in linen, we cooked with wine, / We paid in cash and took no notice" (115)—with the unemployed who surrounded them and whom they were only half aware of: "the queues of men and the hungry chimneys… / Little on the plate and nothing in the post" (116).

As an older generation Bloomsbury writer, Virginia Woolf was an outsider both to Birmingham and to the Auden generation. Her remarks on what she variously termed the "Leaning Tower" writers and "the Brainies" were often scathing ("The Leaning Tower"). Writers such as Julian Symons have called her an "unpolitical aesthete," suggesting that she had nothing in common with the cinematically and politically driven thirties writers I have discussed (42). However, in recent years there has been an end to the myth of Virginia Woolf as a high priestess of modernism, oblivious to the material world and its concerns. In her work of the thirties, Woolf evinces both an awareness of and an anger with the political world. "All politics be damned," she wrote to her nephew, Julian Bell, in 1935 (*L5* 436). Yet this is not a statement of contempt for politics *per se*, but a statement of contempt for the political situation in what Woolf perceived as a male dominated sphere.

In a letter to Stephen Spender shortly after the publication of *The Years* in 1937, Woolf wrote a stark declaration about her own political engagement in the novel. She stated that she had intended "to give a picture of society as a whole; give characters from every side; turn them towards society, not private life; exhibit the effects of ceremonies" (*L6* 116). It is interesting that Woolf is writing to Spender, who had admired the novel and is part of a politically engaged younger generation. Woolf here takes on the mantle of a thirties writer, motivated by much the same anger against society that she attributes to her "Leaning Tower" writers. In this sense we can see the 1940 essay of that name as describing not only the work of Auden and MacNeice and their comrades but of Woolf herself. The writer who expresses hope in this essay "that the world after the war will be a world without classes or towers" is direct in her liberalism and her acceptance of the hopes and forms of modern society (175).

I would argue that as Woolf became more politically engaged, she sought more help from the techniques of the screen to achieve her aim of picturing "society as a whole." In this she was influenced by the younger generation of writers I have discussed in this paper, both working-class and upper-class. There is no doubt that she had read Hampson's novel, despite her initially sceptical reaction to him. In 1924, Leonard Woolf had told William Plomer that he could not decide whether to publish his book because Virginia had to read it first, and she was currently ill (Willis 129); similarly, describing his experience with the Press in the 1930s, John Lehmann wrote that "Virginia read and gave her opinion on all the literary manuscripts offered to the Press" (17). It is clear from her "Leaning Tower" essay that she had read work by Auden and MacNeice.

Woolf, then, was aware of thirties writers who used cinematic technique with a political end, and she herself began to try out a specifically political kind of montage in her *Three Guineas* notebooks, which she was compiling throughout the early 1930s. She juxtaposes two articles from the *Daily Herald* on 1 August 1936, in the first of which an MP urges the public to "Stand up to Dictators" and in the second a woman complains that her husband insists she "call him 'Sir'" (volume 1: 31). Through contrasting the two, Woolf implicitly asks how we can be expected to stand up to dictators if there are mini-dictators ruling in homes throughout England. Later in the book, Hitler's boast that "in battle we have won the German Reich and in battle we shall maintain and guard it" is followed by an article about animals who advertise their fighting qualities to women (2: 20-21). The fact that the animal article, which is placed after the Hitler article, was in fact published two months earlier, indicates that Woolf's montage process is conscious, and that she assembled the articles and then chose the order for her volume, rather than just adding them chronologically.

This conscious montage principle is also employed in the arrangement of quotations in *Three Guineas*, where she often assembles selections of quotes, many of which come from the notebooks. *Three Guineas* grew out of the factual essays planned to alternate with the stories of the Pargiter family in the original novel-essay, *The Pargiters*. Once she decided to abandon the novel-essay, she was able to include more direct quotes from the sources she had assembled in the notebooks, and she employs them using conscious montage and contrast. She juxtaposes Wilfred Owen's desperate plea for pacifism: "Be bullied, be outraged, be killed; but do not kill" with the Lord Chief Justice of England's bellicose "The home of Liberty is in England. And it is a castle indeed—a castle that will be defended to the last" (*TG* 122-23). But it was her novel *The Years*, which grew out of the novel side of *The Pargiters*, that would be the main receptacle for Woolf's use of cinematic technique in a politically charged frame.

A good example of cinematic technique in *The Years* is Eleanor's arrival at Mr Duffus's cottage, which we see not from her point of view but from that of a random neighbour, a woman "leaning out of the windows" who rakes "every cranny for something to feed on" (93). The woman watches the man (later revealed to be Mr Duffus) and his horse and then sees "a tall woman wearing a coat and skirt of grey tweed" come round the corner hastily. It is only in the next paragraph with Eleanor's "Sorry I'm late" that we realise that this woman is Eleanor. In this passage we become aware that Eleanor, a focus of reader identification throughout the book, does not function solely as an individual mind and agent but is always subject to the broader ties of society. It is important that she herself is oblivious to the watching neighbour. The reader is more aware than she is of her ultimate subjugation to the external world. It is interesting that it is a lower-class character who watches her, and that this is repeated in scenes throughout the book. This functions much as the cross-class montage in the other novels I have mentioned to remind us that upper-class characters do not live in a vacuum and that society is comprised of a fuller class spectrum than we might expect from some of Woolf's earlier novels. In this sense, the working-class framing of the scene stands in for some of the wordier expositions about working-class life that Woolf cut from *The Pargiters*, when she turned it into *The Years*.

The use of montage, I think, typifies the growing convergence between the Birmingham working-class writers group and the politically engaged Bloomsbury of the late 1930s. Over the course of the decade, the Birmingham writers' group emerged in parallel with the Auden generation, and the two trajectories often crossed along the way. The Woolfs' publication of Hampson's novel unwittingly began this crossing of paths, and Woolf's later use of cinematic technique suggests that at some point along the way the exchange between Bloomsbury and Birmingham was mutual.

**Works Cited**

Allen, Walter. *As I Walked Down New Grub Street*. London: Heinemann, 1981.
Auden, W.H. *Collected Poems*. Ed. Edward Mendelson. London: Faber and Faber, 1994.
Croft, Andy. *Red Letter Days: British Fiction in the 1930s*. London: Lawrence and Wishart, 1990.
Halward, Leslie. *Let Me Tell You*. London: Michael Joseph, 1938.
Hampson, John. *Saturday Night at the Greyhound*. London: Hogarth, 1986.
Heuser, Alan, ed. *Selected Literary Criticism of Louis MacNeice*. Oxford: Clarendon, 1987.
Lehmann, John. *Thrown to the Woolfs*. London: Weidenfeld and Nicolson, 1978.
MacNeice, Louis. *Collected Poems*. London: Faber and Faber, 1979.
———. *The Strings are False*. London: Faber and Faber, 1982.
Simpson, Mercer F. *Hampson. The Novels of John Hampson*. Diss. University of Wales, 1975.
Symons, Julian. *The Thirties, A Dream Revolved*. London: House of Stratus, 2001.
Taylor, Richard, ed. *The Eisenstein Reader*. Trans. Richard Taylor and William Powell. London: British Film Institute, 1998.
Willis, J.H. *Leonard and Virginia Woolf as Publishers: The Hogarth Press, 1917*-41. Charlottesville: University Press of Virginia, 1992.
Woolf, Virginia. "The Leaning Tower." *A Woman's Essays*. Ed. Rachel Bowlby. London: Penguin, 1992. 159-78.
———. *The Letters of Virginia Woolf*. Ed. Nigel Nicolson and Joanne Trautmann. 6 vols. London: Hogarth, 1975–1980.
———. *A Room of One's Own/ Three Guineas*. Ed. Michèle Barrett. London: Penguin, 2000.
———. *Three Guineas* notebooks. Monk's House Papers, MH/B16f, University of Sussex.
———. *The Years*. Ed. Jeri Johnson. London: Penguin, 1998.

# "The Shock of Love" and the Visibility of "Indecent" Pain: Reading the Woolf-Raverat Correspondence

## by Alyda Faber

The topic of Virginia Woolf and religion has attracted a somewhat wary interest for at least twenty years.[1] Evelyn Haller's remark in a presentation at this conference suggests an even shorter time frame for the possibility of this kind of work: "only in the last five years can we say that Woolf had spiritual interests." Varying accounts of Woolf's mysticism—atheistic, ironic, this-worldly, political, or as interpreted through details of her biography—are used to characterize Woolf's "religious" sensibilities.[2] As a theologian, my interest in Virginia Woolf relates to her understanding of herself as a writer disturbed by "shocks" and "horror," an understanding that resonates with a certain strain of thinking about religious subjectivity in Christian and Jewish theology. That is, a number of philosophers of religion and theologians propose a human subject constituted through a "summons to love," a passionate (suffering and joyous) responsiveness to other human beings, the world, and God. This view disturbs the liberal notion of the subject as a free chooser and complicates optimistic understandings of love.[3] In this essay, I read Woolf's notions of "shocks" and "horror" using the thought of the Jewish German theologian, Franz Rosenzweig (as interpreted by Eric L. Santner), to illuminate Woolf's understanding of religious subjectivity, although in her view, God or Gods appear as necessary fictions. These "shocks," as spasmodic openings of love, do not create a new belief, but revitalize living "in the midst of life" (Santner, *Psychotheology* 15). I explore this dynamic of ethical encounter in her diaries and letters and the recently published correspondence between Woolf and Jacques and Gwen Raverat in the 1920s when Jacques was dying of disseminated (multiple) sclerosis.

### The Shock of Love

In "A Sketch of the Past," Virginia Woolf observes that "the shock-receiving capacity is what makes me a writer" (72). What does she mean by this? It seems to me that some striking resonances exist between what Woolf calls "shocks" and Rosenzweig's modernist understanding of revelation. In Eric L. Santner's reading of this understanding, a "'shock' of love" (*Psychotheology* 84) is a divine summons to love what is unloveable (demonic) in ourselves and other human beings, the "metaethical self" (Rosenzweig 73) in its unruly, repetitive, unintentional, unnameable strangeness. The strangeness of the "metaethical self" emerges in and through "personality" (Rosenzweig 69), the always unfinished efforts at social legitimation and correctness. Love for this self means the desire to stay near another person in their disorientation in the world, their wretchedness, their unloveability—the symptomatic excess of always unfinished efforts at social legitimation. For Rosenzweig, such responsiveness happens in discrete events, with *this* person in front of me, "*one by one*" (Santner, *Creaturely Life* 207, emphasis in original) not as a generalized command to love all persons. As Santner makes explicit with a reference to the unconscious, in these first person encounters, Rosenzweig engages the inchoate expressivity of another person (and himself) rather than belief, thought, or articulated meaning. This ethical encounter in the first person can be accepted or refused (so that choice is reconceived as a matter of an accepted or desired responsiveness).

Woolf's childhood memories of what she calls "shocks" in "A Sketch of the Past" are encounters with human unloveability that also communicate something unnameable (yet meaningful) in herself, others, and the world. During a fist fight with her brother, she suddenly stops hitting him, and thinks, "why hurt another person?" (*MOB* 71). On another occasion, at dinner, she hears that Mr. Valpy, a friend of the family, had committed suicide; later, the apple tree in the garden becomes associated with the horror of his suicide and she cannot pass it (71). In these examples of "shock," Woolf's sense of paralysis and desolation comes as a debilitating responsiveness to the realization that people hurt others and themselves. Another event elicits a different kind of shock, one of delight rather than anguish. She sees a flower in the garden at St. Ives, and understands it to be, somehow, in its concrete particularity, the whole of life (71). Her description amplifies what seems to be at work in the other examples of "shocks": that the empirical particularity of a fleeting event or thing can gain a "revelatory" significance through a loving attention that creates a kind of permanence for it. This resonates with her subsequent account of writing as making severed parts coalesce, writing as making something whole (72), a dynamic that extends beyond her own powers. In a recent essay, Lorraine Sim helpfully elaborates Woolf's sense of this wholeness as a hidden "pattern" that she perceives behind the everyday, a given "metaphysical reality" that awakens, jolts, touches "empirical reality" (38, 41). Sim calls this dynamic interaction Woolf's "belief in the existence of an objective, non-material principle that provides order and meaning to life" (46), and also alludes to this pattern in Platonic terms as "worthy of imitation" or representation. I take this in a slightly different direction, suggesting that meaning or imitation for Woolf seems to be primarily about a certain sensibility rather than belief, a form of life that sustains attention within disorienting shocks.[4]

In the experiences of shock, Woolf details the intense physicality of her response, and a "permanence" given to discrete events that she names "moments of being" (73), of intense anguish or delight. As an adult, the helpless exposure Woolf felt as a child is replaced with a sense that the shocks are valuable, "that it is or will become a revelation of some order" (72). "Revelation" happens through a kind of writing that transforms debilitating shocks into reasoned "explanation[s]" (72) that retain a ragged edge of the unnameable. Woolf names and evokes the unnameable through her writing, an activity she describes as both "given" to her, and made by her (72-73), a paradox best understood, in my view, as loving responsiveness. That is, for Woolf, writing appears to be about a paradoxical, unwanted, unchosen, and yet a desired and accepted responsiveness to beauty as well as unloveability in herself, others, and the world. Woolf's difficult responsiveness, I have been arguing is analogous to a religious subjectivity that disrupts the notion of the liberal free chooser. Accepting "answerability" (Santner, *Psychotheology* 9) to other humans and the world complicates human agency as Woolf's examples of shocks demonstrate: such responsiveness can be debilitating, but it can also release an unnameable "too muchness" (Santner, *Psychotheology* 8) into life and intensify living "in the midst of life" (15).

Woolf's sense of responsiveness—welcomed and valued, yet aversive—opens her to an utter strangeness, an alterity within herself, others and the world. The nonhuman, repetitive, demonic aspect of the human that Rosenzweig calls the "metaethical self" (73) has a counterpart in Woolf's sense of exposure (through shocks) to something that defies description. This comes into view most acutely when her usual functioning is arrested during periods of illness and depression. In a series of diary entries from 1926, she attempts to track the "varieties of horror" she feels: an intense sense of failure, futility, ugliness, incompetence (that have mundane sources, like not having children, or her preference for a certain green paint) (*D3* 110-14). Her recurring sense of unloveability also interests her as an exposure to truth: "There is an edge to it which I feel of great importance.... One goes down into the well & nothing protects one from the assault of truth" (*D3* 112). Woolf is left with what she calls this "odd immeasurable soul," this "queer being" that she imagines will persist into old age when the accolades have gone. In "On Being Ill," published in the same year, Woolf elaborates the terrifying exposure that besets the ill. While the healthy go about making and doing things, the ill experience immense solitude, the absence of consolation, the indifferent, exquisite beauty of nature, all of which amplify the incomprehensibility of life. She ascribes a kind of holiness, or ensoulment, to that within and beyond herself which she cannot control. That which is *not for us*, "nothing to do with human pleasure or human profit" (*E4* 321) nevertheless has a kind of beauty to it. She seeks to engage in other people this "queer being" that forms the ragged edges of social encounters. During a visit with the poet William Plomer, Woolf notices the difficulty of getting beyond the "crust" of his "universal manner fit for all weather & people: [that] tells a nice dry prim story" in order to engage whatever truth his "wild eyes" tell (*D3* 245). In Rosenzweig's terms, this move from "personality" to responsiveness to the demonic "metaethical self" (73) is a space where, as the subtitle of the Woolf-Raverat correspondence implies, "a different sort of friendship" is possible.

While Rosenzweig interprets "shocks of love" as a divine summons to love of neighbour, Woolf regards such shocks as necessary to her life as a writer, however painful her susceptibility to various feelings becomes. She writes, "Happily, I never cease to transmit these curious damaging shocks. At 46 I am not callous; suffer considerably; make good resolutions—still feel as experimental & on the verge of getting at the truth as ever" (*D3* 180). The vibrancy of this painful-pleasurable responsiveness to life is obvious in images used in her letters: she prefers a porous suffering soul to one that has become "shiny" and "enamelled" (*L3* 294). She also uses language of unconsciousness (*L5* 408) or references to God, deployed as a fiction, to describe the responsiveness necessary to writing, an agency not wholly governed by intentionality or choice. Following her assessment that her criticism is often flimsy, she writes, "But there is no principle, except to follow this whimsical brain implicitly, pare away the ill fitting, till I have the shape exact, & if thats no good, it is the fault of God, after all. It is He that has made us, not we ourselves. I like that text" (*D2* 299; reference to Psalm 100:3). Her reference to God gives Woolf a way of conveying her sense that there is more to humans than their own intentions and choices, and that this realization often comes to us in the midst of difficulty, an aspect of life and writing that is a paradoxical "horrid labour" and "rapture" ("A Sketch," *MOB* 75, 72). George M. Johnson makes a compelling argument for Woolf's use of religious language to sound the untracked, inchoate sensations in humans as long as such language does not remove "the shocks and buffetings of experience" (*E3* 320, cited in Johnson 243). Woolf's writing is not an attempt at cathartic expulsion of whatever shocks produce in her (she finds that shocks, however painful, elicit a form of consciousness that she values), nor does she regard herself as progressively strengthened by shocks, as if training the muscles of her will. Rather, her active desire for a life of difficult responsiveness to demonic strangeness in herself, other people, and the world is *necessary* to her writing. Woolf's writing depends upon a keen susceptibility that may capsize her, a liability that is also an ability.

### The Woolf-Raverat Correspondence

The practice of bearing the proximity of another person in their "demonic" intensity, for Rosenzweig love of God as love of neighbour, is powerfully evoked in *Virginia Woolf and the Raverats: A Different Sort of Friendship* (2003). When Woolf and the Raverats renewed their acquaintance through correspondence (1922-1925), Jacques was dying of multiple sclerosis, and he and his wife were living in the south of France in an effort to relieve his declining health. Most of the letters are dictated by Jacques to Gwen, as he was usually unable to write. After his death in early March 1925 at the age of 40, several poignant letters are exchanged between Gwen Raverat and Virginia Woolf.

In one letter, Jacques Raverat tells Woolf that "your letters, particularly the last 3 or 4, have given me something, which very few people have been able to give me, in these last years" (126). What is this unnamed "something" that Woolf was able to give? In what follows, I interpret this "something" as loving attention that allows unloveability to appear, that for Woolf is a necessary practice for the artist akin to Rosenzweig's religious practice of love of neighbour: the desire to bear the proximity, the reality of other humans and oneself, and so to release this pressured intensity into life (Rosenzweig 178-79, 214). In other words, the letters enact an ethical encounter that allows the disorienting strangeness of another human being (and oneself) to be seen through loving attention, a living dynamic that may also call the reader to similar (first person) ethical encounters.

Love becomes an explicit topic in the Raverat-Woolf correspondence as part of a conversation about the shyness of love, of how humans are usually hidden behind masks or in vapours. "[I] can only very very dimly murmur a kind of faint sympathy & love," Woolf writes (113). In spite of love's shyness, it is obvious how love intimates the "eternal in the earthly" to use Hermann Cohen's phrase (cited in Santner, *Psychotheology* 145). Refusing to speculate about the exact nature of the menage à trois of Lytton Strachey, Carrington, and Ralph Partridge, Woolf remarks that she finds private relations boring (99), to which Jacques Raverat replies that he finds personal relations dangerous, always interesting, sometimes "tragic or farcical or devastating or ecstatic & half a hundred other things" but "never never boring" (107). To this Woolf responds with what I consider to be one of her most fascinating sentences. She clarifies that while she has begun to find sexual relations boring, this does not include private relations: she finds "*relations of all kinds more & more engrossing, &* (in spite of being made a fool of so often by one's impulse to surrender everything—dignity & propriety—to intimacy) *final, in some way; enduring; gigantic; & beautiful.* Indeed, I find this in my relations with people, & what I can guess of theirs" (110, emphasis added). Woolf and Jacques Raverat both enact and observe a shared moodiness in their correspondence—within this moodiness, love transfigures relations and becomes "final, in some way; enduring; gigantic; & beautiful." That is, love transfigures relations just as Woolf's "shocks" transfigure, through writing, the everyday into "moments of being." The contingent and fleeting is given a kind of permanence in love, and in writing, without becoming consolation. Love and writing both bear witness to a possible responsiveness to the strange, repetitive, demonic aspect of humanness.

In one letter, Jacques Raverat gives an apt description of attention to the "demonic" in the novelist Stella Benson's "power for laying bare all the things one is so dreadfully ashamed of in human nature & human life. It really makes one writhe sometimes" (73). This "laying bare" also happens in the Woolf-Raverat correspondence. In a 1922 letter that begins the correspondence, Woolf writes about "laying bare" as a quality that a letter must have: "you must write me a proper letter, & expose yourself as I hereby expose myself" (47). The exposure can only happen in the presence of love, as other letters imply by the unflattering accounts Woolf and Raverat offer of themselves. Woolf exposes her malicious tendencies, both by identifying this as a means of self-flattery as she contrasts herself favorably with other people, as well as practicing it with her vivid, sometimes mean-spirited descriptions of other people. She describes herself as vain, as always wanting praise. Throughout the correspondence, Jacques Raverat replies with his own secrets: how he despises the healthy and is jealous of them, his melancholy, chagrin, and despair about what his illness and impending death have robbed him of. Woolf keeps encouraging an encounter with the widest possible range of Jacques Raverat's sensations and passions as indicated by her description of the autobiography he must write: "let it be the waste paper basket, conduit pipe, cess pool, treasure house, & larder & pantry & drawing & dining & bed room of your existence" (125). Like the other letters, Jacques's last letter shows this range, conversationally engaging Woolf on Sapphism and sodomy, mutual acquaintances, parties, happiness, and melancholy. He writes that his latest work is his best, and now, instead of twenty or thirty more years to work, he faces death. "I think *I* should have had a certain gift for happiness also; but destiny or fate or whatever you call it has broken me to bits instead. An awful waste" (152).

In a similar way, after Jacques's death, Gwen, who, as her husband's scribe, has "overheard" the conversation between Jacques and Virginia, interprets love as the possibility of exposing indecent pain. "There are some things in life, that some of us know about, but that is indecent to write about—some kinds of pain I think" (165). Immediately she adds that such "indecent" pain must be ignored if life is to go on. Her next paragraph, however, says the opposite. She refers to Goya etchings, parts of Shakespeare, or the dying cry of Christ, "My God, my God, why hast thou forsaken me?" as examples of such pain that most people fail to notice, or are afraid to notice, because it shatters life into a "heap of wreckage" to use Rosenzweig's phrase (cited in Santner, *Psychotheology* 15). But not everyone can pretend that indecent pain does not exist Gwen writes (alluding to Woolf's madness), "only one has to be awfully careful how one writes or talks about it" (165). Her own confession, in a letter immediately following Jacques's death, tells the "mad nightmare" of the last days of his life as a terrible, indecent pain that "nobody knows or guesses" (164); an excruciating pain of desiring to live as "he was dying & partly dead—the slow tearing apart of us—I hurt him infernally" (165). In a subsequent letter, Gwen returns to the subject of decency with reference to scenes of Septimus Smith's madness in *Mrs. Dalloway* that she was unable to read with Jacques. The horror, while true, was too intense: "it isn't squeamishness, it is that certain things—horrors or intimacies or heroisms or madness—have to be written about with very great restraint else they get out of key" (175). Woolf responds that the scenes about madness are "a subject that I have kept cooling in my mind until I felt I could touch it without bursting into flame all over. You can't think what a raging furnace it is still to me—madness & doctors & being forced" (181). This indecent pain or "demonic" humanness is at once that which compels writing and makes it terribly difficult, just as it compels love—in all its modulations, moodiness, strangeness. Love befalls us and remains difficult to inhabit, to stay near.

Just how difficult it is to inhabit our loves is clear from a few letters exchanged between Woolf and Gwen Raverat about three years after Jacques's death. The difficulty of remaining open to the intensity of other people, particularly face to face, is suggested in Woolf's diary entries about visits with Gwen Raverat (184). The exposure to indecent pain that shocks of love allow alters considerably in a letter from Gwen. She refers to having been unable to read for two and a half years, a condition she calls "madness," and continues "What I really wanted to say (and the reason I didn't write before is that its so difficult to express)—is that being *unhappy* is to my mind both *so boring and so disgusting*, that I feel I would like to apologize to the world for being so, or only it were not so ridiculous to do it" (188, emphasis added). It becomes obvious near the end of the letter that the apology is intended for Woolf, not the world at large: "it must have been rather horrid (and dull) for you" (189). Gwen Raverat's apology for her "boring" and "disgusting" depression is the kind of "indecent" pain that required no apology in previous correspondence with Woolf. In her response, Woolf mentions missing Gwen's latest exhibition, and shifts from a reference about the possibility of their meeting in the summer to this: "It is an almost impossible achievement. Human beings are so terrified of each other" (190).

The meeting of two people that Woolf considers an "almost impossible achievement" is actualized as a possible impossibility in the frank, teasing, loving conversation of the Woolf-Raverat correspondence. For Woolf, the satisfaction and terror of these encounters with other human beings is a vital aspect of her attempts as a writer "to break every mould & find a fresh form of *being*, that is of *expression*, for everything I feel and think" (*D4* 233, emphasis added). As she continues the diary entry, this work gives her a sense of being fully alive: "But this needs constant effort, anxiety & risk" (*D4* 233). As I have argued, a religious sense of subjectivity, without God or Gods, except as necessary fictions, allows Woolf to express her sense of herself as a writer making precarious and necessary efforts to love other humans. As such, her writing, and here, the correspondence with the Raverats, gives the reader an opening to a kind of engagement that moves beyond seeing others as "emanations from ourselves" (*L3* 245) to the "constant effort, anxiety & risk" of ethical encounter with unloveabilty, the demonic in other humans.[5] That is, a difficult responsiveness to the inchoate, the unnameable, the unclassifiable in ourselves, other humans, and the world. For Woolf, this kind of engagement is necessary for a writer, as it creates space for "a different kind of friendship." For Rosenzweig, it is selfhood exposed to love for other humans: the central task of religious life that disrupts static, clichéd religious formulations with keen, revelatory "shock[s] of love." Both draw us beyond the liberal ethos of the self as free chooser and its reiterations of the happy endings of love. In so doing, Rosenzweig and Woolf take us into a sharper kind of love that places us in the middle of life (and death).

### Notes

1    The research for this essay was supported by the Lilly Theological Research Grants Program. I am grateful to Pat Saunders, Kathleen Skerrett, David Heckerl, and Diana Swanson for conversations that contributed to this essay.

2    Some key works in this area include the following: Jane Marcus, "The Niece of a Nun: Virginia Woolf,

Caroline Stephen, and the Cloistered Imagination," in *Virginia Woolf: A Feminist* Slant, ed. Jane Marcus (Lincoln: University of Nebraska Press, 1983), pp. 7-36; Madeline Moore, *The Short Season Between Two Silences: The Mystical and the Political in the Novels of Virginia Woolf* (Boston: George Allen & Unwin, 1984); Mark Hussey, *The Singing of the Real World: The Philosophy of Virginia Woolf's Fiction* (Columbus: Ohio State UP, 1986), and Martin Corner, "Mysticism and Atheism in *To the Lighthouse*" in *Virginia Woolf's* To the Lighthouse, ed. Harold Bloom (New York: Chelsea House, 1988), pp. 43-58. The issues that concern me—selfhood, attention, suffering, and representations of the obscurity of life, human and otherwise—appear in these works as well.

3   In his book, *Lost Icons: Reflections on Cultural Bereavement* (New York: Morehouse, 2000), Rowan Williams argues that religious subjectivity is a "lost icon" in North Atlantic culture given consumer practices that consistently reinforce the attractions of the subject as free chooser.

4   In *Contesting Spirit: Nietzsche, Affirmation, Religion* (Princeton: Princeton UP, 1998), Tyler T. Roberts contrasts the modern fascination with meaning in terms of intellectual significance (following the loss of a sense of inherent meaning in the world or in humans) with the way that Nietzsche reclaims both classical philosophy and religious asceticism wherein meaning is "a lived, embodied, practiced relation to the world" (197). Woolf also distrusts schematic intellectual meaning, which her writing about the practice of writing amplifies.

5   Woolf also uses the image of screens to convey how people resist seeing others in their peculiar particularity (*D3*: 104).

## Works Cited

Johnson, George M. "A Haunted House: Ghostly Presences in Woolf's Essays and Early Fiction." *Virginia Woolf and the Essay*. Ed. Beth Carole Rosenberg and Jeanne Dubino. New York: St. Martin's Press, 1997. 235-54.

Rosenzweig, Franz. *The Star of Redemption*. Trans. William W. Hallo. Notre Dame: University of Notre Dame Press, 1985.

Santner, Eric L. *On Creaturely Life: Rilke, Benjamin, Sebald*. Chicago: University of Chicago Press, 2006.

___. *On the Psychotheology of Everyday Life: Reflections on Freud and Rosenzweig*. Chicago: University of Chicago Press, 2001.

Sim, Lorraine. "Virginia Woolf Tracing Patterns through Plato's Forms." *Journal of Modern Literature* 28/2 (Winter 2005): 38-48.

Woolf, Virginia. *The Diary of Virginia Woolf*. Ed. Anne Olivier Bell with Andrew McNeillie. 5 vols. New York: Harcourt Brace Jovanovich, 1977-1984.

___. *The Essays of Virginia Woolf*. Ed. Andrew McNeillie. 4 vols. to date. London: Hogarth, 1986-1994.

___. *The Letters of Virginia Woolf*. Ed. Nigel Nicolson and Joanne Trautmann. 6 vols. New York: Harcourt Brace Jovanovich, 1975-1980.

___. "A Sketch of the Past." *Moments of Being*. Ed. Jeanne Schulkind. 2nd ed. London: Harcourt, 1985. 64-159.

___ and Jacques and Gwen Raverat. *Virginia Woolf & the Raverats: A Different Sort Of Friendship*. Ed. William Pryor. Bath: Clear Books, 2003.

# KILLING THE ANGEL IN THE HOUSE: VIRGINIA WOOLF, D. H. LAWRENCE, AND THE BOUNDARIES OF SEX AND GENDER

## *by Susan Reid*

Virginia Woolf famously condemned the Angel in the House as the enemy of female creativity and although it is now a critical commonplace that she killed her Angel in *To the Lighthouse* (1927), Woolf felt she had yet to solve the problem of "telling the truth about [her] experiences as a body" (*DM* 241). While her dilemma has already received much critical attention, this essay focuses on comparable difficulties in the writing of D. H. Lawrence, who also killed his Angel/mother in *Sons and Lovers* (1913). Although Lawrence is notorious for writing about the body, his attempts to convey embodied experience are laden with ambiguity and contradictions. For example, Woolf herself observed of *Sons and Lovers* that "bodies become incandescent," "possessed of a transcendental significance," with the effect that "stability is never reached" and there can be no bringing "the separate parts into a unity" (*CE1* 354). This essay will illustrate a tendency towards transcendence in works by both writers and relate this to the authors' ambivalence towards the figure of the Angel in the House. For despite their disparagement of the Angel as a figure which contained women within an ideal of selfless domesticity and maternity, writers like Woolf and Lawrence remained attracted to her implied sexlessness and disembodiment and often created a variation of the Angel ideal in their own fiction. In Woolf's case, this has been characterized by Elaine Showalter as a (hotly contested) "flight into androgyny," "the sphere of the exile and the eunuch" and a response to "feelings too hot to handle" (285, 286), while in Lawrence's case, there has been relatively little exploration of such ideas. This essay, then, explores the extent to which certain texts by Woolf and Lawrence challenge the boundaries of sex and gender but risk leaving behind the body for a state of transcendence: a state which seems to foreshadow the androgynous angel of Luce Irigaray's writings. In particular, how might their troubling revisions of the Angel ideal, as an imaginative if not physical combination of "male" and "female," challenge conventional thinking about the body?

Despite objections that the Angel in the House has also been done to death by literary critics, her place in Lawrence's novels has been oversimplified or simply overlooked. Her importance in Lawrence's work suggests that the figure loomed also over the working classes and affected men as well as women. Confining discussion of the Angel in the House to issues of "female" creativity and emancipation, however important, has restricted the debate in terms of modernism more generally and of modernist masculinities more specifically. Lois Cucullu's recent study, *Expert Modernists, Matricide, and Modern Culture* (2004), is a welcome exception. Cucullu's analysis of Woolf, E. M. Forster and James Joyce posits a double-sided attack on domestic ideology, which undermines the usual assumption that male and female modernists were polar opposites and suggests that the Victorian legacy of separate "male" and "female" spheres was breaking down, allowing greater fluidity of "male" and "female" roles. Cucullu concludes that dethroning the Angel in the House was one means by which modernist writers established themselves as part of "expert culture and specialized knowledge" and while her specific argument is beyond the scope of this essay, it helpfully points up a tension between modernism's complicity with and opposition to the reorganization of these domains and the associated domains of gender and sexuality (65).

While Woolf's famous argument with the Angel in the House is set out in "Professions for Women" (1931), the nature of Lawrence's quarrel demands some further introduction. The following quotation is from an unpublished fragment by Lawrence, assumed to have been written shortly before his death in 1930, providing both a useful proximity to Woolf's essay and an interesting distance from *Sons and Lovers* (1913), which it seems to describe:

> My mother's generation was the first generation of working-class mothers to become really self-conscious…the woman freed herself at least mentally and spiritually from the husband's domination, and then she became that great institution, that character-forming power, the mother of my generation. I am sure the character of nine-tenths of the men of my generation was formed by the mother: the character of the daughters too.
> …The woman felt herself the higher moral being: and justly, as far as economic reality goes. She therefore assumed the moral responsibility for the family, and the husband let her. So she proceeded to mould a generation. (*Phoenix* 818)

Although Lawrence does not use the term Angel in the House, she is nevertheless recognizable in the "character-forming institution" who "assumed the moral responsibility for the family." Lawrence's version of the Angel in the House shares with Woolf's renditions the fundamental characteristics of self-consciousness, self-sacrifice, and character-moulding, characteristics which are unwittingly destructive of those around them, men as well as women. In *Sons and Lovers*, Mrs. Morel's drive to improve her family leaves her husband an empty "husk" (62), her first son William dead, and her youngest son, Paul, struggling against a death-wish. In *To the Lighthouse*, although Mrs. Ramsay seems to be dominated by her husband, she nonetheless infantilizes him, while her domesticating drive results in a sham marriage for the Rayleys and a premature death in childbirth for her daughter, Prue. And yet, while both novels kill their Angel/demon, neither finally condemns the woman herself: what is actually contested is the institution of heterosexual marriage and particularly the institution of motherhood. Lawrence's repeated attacks on the "*magna mater*" are usually interpreted as misogynistic, although they also bear some resemblance to Luce Irigaray's critique of the ideology of motherhood, whereby "'Femininity' fades away before maternity, is absorbed into maternity" and "the mother once again…masks the woman" (*Speculum* 74,117).

In contrast to the outward self-denial of the mother figures in *Sons and Lovers* and *To the Lighthouse*, both novels reveal an inner essence of being which could access a very different life than that of duty and social convention followed by Mrs. Morel and Mrs. Ramsay: what Woolf describes as "a wedge-shaped core of darkness" which "could go anywhere, for no one saw it" (*TTL* 69). And yet this potential transcendence of the physical body is problematic for sex and gender identities, as a comparison of two passages from the novels will illustrate. In the first passage, from the opening chapter of *Sons and Lovers*, a pregnant Mrs. Morel has been locked out of the house during a bitter argument with her husband. After half an hour in a "delirious condition," she becomes aware of "the tall white lilies…reeling in the moonlight…the air was charged with their perfume, as with a presence":

> Mrs Morel leaned on the garden gate, looking out, and she lost herself awhile. She did not know what she thought. Except for a slight feeling of sickness, and her consciousness in the child, her self melted out like scent into the shiny, pale air. After a time, the child too melted with her in the mixing-pot of moonlight, and she rested with the hills and lilies and houses, all swum together in a kind of swoon. (34)

In the next passage, from *To the Lighthouse*, Mrs. Ramsay has finished reading to her youngest son, James, and has a brief respite from the demands of her numerous family and house guests:

> She saw the light again. With some irony in her interrogation, for when one woke at all, one's relations changed, she looked at the steady light, the pitiless, the remorseless, which was so much her, yet so little her, which had her at its beck and call (she woke in the night and saw it bent across their bed, stroking the floor), but for all that she thought, watching it with fascination, hypnotised, as if it were stroking with its silver fingers some sealed vessel in her brain whose bursting would flood her with delight, she had known happiness, intense happiness, and it silvered the rough waves a little more brightly, as daylight faded, and the blue went out of the sea and it rolled in waves of pure lemon which curved and swelled and broke upon the beach and the ecstasy burst in her eyes and waves of pure delight raced over the floor of her mind and she felt, It is enough! It is enough! (71-72)

Both passages begin with the women looking out, but sight, the sense most associated with mind and consciousness, leads to a different sort of vision. Mrs. Morel and Mrs. Ramsay, both of whom suffer from excessive consciousness, relinquish their exterior, social selves and experience an inner self in harmony with the external world. And yet what are we to make of this solitary state of transcendence, a state accessed through sensuous experience, but experienced finally in the mind? Transcendence is usually interpreted as a "male" goal, in its subjection of the body (traditionally gendered female) to the mind (gendered male). However, Molly Hite's reading of Woolf suggests a transcendence of the social body to what she terms the "visionary body," defined as "a second physical presence in fundamental respects different from the gendered body constituted by the dominant social order" (3). And yet, as Hite concedes, while the "visionary body" "is the site of the most acute sensations," it is "enclosed," "is almost by definition out of social contact with other bodies" (7, 10). In the quoted passages, both Mrs. Morel and Mrs. Ramsay appear to exhibit this type of visionary self-embodiment, in parallel to their social selves. In other words, there remains a split between interior and exterior being, a split which both novels represent as threatening to the physical body: both Angels die and their protégés are also threatened if not overcome by death. Merger or dissolution of self is what the Angel in the House figure seems to promise for others: as Mrs. Ramsay reflects "the whole of the effort of merging and flowing and creating rested on her" (*TTL* 91). The danger of this type of dissolution of the self, mediated by the Angel figure, is felt most acutely by Lily Briscoe and Paul Morel. In contrast to Mrs. Ramsay and Mrs. Morel, Lily and Paul attempt to foreground the body—"It was one's body feeling, not one's mind" (*TTL* 194)—but both must fight an impulse to merge with the beloved:

> What art was there, known to love or cunning, by which one pressed through into those secret chambers? What device for becoming, like waters poured into one jar, inextricably the same, one with the object one adored? Could the body achieve it, or the mind, subtly mingling in the intricate passages of the brain? Or the heart? (*TTL* 57)

This imaging of the body as a vessel, prone to intrusion and appropriation, reaches its apotheosis in the possessive love of Gerald Crich and Gudrun Brangwen in Lawrence's *Women in Love* (1920), but is foreshadowed in *Sons and Lovers* by Paul's precarious sense of self, threatened with a desired dissolution. In the crisis of the final chapter, "Derelict," Paul is almost overcome by grief for his dead mother and by the dissolution of self that the Angel ideal represents: there are repeated references to his body lying abandoned and his desire to follow his mother into the darkness. Although Paul senses earlier in the novel that his life is a "toppling balance" (260), he is less successful than Lily in striving to shape and balance experience. Lily knows that she must find balance in order to complete her painting and she therefore struggles to reconcile the opposing forces of Mr. and Mrs. Ramsay, of "male" and "female:" "For whatever reason she could not achieve that razor edge of balance between two opposite forces; Mr Ramsay and the picture; which was necessary" (*TTL* 209).

While Lily ultimately achieves her vision in *To the Lighthouse*, *Sons and Lovers* is more ambivalent and it is Lawrence's next novel, *The Rainbow* (1915), which begins to envision a way beyond the problem of desired subjection to the Angel in the House. Lydia Brangwen represents a more balanced vision of matriarchy: she resists her husband Tom's dependence upon her and prompts his realization that physical consummation is the vehicle to a separate state which allows integral selfhood and imaginary unity with the other: "when a man's soul and a woman's soul unites together—that makes one angel" (129). Associated by Tom with marriage, this Platonic ideal may also be a spiritual state achieved by a personal reconciliation of "male" and "female" forces, resulting, for example, in Ursula Brangwen's private vision of the rainbow at the end of the novel. This alternative "angel" state is also described in Lawrence's *Study of Thomas Hardy*, as something which may be both physical and purely spiritual:

> What we call the Truth is, in actual experience, that momentary state in living [when] the union between the male and the female is consummated. This consummation may also be physical, between the male body and the female body. But it may be only spiritual, between the male and female spirit. (72)

Importantly, Lawrence is moving away from the idea of merger as promised/threatened by the Angel in the House towards an ideal of union, a connection between discrete identities rather than a blurring of boundaries. Lawrence's ideal receives its most famous expression in Rupert Birkin's notion of "star equilibrium" in *Women in Love*: "What I want is a strange conjunction with you—not meeting and mingling...but an equilibrium, a pure balance of two single beings:—as the stars balance each other" (148). This idea has some resonance with Irigaray's later writing, in which she focuses on the heterosexual couple as having the potential to redeem society, asserting that in order to celebrate marriage "a harmonious passage from the exterior to the interior, from the interior to the exterior of bodies...is needed. That the two be here and there at the same time, which is not to say that they merge" (*Nietzsche*, 124-25). Irigaray is often invoked in Woolfian studies, but her exploration of the heterosexual couple as the ground of a genuine sexual difference that will entail an ethical relation to the other bears some similarity to Lawrence's later work with its increasing emphasis on sexual difference.

However, *Women in Love* also works to undermine any revised ideal of heterosexuality, ending with Birkin lamenting the death of Gerald Crich and their failure to achieve "another kind of love" (481). The search for a male friend, which recurs through Lawrence's fiction, is usually interpreted as a homosexual subtext, but may also represent an attempt to balance male and female relationships, just as Lily Briscoe must balance Mr. and Mrs. Ramsay in order to "complete" her vision/picture. Indeed, as Leo Bersani observes, "there seems to be a profound tendency in Lawrence to get rid of sex altogether" (169) and in its avoidance of the frictional opposition of conventional male/female relations, Ursula and Birkin's relationship in *Women in Love* seems to peter out into a stillness caused by the absence of difference. And it is this question of difference that is so troubling to theories of gender and sexuality: without difference are we once again reduced to what Luce Irigaray, among others, would excoriate as the phallocentric doctrine of the same? Without sexual difference are we, like Irigaray, haunted by the androgynous figure of the angel as the "most beautiful" of the many "consequences of the nonfulfillment of the sexual act," "messengers who never remain enclosed in a place, who are also never immobile" (*Ethics* 15)? Is this the type of angel ideal that Woolf and Lawrence risk creating in their texts?

Woolf's later work remains committed to breaking down the boundaries of sex and gender, most successfully perhaps in *The Waves* (1931). For example, Andrea Harris asserts that Bernard "becomes a differently gendered being, one in whom masculine and feminine coexist" and concludes that "Woolf sketches the contours of a new state of being in which difference no longer represents an obstacle or battlefield but instead a fertile ground of exchange" (354, 355). And Miriam Wallace traces Woolf's image of the "seven-sided flower" as a vision of the merged subject (135-36). But what of the underlying anxiety about corporeality betrayed by images like this and by Birkin's abstract idea of "star equilibrium"? In his work after *Women in Love*, Lawrence seems to strive to redress the balance with the body through an increased emphasis on sexual difference. Feminists, from Simone de Beauvoir onwards, have criticised Lawrence's doctrine of "phallicism," which is perceived as privileging the male. And yet, this ignores the ethics of "otherness," inherent throughout Lawrence's writing, but most clearly expressed in his later works. For example, in *Fantasia of the Unconscious* (1922), Lawrence asserts that "The whole mode, the whole everything is really different in man and woman...the vital sex polarity...the magic and the dynamism rests on otherness" (103). And the following, perhaps seminal, statement of Lawrentian "otherness" is drawn from *Studies in Classic American Literature* (1922):

> But the triumph of love, which is the triumph of life and creation, does not lie in merging, mingling, in absolute identification of the lover with the beloved. It lies in the communion of beings, who, in the very perfection of communion, recognise and allow the mutual otherness. There is no desire to transgress the bounds of being. Each self remains utterly itself—becomes, indeed, most burningly and transcendently itself in the uttermost embrace or communion with the other. (240)

As Neil Roberts observes, for Lawrence "the self is 'most burningly and transcendently itself' in communion with the other, but the other is not constitutive of the self," a crucial distinction from standard feminist criticism of Lawrence (21). This is not an attempt to recuperate Lawrence from feminist attack, but to argue that Lawrence's vision of masculinity balances rather than opposes and negates the "otherness" of woman. Lawrence seems, then, to approach the problem of sexual difference from the other side of the sexual divide from Irigaray, who writes that

> Sexual difference would constitute the horizon of worlds more fecund than any known to date—at least in the West—and without reducing fecundity to the reproduction of bodies and flesh. For loving partners this would be a fecundity of birth and regeneration, but also the production of a new age of thought, art, poetry, and language: the creation of a new poetics. (*Ethics* 5)

And yet, despite his apparent avowal of sex and the body, Lawrence, like Woolf, remains attracted to an ideal of disembodiment. In his writing, as Marianna Torgovnick has remarked, "sex is not the point, is no more than a means to an end, an expression of larger, cosmic, unities" (164). Thus, even in his final, famously "dirty" book, *Lady Chatterley's Lover* (1929), the message is one of "tenderness," of a "democracy of touch," rather than sexual passion. As suggested in the extract above from *Studies in Classic American Literature*, transcendence seems to remain the ultimate goal.

And yet, may the idea of transcendence through communion, inherent in texts by Woolf and Lawrence (and indeed by Irigaray), demand a new way of thinking about the body? What if, as Gilles Deleuze and Félix Guattari suggest, the body is not an organic whole but a "desiring machine" connected in "fusional multiplicity" with the world? While Irigaray, like many feminists, remains suspicious that concepts such as "becoming-woman" and "desiring machines" represent new forms of male appropriation, Elizabeth Grosz, in particular, has argued that the Deleuzian interest in the question of difference may be productive for both men and women. Grosz suggests that "In conceptualizing a difference in and of itself, a difference that is not subordinated to the identity or the same, Deleuze and Guattari invoke two forms of energy and alignment: the processes of becoming and the notion of multiplicity" (192). This leads to a very different notion of the body, one which evades the binary polarizations of mind/body and self/other and which posits the body as "a discontinuous, nontotalized series of processes, organs, flows, energies, corporeal substances and incorporeal events" (Grosz 193-94). These are ideas which, as Deleuze and Guattari frequently acknowledged, have some resonance with the writings of Woolf and Lawrence.

In drawing towards a close, it may seem that this essay has only demonstrated the complexity of the problem it commenced with: that killing the Angel in the House did not solve the problem of telling the truth about experiences of the body for either Woolf or Lawrence. Or rather that their rejection of the essentialism seemingly embodied by the Angel in the House did not suppress a desire for disembodiment also inherent in the Angel ideal. This is perhaps unsurprising given a similar tension in the contested field of gender and sexuality which continues to perplex us today. And yet, what does emerge from texts by Woolf and Lawrence is a resistance to polarity or fixity: a possibility of multiple selves as an alternative to the rigidly individualized subject and the pleasure/terror of a merged subject.

## Works Cited

De Beauvoir, Simone. *The Second Sex*. Trans. and ed. H. M. Parshley. London: Cape, 1953.
Bersani, Leo. *A Future for Astyanax: Character and Desire in Literature*. Boston: Little, Brown, 1969.
Cucullu, Lois. *Expert Modernists, Matricide and Modern Culture: Woolf, Forster, Joyce*. Basingstoke: Palgrave, 2004.
Deleuze, Gilles and Félix Guattari. *Anti-Oedipus: Capitalism and Schizophrenia*. Trans. Robert Hurley, Mark Seem, and Helen R. Lane. London: Athlone, 1984.
Grosz, Elizabeth. "A Thousand Tiny Sexes: Feminism and Rhizomatics." *Gilles Deleuze and the Theater of Philosophy*. Ed. Constantin V. Boundas and Dorothea Olkowski. London: Routledge, 1994. 187-210.
Harris, Andrea L. "'This Difference ... This Identity ... Was Overcome': Merging Masculine and Feminine in Virginia Woolf's *The Waves*." *Virginia Woolf and the Arts: Selected Papers from the Sixth Annual Conference on Virginia Woolf*. Ed. Diane F. Gillespie and Leslie K. Hankins. New York: Pace UP, 1997. 350-57.
Hite, Molly. "Virginia Woolf's Two Bodies." *Genders* 3 (2000). <http://www.genders.org/g31>.
Irigaray, Luce. *Amante Marine de Friedrich Nietzsche*. Paris: Editions de Minuit, 1980.
——. *An Ethics of Sexual Difference*. Trans. Carolyn Burke and Gillian C. Gill. Ithaca: Cornell UP, 1993.
——. *Speculum of the Other Woman*. Trans. Gillian C. Gill. Ithaca: Cornell UP, 1985.
Lawrence, D. H. *Fantasia of the Unconscious and Psychoanalysis of the Unconscious*. Harmondsworth: Penguin, 1971.
——. *Phoenix: the Posthumous Papers of D. H. Lawrence*. Ed. Edward D. McDonald. London: Heinemann, 1936.
——. *The Rainbow*. Ed. Mark Kinkead-Weekes. Harmondsworth: Penguin, 2000.
——. *Sons and Lovers*. Ed. Helen Baron and Carl Baron. Harmondsworth: Penguin, 2000.
——. *Studies in Classic American Literature*. Ed. Ezra Greenspan, Lindeth Vasey, and John Worthen. Cambridge: Cambridge UP, 2003.
——. *Study of Thomas Hardy*. Ed. Bruce Steele. Cambridge: Cambridge UP, 1985.
——. *Women in Love*. Ed. David Farmer, Lindeth Vasey, and John Worthen. Harmondsworth: Penguin, 1995.
Roberts, Neil. *D.H Lawrence, Travel and Cultural Difference*. Basingstoke: Palgrave, 2004.
Showalter, Elaine. *A Literature of Their Own: From Charlotte Bronte to Doris Lessing*. London: Virago, 1999.
Torgovnick, Marianna. *Gone Primitive: Savage Intellects, Modern Lives*. Chicago: Chicago UP, 1990.
Wallace, Miriam L. "Imagining the Body: Gender Trouble and Bodily Limits in *The Waves*." *Virginia Woolf and Emerging Perspectives: Selected Papers from the Third Annual Conference on Virginia Woolf*. Ed. Mark Hussey and Vara Neverow. New York: Pace UP, 1994. 132-39.
Woolf, Virginia. *Collected Essays*. Ed. Leonard Woolf. Vol. 1 London: Hogarth, 1968.
——. "Professions for Women." *The Death of the Moth, and Other Essays*. New York: Harcourt Brace Jovanovich, 1942. 235-42.
——. *To the Lighthouse*. Ed. Stella McNicholl. Harmondsworth: Penguin, 1992.
——. *The Waves*. Ed. Gillian Beer. Oxford: Oxford UP, 1992.

# Real Bodies and the Psychology of Clothes: *Three Guineas* and the Limits of Sartorial Reasoning

## by Randi Synnøve Koppen

To glance at the photographic images that accompany Woolf's argument in *Three Guineas* is to be reminded at once of its topic and its topos, of that boundary and mediacy which is signified by the sartorial, and where Woolf's analysis of patriarchal society and its psychology of war is concentrated. Deceptively trivial, clothes represent all those cultural symbols and artefacts which consistently veil their involvement in a signifying fabric and habitually belie their importance. The banality of dress, much like the banality of the male vanity which preoccupies Woolf in this essay, effectively masks what is really at issue. Doubly constituted, as limit and mediacy, dress fashions and disciplines bodies; it symbolises, interprets, and inscribes subjects in signifying systems and hierarchies; and it describes relations between inside and outside, self and surface, in ways which may be taken as synecdochic or allegorical, as representative or non-representative. The sartorial, as trope, embodied practice, and symbolic system, allows Woolf, as reader of patriarchal culture, to examine the symbolic order as a fabric in which a complexity of threads cross and recross. The sartorial also informs her rhetoric—a patchwork of the ostensibly serious and the deceptively trivial—and it inspires her proposed strategy of resistance: to withstand the seduction of the Symbol, and to practise modes of signification which are not represented by "sartorial splendour" but by dress as one of "the little arts" of human intercourse (*TG* 40). Of all these threads in Woolf's argument the photographs stand as a visual shorthand.

The points I have made so far are little more than reminders of what is already well known. Critics, notably in the valuable collection of essays edited by Merry M. Pawlowski, *Virginia Woolf and Fascism* (2001), have made the connection between sartorial display and other types of visual and verbal symbolism, taking the seductiveness of the sartorial spectacle as indicative of a general "susceptibility to symbols" (the flag, the swastika, Bradshaw's Proportion and Conversion) whose modus operandi is the generation of emotional response and automatised behaviour (loyalty, submission, faith) (Rosenfeld 126). These critics place Woolf's analytic gaze at the masculine vanity informing academic, ecclesiastical, and judicial processions in its proper context, focussing on the choreographed and fashioned bodies performing in the fascist aestheticisation and masculinisation of culture. Vara Neverow, in a particularly illuminating essay, is concerned with Woolf's grasp of the phallic logic of the symbolic order, its organisation and dependence on the principle of the phallus as privileged symbol and transcendental signifier. Reading the photographs in *Three Guineas*, Neverow focuses on the presence in each image of at least one "ritual object that represents male authority and resembles a phallic signifier": "an erect feather," "elongated trumpets," "large ceremonial staffs," "a dangling cord at the waist," and so on (58). Here, then, is Woolf's visual demonstration of male fetishisation of the phallus and patriarchal legitimation of male dominance by the fiction of genital privilege (having, as opposed to lacking, the penis). The obverse of such privilege, of course, is castration anxiety, dispelled only by the assurance of women's penis envy and desire. Woolf's tactic, however, as Neverow shows, is to substitute mockery for desire and to emphatically refute the Freudian theory of penis envy.

The source for Woolf's ideas on what she terms "infantile fixation" in *Three Guineas* is identified by Neverow as Freud, or rather as the Freudian theories circulating within contemporary progressive culture. Whilst this is obviously true, a further likely influence on Woolf's understanding of the phallic value of clothing is the work of the psychologist J. S. Flügel, who published his *Psychology of Clothes* with the Hogarth Press in 1930 and *The Psycho-Analytic Study of the Family* in 1921. With Leonard Woolf (as well as Bertrand Russell, H. G. Wells, and Rebecca West), he was one of twenty-two Vice-Presidents of the Federation of Progressive Societies and Individuals (the FPSI), an umbrella organisation for several groups with a shared commitment to social and economic reform. Flügel was a co-author of the Federation's 1934 Manifesto, contributing an essay entitled "A Psychology for Progressives—How Can They Become Effective?" Throroughly steeped in Freudian psychoanalytic theory Flügel's work explores clothing in its full psychological range, from the protective/maternal to the phallic/paternal, from sublimation of narcissism to cultural discipline and constraint. Assuming a causal relationship between the corporeal discipline effected by clothing and a conservative disposition, he proposes dress reform (as advocated by the Men's Dress Reform Party) and ultimately nudity (the ideal of the trans-European nude culture movement) as effective progressive strategy.

The purpose of introducing Flügel into the argument of *Three Guineas* is not simply to show how Woolf appropriates and revises Flügel's thinking on sartorial psychology. It is also, and more importantly, to throw light on *Three Guineas* as Woolf's engagement with contemporary progressive discourse and tactic as much as with British or Italian/German fascism. Pawlowski's collection of essays decisively makes clear the connection between an obsessively phallocentric culture and phallologocentric language (the fascist poem and the masculine metaphors defining modernist aesthetics), as well as between individual bodies and the body politic (physically efficient bodies functioning in the machinery and spectacle of the organically unified nation). It further demonstrates that the rhetoric of organicism and "coordinated, cooperative and controlled" action also informed supposedly progressive political thought, as evidenced in Labour Party and New Party writings of the late 1920s and early 1930s (Berman 110). Jessica Berman's reading of the New Party journal *Action*, whose editor Harold Nicolson was one of Mosley's strongest early supporters, reveals its aim of "creating a modern State as organic as the human body…. A State in which energy and efficiency are always rewarded, and in which the bungler and the sluggard must go to the wall" (Berman 120). As Berman points out, many early supporters made a quick defection from the New Party, and, one would think, from its proto-fascist tropology, when Mosley's fascist aspirations became known. What is striking, however, and what a focus on the sartorial as trope and theory brings clearly to light, is the extent to which progressive discourse was constructed on, and continued to participate in, appropriations of the body and, more to the point, a body-clothing dichotomy which validates the body as positive term, as principle of modernity, transparency, and truth. Moreover, foregrounding this dichotomy reveals the limits of the progressive analysis of the relation between gendered bodies and socio-symbolic fabrics, and of the civilising and modernising tactics which ensued from it. It also shows Woolf as an unusually sophisticated reader of culture and of the displacements and condensations which make the tangles and infiltrations of discursive networks.

In his contribution to the FPSI Manifesto, Flügel defines the "psychology" that unites the variety of societies and individuals comprised by the federation, as well as setting down the strategy by which such a psychology may be rendered useful. Flügel finds this common psychological foundation in the word "progressive"—a mental attitude described as predominantly scientific and psychological, in contradistinction to the "moral" attitude of other regimes, the "blind reliance on outworn loyalties, conventions, and taboos" necessary to societies run on "rigidly conservative, communist, or fascist lines" ("A Psychology" 302-3). Originating in the super-ego and the primitive instincts of the id, the "moral" attitude is by definition a "rigid and archaic one, which adapts itself only with the utmost difficulty to the changing conditions of modern life" ("A Psychology" 296). The aim of the progressive, like the aim of psychoanalysis, is to modernise the mind by strengthening the control of the ego over the super-ego and the id, making conscious and sublimating the primitive and archaic elements which stand in the way of progress. Creating modern subjects is to achieve a freer, less oppressive society run on principles of reason and science, and ultimately to prevent war.

The civilised modernity represented by conscious reason is asserted by other progressives concerned with the psychology of peace (as opposed to the primitive unreason of the psychology of war), notably in *The Intelligent Man's Way to Prevent War* (1933), edited and introduced by Leonard Woolf. Pointing to "human psychology, the beliefs and desires of human beings," as the ultimate reason for war, the book's contributors propose to consider "these psychological factors and the part which education must play in creating the psychology of peace" (16). Leonard Woolf's related attack on metaphysics and the dangers of the symbol in *Quack, Quack!* (1935) participates in the same promotion of reason and the intellect as protection against resurfacing primitive instincts and morality. *Quack, Quack!* is a tract against quackery, the return of the superstitions of the savage, threatening to displace classical intellectual integrity since the early nineteenth century. Leonard traces such anti-rational tendencies through the Hegelians, Carlyle, Nietzsche, and Bergson, to their culmination in fascist ideology: "the supreme example in modern times of the reversion to savagery and the belief in political magic" (*Quack, Quack!* 37). What a "civilised" man such as Bergson has in common with the fascists and the "quacks"—the god-inspired kings of primitive cultures—is a claim to inspiration combined with symbolic obscurity, the fiction of synthetic intuitions communicable only by symbolisation and analogy. In conveying such intuitions, "the oracle itself has lost all perception of what is imagery and metaphor and simile and what is the truth which it is seeking to express through imagery, metaphor, or simile…the quack himself can no longer distinguish between the symbol and the thing symbolized" (*Quack, Quack!* 133). The state of "inspiration" claimed by the primitive and the fascist Führer alike manifests itself corporeally (as embodiment/performance) and as verbal and visual symbols which deliberately confuse sign and referent and demand instinctive, emotional response. Thus, writes Leonard:

> As soon as the god had entered the king or priest, "the latter became violently agitated, and worked himself up to the highest pitch of apparent frenzy, the muscles of the limbs seemed convulsed, the body swelled, the countenance became

terrific, the features distorted, and the eyes wild and strained".... The Polynesian Führer sometimes "continued for two or three days possessed by the spirit or deity; a piece of native cloth, of a peculiar kind, worn round one arm, was an indication of inspiration, or of the indwelling of the god with the individual who wore it".... In Germany and Italy the inspiration of Hitler and Mussolini is permanent. Hence the wearing of a piece of cloth of a peculiar kind (e.g. inscribed with the swastika) has also become permanent and has been extended from the god-inspired leader to the leader-inspired followers, for it indicates that the wearer has accepted the inspiration either directly or indirectly. (*Quack, Quack!* 45-47; internal quotations from Frazer's *The Golden Bough*).

So far we have seen that both Flügel and Leonard Woolf are concerned with the relations between mind/psychology, discourse/symbolic systems (including visual and verbal symbols), and the body. Their modernising projects spring from the conviction that the "symbol" upholds its authority by the combined forces of id and super-ego, and consist in liberating the conscious mind from the primitive, archaic instincts of the body and the moral response of the super-ego. While Leonard Woolf emphasises the education of the rational mind as a counter-measure to the Nazi's primary object of education, "the rearing of strong bodies" (*Quack, Quack!* 81), Flügel is particularly concerned with the idea that modernising the mind effectively depends on modernising the body. Hence the project of the clothes psychology, of describing how bodies and minds are fashioned by clothing; how bodies signify and perform within a culturo-symbolic order; and how it is possible to sublimate states of interiority onto a bodily exterior.

Integrating clothing into a general theory of human development, Flügel understands dress as a gendered discourse invested with narcissistic/exhibitionistic and phallic symbolic value. On the journey from naked infant to clothed and civilised adult, clothing emerges as an important component in drawing the infant out of the primary, id-dominated condition. Simplified, clothing mediates paternal law, the prohibition placed upon the narcissistic and auto-erotic pleasures the infant gains from his or her naked body. Clothing also signifies the individual's position with respect to the phallus. The case among primitive people for men to be more decorated than women, and the remnants of this in some European customs, suggests that men are inherently more inclined to decoration and women more inclined to modesty in dress. Traces of the primitive state are seen in military and ecclesiastical hierarchies and in academic robes, also in the forms of social convention which require men to temporarily remove a garment as a sign of respect, for example the hat on entering a church. Thus, "In men, castration itself is symbolised by the removal of garments, while the possession or display of the corresponding garments serves, in virtue of their phallic symbolism, as a reassurance against the fears of castration" (*Psychology of Clothes* 104-5).

In modern times, according to Flügel, sexual difference divides along different lines. Apart from the anachronistic remnants of primitive phallic display referred to above, modern males are ruled by clothes regimes abounding "in features which symbolise [man's] devotion to the principles of duty, renunciation, self-control" (*Psychology of Clothes* 113), effectively preventing sublimation of infantile narcissism onto clothing. Sublimated narcissism of this kind is understood to be of benefit to the individual and culture, carrying a certain ego-liberating, hence progressive, potential. In contrast to male renunciation of narcissism, the so-called "sartorial emancipation" of women, as Flügel theorises it, has introduced modes of dress which combine a principle of decorative clothing with exposure of the naked body (as with the décolleté) (*Psychology of Clothes* 105). This is to say that women's fashion allows for sublimated narcissism as well as the auto-erotic pleasures, the skin-and-muscle eroticism, of actual exposure. The auto-erotic element, argues Flügel, brings women's fashion into line with the rationale of the nude culture movement and its emphasis on the auto-erotic constituents of the pleasures connected with the naked body—a modern attitude to the relations between clothes and body "that appears to be quite foreign to the primitive mind" (*Psychology of Clothes* 225).

The route to modern bodies and progressive psychology as Flügel maps it, goes via modes of dress which permit sublimation while removing undue elements of corporeal discipline and primitive phallic display. The final step, however, depends on realising the reality principle of "the natural corporeal body," persisting under our artificial sartorial one, as the "essential, permanent, and inescapable element of our being"—a reality principle, moreover, to which "the new science of eugenics, emphasising the importance of sexual selection for future human welfare, adds its own argument" (*Psychology of Clothes* 222-23). Flügel's prediction of a nude future and his ideas on the connection between nudity and modern, civilised and pacifist subjects, was supported by other theorists of clothing in the 1920s and 30s (including Havelock Ellis, Gerald Heard, and John Langdon Davies), as well as by the Gymnic and nudist movement which was among the affiliated societies of the FPSI. By 1933 the British Gymnic Association was expressing concern that Hitler's suppression of *Freikörperkultur* and *Nacktkultur* in Germany was a prelude to "a revival of war-fervour" (*Gymnos* 12). Civilised nudity, as Flügel and the FPSI saw it in 1933, was an attitude correlative with mother-regarding, rather than father-regarding feelings towards the surrounding environment and the State, hence with the protective, nourishing and democratic associations of Mother Nature and the Mother country, rather than with the repressive paternalism of *das Vaterland*.

Returning to *Three Guineas* from progressive discourse in the early 1930s, it is clear that what may at one point have seemed like Woolf's idiosyncratic patchwork of sartorial symbolism, narcissism, castration fears, the Pauline precept, patriarchal power, and fascism, has both precedents and analogues. In some respects, notably in her semiotic analysis of ceremonial dress, and of clothing as an alternation of modesty and display centred on the principle of the phallus, Woolf's argument can be seen to resemble Flügel's. Woolf's radical intervention in this theory, however, occurs through two acts of substitution: the everyday word "vanity" for the psychoanalyst's "narcissism," and the history of chastity for the history of female sartorial emancipation. Firstly, calling narcissism vanity is in a sense to unclothe it by recalling its trivial and effeminising connotations. Woolf places vanity in its male and female forms in a gendered economy of exchange value, in which the modes of display which advertise women's value on the marriage market or as trophies and accessories to the male, are essentially no different from the way educated men wear their robes and regalia—like "the tickets in a grocer's shop"—to exhibit their value to the gross national product (*TG* 24). Dress as women use it "is comparatively simple. Besides the prime function of covering the body, it has two other offices—that it creates beauty for the eye, and that it attracts the admiration of [the male] sex. Since marriage until the year

1919...was the only profession open to us, the enormous importance of dress to a woman can hardly be exaggerated" (*TG* 24). Male dress has a similar "advertisement function," as the essay shows by juxtaposing the stars and ribbons which advertise men's intellect to powder and paint, a woman's chief method of advertising her professional asset, and by setting the sum paid for a knighthood next to the sum paid for a yearly dress allowance.

The argument is not against taking pleasure in beauty or aesthetic display. However, when what is displayed is power and privilege, and when exhibitionism depends on casting the other in a subordinate role, vanity emerges as the symptom of a pathology which mars individual as well as cultural history. The essayist's appropriation of psychoanalytic terms traces the origin of male vanity in "subconscious ideas of woman as 'man manqué,'" in infantile fixation (on the phallus), and in the castration complex (*TG* 144). Woolf reflects at length on the Pauline precept as a primal scene of law, revealing the subconscious motivations behind St. Paul's "famous pronouncement upon the matter of veils" (the foundational text for the ruling Western conception of chastity) in the castration fears "of the virile or dominant type, so familiar at present in Germany":

> Chastity then as defined by St. Paul is seen to be a complex conception, based upon the love of long hair; the love of subjection; the love of an audience; the love of laying down the law, and, subconsciously, upon a very strong and natural desire that the woman's mind and body shall be reserved for the use of one man and one only. (*TG* 186-87)

As the woman is of and for the man, according to St. Paul, "for this cause ought the woman to have a sign of authority on her head" (*TG* 187). For him to be in secure possession of the phallus she must bear the sign of his authority.

Woolf goes on to trace the manifestations of infantile fixation—culturally sanctioned and supported—in a range of areas and discourses. Her concern, undoubtedly, is to show that the Pauline argument and its infiltration with the ideological and material interests of patriarchy is a web which still traps us. It is this historical continuum of unacknowledged desire and castration fears which makes her sceptical of progressive schemes of modernising the ego. The clothes regimes Flügel describes as remnants of a primitivism destined to be dispelled by modernity's liberating force, are shown by Woolf to have continued actuality. Women's sartorial emancipation is revealed as the modern obverse of chastity, involved in the same economy of demand and exchange. In the nineteenth century to be veiled was to be "accompanied by a male or a maid" (*TG* 188). To the maid acting as veil in public, the knowledge that "she was putting into practice the commands laid down by St. Paul [and] doing her utmost to deliver her mistress's body intact to her master" may have offered some solace but even so, "in the darkness of the beetle-haunted basement she must sometimes have bitterly reproached St. Paul on the one hand for his chastity, and the gentlemen of Piccadilly on the other for their lust" (*TG* 186). Nowadays, concedes Woolf, "chastity has undergone considerable revision," though not to the point of a real emancipation. In fact, as she notes ironically, "there is said to be a reaction in favour of some degree of chastity for both sexes. This is partly due to economic causes; the protection of chastity by maids is an expensive item in the bourgeois budget" (*TG* 189). The threads and filaments of desire, phallic power, and the economic as well as psychological advantages of marking women's bodies as the property of one man and hence prohibited to others, still persist.

*Three Guineas*'s second letter, asking for the second guinea, comes as a request for cast-off garments for "women whose professions require that they should have presentable day and evening dresses which they can ill afford to buy" (*TG* 179). Debating with herself whether to contribute her guinea to dressing women for the professions, with the prospect of one day being allowed to wear a judge's wig, an ermine cape, a military uniform, the essayist reflects that opening the professions to women is in effect to substitute one system of exchange value (work) for another (sex). Moreover, this new exchange system comes with a set of ties—dog collars, ribbons, and badges inscribed with the duties of God and Empire—which chastity did not have. With a choice between the veil and the dog collar, and the recognition of a degree of freedom behind the veil—the freedom of "derision" as well as freedom from "unreal loyalties" (*TG* 90)—chastity is a real option. In the end, the essayist's guinea comes with the condition that bodily chastity is translated, not into Flügel's narcissism and nudity, but into mental chastity: the state of dressing for the professions without marrying them, of remaining sceptical of patriarchy's symbolic systems and their enunciative force, retaining the defamiliarizing gaze from behind the veil.

In some sense Virginia's "mental chastity" would seem to coincide with Leonard's recommended tactic of setting sceptical reason against the susceptibility to symbols—the piece of cloth around the arm or the intuition conveyed as trope or analogy. In light of Virginia's thinking on language, however, the impossibility of such coincidence becomes apparent. It is hardly surprising that Virginia has a different conception of the traffics of language than Leonard. She knows that words are "out and about" and that they consummate their own "swift marriages," as she puts it in "Craftsmanship"(*DM* 129, 132). It is a marriage of this kind—brought about by the rhythmic, intertextual, syntagmatic flux of the unselfconscious mind, freed from the grip of vanity—that she sets against the fascist "abortion" and the capitalised Symbol in *A Room of One's Own*: "a girl in patent leather boots" and "a young man in a maroon overcoat" swept together by the current of traffic to "celebrate their nuptials in darkness" (98, 92, 99). In Leonard's thinking, naked language, the vehicle of transparent reasoning, is what redeems civilisation from the inspired bodies of metaphysical and ideological quackery, and from the useful bodies of the fascist machinery of war. Virginia's understanding of linguistic mediacy and writerly *texere* allows her to see that Symbols will not be dispelled by decree of reason, civilisation, or the ego, nor in the name of a rhetoric of transparency in which the relations between symbol and referent are unequivocally clear. Boundaries between Symbol and symbol, naked and dressed language, the speaking subject and the symbolic order, will not let themselves be upheld. What this amounts to, as we know, is that the artist's understanding of language and the feminist's commitment to an analysis of power make Virginia an unusually sophisticated reader of signifying fabrics and discursive webs. Thus, where Flügel and other progressives assume a relatively simple boundary between, on the one hand, disciplined bodies and primitive minds in the service of the *Vaterland*, and on the other, modernised bodies and civilised minds as agents in the Mother country, Virginia reveals transnational tangles of dressed bodies under the sign of the phallus.

The question remains, then, what type of symbolic practice is involved in the strategy of "mental chastity." Partly, this practice is suggested by the rhetoric of *Three Guineas* itself—

the patchwork of the serious and the trivial, the public and the private, past and present, fact and fiction, which uncovers and untangles threads. Further, it is suggested by the education in signification the essayist envisages for the poor college, where will be taught

> the arts of human intercourse; the art of understanding other people's lives and minds, and the little arts of talk, of dress, of cookery, that are allied with them. The aim of the new college, the cheap college, should be not to segregate and specialize, but to combine. It should explore the ways in which mind and body can be made to cooperate; discover what new combinations make good wholes in human life. (*TG* 40)

What seems to be envisaged here is a redefined humanism and a signifying practice based on combinations rather than boundaries, on human intercourse rather than the dominance of the phallus, and, ultimately, on the ethics and aesthetics of the gift. Perhaps we may imagine it in the flux and flow of Clarissa Dalloway's mermaid dress, at once transformative and unifying, or in the hat, the little work of art, made by the Italian milliner and the victim of war, not to deck out the woman as a spectacle for consumption or to advertise her value, but as a gift of beauty. Here, it seems, the sartorial has moved out of the shadow of the phallus to take up its place at last as one of the "little arts."

**Works Cited**

Berman, Jessica. "Of Oceans and Opposition: *The Waves*, Oswald Mosley, and the New Party." Pawlowski 105-21.
Flügel, J. S. "A Psychology for Progressives: How Can They Become Effective?" Joad et al. 292-313.
———. *The Psychology of Clothes*. The International Psycho-Analytical Library No. 18. London: Hogarth, 1930.
———. *The Psycho-Analytic Study of the Family*. The International Psycho-Analytical Library No. 3. London: Hogarth, 1921.
*Gymnos: The Official Organ of the Gymnic Association of Great Britain*. Vol. 1. No. 4. London: May 1933.
Joad, C.E.M. et al. *Manifesto: Being the Book of the Federation of Progressive Societies and Individuals*. London: Allen and Unwin, 1933.
Neverow, Vara. "Freudian Seduction and the Fallacies of Dictatorship." Pawlowski 56-72.
Pawlowski, Merry M., ed. *Virginia Woolf and Fascism: Resisting the Dictator's Seduction*. London: Palgrave, 2001.
Rosenfeld, Natania. "Monstrous Conjugations: Images of Dictatorship in the Anti-Fascist Writings of Virginia and Leonard Woolf." Pawlowski 122-36.
Woolf, Leonard, ed. *The Intelligent Man's Way to Prevent War*. London: Gollancz, 1933.
———. *Quack, Quack!* New York: Harcourt, Brace, 1935.
Woolf, Virginia. *The Death of the Moth and Other Essays*. London: Hogarth, 1942.
———. *A Room of One's Own*. London: Granada, 1977.
———. *Three Guineas*. London: Hogarth, 1991.

# Woolf, Rooks, and Rural England

## by Ian Blyth

Perfect day; completely blue without cloud or wind, as if settled for ever. Watched dog herding sheep. Rooks beginning to fly over the trees, both morning & evening. (*D1* 48)

The rook (*Corvus frugilegus*) is a member of the crow family, in fact it is often mistaken for a crow: the name scarecrow and the expression "as the crow flies" both having their origins in the habits of rooks, rather than their more well-known cousins (Greenoak 192). A rook is about the same size as a carrion crow, but with glossy black plumage which, in the right conditions, reflects the sun in oily patches of blue, green, reddish-brown, and violet-tinged purple. Rooks have a small tufted peak at the crown of the skull and loose feathers, resembling baggy shorts, round the tops of their legs. Their most distinguishing feature is a bare, grey-white, bone-coloured patch on the face, which generally extends about halfway along the beak. Rooks are gregarious creatures, gathering with other birds in large woodland roosts for the winter, and for much of the year can be found in rookeries—colonies of nests perched in the very topmost branches of a row of trees, traditionally elms, though oak and ash also have a long history of use (Jefferies 265). A typical rookery can be home to up to a hundred birds, sometimes considerably more.[1] The strangely harmonious cacophony that results is reflected in some of the collective nouns associated with rooks: a parliament, a building, a clamour, a congregation, a storytelling. The main call, or caw, of the rook is softer, less harsh than that of a crow: the rook's Scots dialect name, *craa*, is as good an approximation as any (Cocker and Mabey 413). Though not adverse to carrion, the rook's diet mainly consists of seeds and insects, with apples and acorns as seasonal supplements (Coombs 106). Like the lapwing and skylark, it is a bird of the rural landscape—cleared woodland, rich pasture, tilled earth; rooks are rarely, if at all, seen in great numbers in urban sprawls or remote wilderness locations (Cocker and Mabey ix, 414). The rook is a very British bird. It is perhaps the most British of all birds, for while they are found in much of Europe, as E. M. Nicholson observed in 1951: "Except in a few parts of France I have never personally found rooks on the Continent…in numbers which would be considered normal in England. Whether to be thronged with rooks is a blessing or a curse, it is certainly something which the British Isles enjoy or suffer beyond all experience elsewhere" (41–42).

Woolf's writing also throngs with rooks. Of the books published in her lifetime, only *Monday or Tuesday*, *A Room of One's Own*, the first *Common Reader* and *Roger Fry* are *sans* rooks. Now, it must be admitted that various other birds appear from time to time—sparrows, woodpigeons, swallows, starlings—but none occurs with the consistent regularity of Woolf's rooks. For instance, rooks are the only species of bird present in every one of her novels. Sometimes they have minor roles, tucked away in the background. Sometimes they are right there in the foreground, invested with significance. Think of Ralph Denham's pet rook in *Night and Day*; or the section of *Jacob's Room* given over to a description of rooks settling down for the night (*JR* 73–74); or Joseph and Mary in *To the Lighthouse*; or Orlando's reaction upon hearing Shelmerdine's name for the first time:

> "I knew it!" she said, for there was something romantic and chivalrous, passionate, melancholy, yet determined about him which went with the wild, dark-plumed name—a name which had, in her mind, the steel-blue gleam of rooks' wings, the hoarse laughter of their caws, the snake-like twisting descent of their feathers in a silver pool. (*O* 239)

Woolf's love of rooks can be traced to her childhood, to her earliest memories. In "A Sketch of the Past" she recalls hearing both "the waves breaking" and "the caw of rooks falling from a great height" above Talland House (*MOB* 66), and it is surely no coincidence that the rookish part of this memory resurfaces at the start of *To the Lighthouse*: the sound of "rooks cawing" being one of the things "so coloured and distinguished in [James Ramsay's] mind that he already had his private code, his secret language" (*TTL* 7). It is there again, in *Three Guineas*, when Woolf—having called for a rejection of patriotism—describes a lingering "drop of pure, if irrational" national feeling; a feeling, she explains, that takes the form of "some love of England dropped into a child's ears by the cawing of rooks in an elm tree, by the splash of waves on a beach, or by English voices murmuring nursery rhymes" (*TG* 234). Woolf's diffuse sense of Englishness is in tune with the natural world. Her rooks appear to function as a form of metonymy, a shorthand for rural England. They find their way into the most unlikely of places, such as the thoughts of an elderly English couple who have just eaten lunch in a South American hotel:

> There was then a very long pause, which threatened to be final, when, mercifully, a bird about the size of a magpie, but of metallic blue colour, appeared on the section of the terrace that could be seen from where they sat. Mrs Thornbury was led to enquire whether we should like it if all our rooks were blue—"What do *you* think, William?" she asked, touching her husband on the knee.
> "If all our rooks were blue," he said,—he raised his glasses; he actually placed them on his nose,—"they would not live long in Wiltshire." (*VO* 277–78)

Again and again, when Woolf wishes to convey, in a single brushstroke, some sense of rural England, she turns to "the usual country gabble" (*TW* 224): "rooks flaunting up and down in the pink evening light" (*MD* 29–30), "rooks dropping cool cries from the high blue" (*TTL* 19), "homing rooks" (*O* 15), "rooks rising and falling, and catching the elm-trees in their net" (*TW* 119), "rooks, sitting huddled black on the tree-tops" (*TY* 207), rooks who would "now and then let fall a queer little croak" (*TY* 287). Yet these most scruffy and unglamorous of British birds are also present at moments of great national significance. For instance, Woolf's diary entry for Armistice Day, 11 November 1918, begins thus:

> Twentyfive minutes ago the guns went off, announcing peace. A siren hooted on the river. They are hooting still. A few people ran to look out of windows. The rooks wheeled round, & were for a moment, the symbolic look of creatures performing some ceremony, partly of thanksgiving, partly of valediction over the grave. (*D1* 216)

G. K. Yeates, who in the 1930s was the first person to conduct a year-long survey of the rook's life cycle, remarks that he "would not exchange a 'seat' at a rookery for the best entertainment in London"; "all the time," he explains, "there is life and action" (20). Gilbert White delighted in seeing them "sport and dive in a playful manner," or hearing them make "a pleasing murmur, very engaging to the imagination, and not unlike the cry of a pack of hounds in hollow, echoing woods…or the tumbling of the tide upon a pebbly shore" (270). Richard Jefferies includes various anecdotes about personal encounters with rooks in *Wild Life in a Southern County* (1879)—the county in question being Mr. Thornbury's Wiltshire. Any excuse to introduce rooks is taken up. W. H. Hudson's *Birds in London* (1898) is as much concerned with the birds that are absent from the city as with those that live there; "utter, irretrievable disaster has fallen on the inner London rookeries," he writes, before giving a detailed account of tame rook found "injured in a park in Oxfordshire" and adopted by an elderly lady who would visit London in the summer:

> Early every morning he flew into her bedroom by the open window, and alighting on her bed would deposit a small offering on the pillow—a horse-chestnut bur, a little crooked stick, a bleached rabbit bone, a bit of rusty iron, which he had picked up and regarded as a suitable present. Whatever it was, it had to be accepted with demonstrations of gratitude and affection. If she took no notice he would lift it up and replace it again, calling her attention to it with little subdued exclamations which sounded like words, and if she feigned sleep he would gently pull her hair or tap her cheek with his bill to awake her. Once the present was accepted he would nestle in under her arm and remain so, very contentedly, until she got up…. One day his mistress was walking in the Row, at an hour when it was full of fashionable people, and the rook, winging his way homewards from the gardens spied her, and circling down, alighted on her shoulders, to the amazement of all who witnessed the incident. "What an astonishing thing!" exclaimed some person in the crowd that gathered round her. "Oh, not at all," answered the lady, caressing the bird with her hand, while he rubbed his beak against her cheek; "if you were as fond of the birds as I am, and treated them as well, they would be glad to come down on to your shoulders, too." (52, 54–56)

It is quite possible this account served as the inspiration for Ralph Denham's pet rook in *Night and Day*—the coincidence of imagery is certainly striking.[2] Like Hudson's "injured" Oxfordshire rook, Ralph's was rescued after "A cat had bitten one of its legs" (*ND* 400). Again like Hudson's rook, we are told that "The bird, encouraged by a scratch behind the ear, settled upon Denham's shoulder," and then stays there, for "some minutes, in the course of which neither he nor the rook took their eyes off the fire" (21). Ralph later tries to show Mary how he can get one of the sparrows in Lincoln's Inn Fields "to sit on [his] arm" (164); and for Katharine, whose "attention" is first drawn to Ralph's rook by its making "A little dry chirp from the corner of the room" (399), it is the emphasis placed on this encounter that reveals to her mother the truth about her daughter's feelings:

> Mrs Hilbery elicited the facts that not only was the house of excruciating ugliness, which Ralph bore without complaint, but it was evident that everyone depended on him, and he had a room at the top of the house, with a wonderful

view of London, and a rook.

"A wretched old bird in a corner, with half its feathers out," she said, with a tenderness in her voice that seemed to commiserate the sufferings of humanity while resting assured in the capacity of Ralph Denham to alleviate them, so that Mrs Hilbery could not help exclaiming:

"But, Katharine, you *are* in love!" (506–7)

When not appearing in person, Woolf's rooks are a rich source of simile. An acquaintance, W. J. Turner, is described as being "like a tipsy rook" (*L3* 330); the arrival of "a great many old friends," including Desmond MacCarthy and E. M. Forster, is referred to as "the homing of the rooks: we're all settling on the trees" (*L5* 160). Flush encounters an Inner London slum dwelling, a "Rookery," where "human beings swarmed on top of each other as rooks swarm and blacken tree-tops" (*F* 53).[3] Eleanor Pargiter watches from the top of a London bus as the women shopping in the street below move about "like rooks swooping in a field, rising and falling" (*TY* 91); the image returns to her when she goes to watch Morris in the courtroom (104–5), whereas for her cousin Kitty, it is the audience at the opera house who "were like birds settling on a field" (173). And then, at the conclusion of the pageant in *Between the Acts*, when the Reverend Streatfield appears on the stage, it is "As if a rook had hopped unseen to a prominent bald branch" (171).

As a letter to her sister on 18 May 1929 reveals, Woolf found the antics of rooks to be an endless source of fascination: "the gossip is coming, though I'm very cold, sitting in my lodge, looking at the rooks building—but that you dont want to hear about—Whats Rooks to me, or me to Rookeries you say, quoting Shakespeare, as your way is" (*L5* 58).[4] In her writing about rooks, Woolf can be seen struggling to bridge the gap between image and word. For instance, consider Mrs. Ramsay, watching Joseph and Mary: "the air was shoved aside by their black wings and cut into exquisite scimitar shapes. The movement of the wings beating out, out, out—she could never describe it accurately enough to please herself—was one of the loveliest of all to her" (*TTL* 66–67). Or Woolf herself, writing in her diary at Monk's House on 12 August 1928:

> Even now, I have to watch the rooks beating up against the wind, which is high. & still I say to myself instinctively "Whats the phrase for that?" & try to make more & more vivid the roughness of the air current & the tremor of the rooks wing <deep breasting it> slicing—as if the air were full of ridges & ripples & roughness; they rise & sink, up & down, as if the exercise <pleased them> rubbed & braced them like swimmers in rough water. But what a little I can get down with my pen of what is so vivid to my eyes. (*D3* 191)

Imperfect it may be, but such "imperfection" is grounded in the limits of language rather than in the shortcomings of the writer. By anyone's standard, this is a meticulously observed, beautifully described short passage of nature writing—one of many such passages scattered throughout Woolf's work. As those who have been lucky enough to see such a performance for themselves can testify, "swimmers in rough water" is an excellent attempt at what is in truth impossible: conveying in words the shapes in the sky made by rooks when flying—or rather "playing"—in high winds.[5] Indeed, I would argue that Woolf's description stands up to comparison with any other in the field. Here is Richard Jefferies's account of a similar scene:

> At another time a flock will go up and wheel about in the strangest irregular manner. Every now and then one will extend his wings, holding them rigid, and dive downwards, in his headlong descent wavering to and fro like a sheet of paper falling edge first. He falls at a great pace, and looks as if he must be dashed to pieces against a tree or the earth; but he rights himself at the last moment, and glides away and up again with ease. Occasionally two or three rooks may be seen doing this at once, while the rest whirl about as if possessed; and those that are diving utter a gurgling sound like the usual cawk prolonged—"caw-wouk." (276–77)

Like all good nature writing, Woolf's emerges from a day by day, week by week, year by year familiarity with her subject. "I think both Jefferies and Hudson succeed because they are very careful about what they observe," she advises her nephew Julian Bell on 16 October 1927, adding: "I mean they do not make a catalogue of things, but chose this that and the other" (*L3* 432). Woolf would have had plenty of opportunity to follow her own advice. The letters and diary entries in which she describes watching rooks were all written in Sussex.[6] It is also probable, with the notable exception of *Night and Day*, that the detailed descriptions of rooks in her essays and fiction were—at the very least—initially drafted in this rural locality.[7] This is significant, because whether she was staring out of the window of her writing lodge, playing bowls on the lawn, or walking across the Downs, the sight and sound of rooks would have been an integral part of Woolf's day. As was indicated above, these are agricultural birds: birds whose presence in the rural landscape is as commonplace as that of buses, streetlamps, and human beings in an urban vista. Their presence might not always be registered on a wholly conscious level, but they are missed when absent. It is little wonder, then, that rooks are to be found at the heart of Woolf's vision of rural England, a vision expressed in her diary entry for 27 March 1937 (written, of course, at Monk's House in Rodmell):

> Merely scribbling here, over a log fire, on a cold but bright Easter morning; sudden shafts of sun, a scatter of snow on the hills early; sudden storms, ink black, octopus pouring, coming up; & the rooks fidgetting & pecking in the elm trees.... Curiously a combination, this garden, with the Church, & the cross of the Church black against Asheham Hill. That is all the elements of the English brought together, accidentally. (*D5* 72)[8]

**Notes**

1. Nicholson records that "in England...a colony of 500 nests is exceptional.... Yet in Scotland there are plenty of colonies running up to 1,000 nests or more, and the rookery in Crow Wood at Hatton Castle near Turiff in Aberdeenshire gave a total of 6,085 nests at the 1945 count. This is probably the largest breeding colony of any land bird in Great Britain" (40–41).
2. One factor that might argue against this suggestion is that the copy of *Birds in London* found in the Woolfs' library is the 1924 reprint (King and Miletic-Vejzovic 108), but then Woolf was certainly reading Hudson prior to this—she reviewed his autobiography, *Far Away and Long Ago*, for the *TLS* on 26 September 1918 (see *E2* 298–303)—and the presence of this 1924 reprint does not in itself rule out the possibility that she read the 1898 first edition at some point prior to writing *Night and Day*.
3. In this instance, Woolf is also drawing on the work of Thomas Beames, whose *The Rookeries of London: Past, Present and Prospective* (1850) she recommends to those seeking "an account of London Rookeries" (*F* 107).

4. The allusion is to *Hamlet*, 2.2.553: "What's Hecuba to him, or he to her." I am grateful to a member of the audience in Birmingham for pointing this out.
5. On this question of "play," Coombs notes: "Rooks sometimes make tumbling dives…most commonly in windy weather.…This seems to be 'play' as several species may take part, mixed flocks of rooks and jackdaws, sometimes with ravens and carrion crows, and even herring gulls fly to and fro along the hillside, rising with the updraught and diving and turning down again" (91).
6. See *L2* 64, *L4* 58, *L6* 316, *D1* 48, *D1* 216, *D3* 190–91, *D4* 41, *D5* 72.
7. See, for example, *JR* 73–74, *TTL* 66–68, *O* 236–37, *DM* 9; see also the fleeting reference to "the rooks of Gray's Inn passing overhead" (*JR* 121). The last of the Inner London rookeries, the Gray's Inn rookery dated back to at least the sixteenth century, and Woolf would have seen these rooks on many occasions during her early years in the city; however, their presence in *Jacob's Room* is an "historical" reference: the rookery was abandoned in 1915 (see Nicholson 46).
8. This essay was prepared for publication during an AHRC-funded research fellowship in the School of English, St Andrews. My thanks to Fiona Benson, Annie Kelly, Rich King, Jim Stewart, Emma Sutton, Beth Wright and everyone else who commented on the text and passed on items of folklore, poems, etchings and sightings of rooks.

## Works Cited

Beames, Thomas. *The Rookeries of London: Past, Present and Prospective*. London: Bosworth, 1850.
Cocker, Mark and Richard Mabey. *Birds Britannica*. London: Chatto & Windus, 2005.
Coombs, Franklin. *The Crows: A Study of the Corvids of Europe*. London: Batsford, 1978.
Greenoak, Francesca. *British Birds: Their Folklore, Names and Literature*. London: Christopher Helm, 1997.
Hudson, W. H. *Birds in London*. London: Dent, 1898. Rpt. 1924.
Jefferies, Richard. *Wild Life in a Southern County*. London: Nelson, 1879. Rpt. 1918.
King, Julia and Laila Miletic-Vejzovic. *The Library of Leonard and Virginia Woolf: A Short-Title Catalog*. Pullman: Washington State UP, 2003.
Nicholson, E. M. *Birds and Men: The Bird Life of British Towns, Villages, Gardens & Farmland*. London: Collins, 1951.
White, Gilbert. *The Natural History of Selborne*. London: Oxford UP, 1971.
Woolf, Virginia. *Between the Acts*. Ed. Frank Kermode. Oxford: Oxford UP, 2000.
———. *The Death of the Moth and Other Essays*. Ed. Leonard Woolf. London: Hogarth Press/Readers Union, 1943.
———. *The Diary of Virginia Woolf*. Ed. Anne Olivier Bell with Andrew McNeillie. 5 vols. London: Hogarth, 1977–1984.
———. *The Essays of Virginia Woolf*. Ed. Andrew McNeillie. 4 vols. to date. London: Hogarth, 1986-1994.
———. *Flush*. Ed. Kate Flint. Oxford: Oxford UP, 2000.
———. *Jacob's Room*. Ed. Kate Flint. Oxford: Oxford UP, 2000.
———. *The Letters of Virginia Woolf*. Ed. Nigel Nicolson and Joanne Trautmann. 6 vols. London: Hogarth, 1975–1980.
———. *Moments of Being*. Ed. Joanne Schulkind. 2nd ed. San Diego: Harcourt Brace, 1985.
———. *Mrs. Dalloway*. Ed. David Bradshaw. Oxford: Oxford UP, 2000.
———. *Night and Day*. Ed. Suzanne Raitt. Oxford: Oxford UP, 2000.
———. *Orlando: A Biography*. Ed. Rachel Bowlby. Oxford: Oxford UP, 2000.
———. *A Room of One's Own* and *Three Guineas*. Ed. Michèle Barrett. London: Penguin, 1993.
———. *To the Lighthouse*. Ed. David Bradshaw. Oxford: Oxford UP, 2006.
———. *The Voyage Out*. Ed. Lorna Sage. Oxford: Oxford UP, 2001.
———. *The Waves*. Ed. Gillian Beer. Oxford: Oxford UP, 1998.
———. *The Years*. Ed. Hermione Lee. Oxford: Oxford UP, 2000.
Yeates, G. K. *The Life of the Rook*. London: Philip Allan, 1934.

# WOOLF AND THE OTHERS AT THE ZOO

## by Richard Espley

This enquiry into Virginia Woolf at London Zoo is part of wider research into the significance of the Zoo for modernist writers and artists. Woolf, however, is perhaps pre-eminent in the group I am studying, in reputation but also in persistence of interest in this ambiguous animal space in the city. Mentioned not only throughout her diaries and letters, but also *Hyde Park Gate News*, the Gardens were known to her all her life. Her father, Sir Leslie Stephen, was a Fellow of the Zoological Society for over forty years, and Woolf later purchased Fellowship for Leonard, suggesting that it would be a "refuge…to sit with the baboons" (*L4* 269). Moreover, as Kate Flint phrases it, "Animals—real, imaginary, and metaphorical—were a constant presence in Virginia Woolf's life" (xii). This quotation provides an excellent first reason for focussing on the Zoo in particular, in the need to unpack those three categories. In the inter-war years London Zoo offered the visitor an unparalleled display of "real animals." However, certainly outside the Zoo gates and perhaps inside them, that animal ran, and runs, with an imaginary and metaphorical pack that threatens to obscure it utterly. These notions are often so pervasive in the culture as to pass unnoticed, so that Flint states that Woolf sometimes uses animals "to express anger, or passion, or violence: elemental responses which exist across species" (xv). This assumed commonality of strong emotion may be a widespread idea, but it is highly tendentious nonetheless. It is true that human violence and human sexual passion, and their capacity to disrupt an ordered human society, are ubiquitously expressed through the animal. However, this is reliant upon a confident assumption of knowledge of the interiority of the animal, a certainty that these alien creatures are motivated by drives with which we can empathise. As Erica Fudge notes, it is a "powerful desire of all humans—children and adults—to get into the minds of animals" (75). However, George Bataille, after a lifetime of considering the significance of the animal, insisted that to attempt to perceive the world of the animal was to "only call up a vision in which we see nothing" (21). Indeed, he stated that "nothing…is more closed to us than this animal life from which we are descended" (22). However, he simultaneously conceded that the "animal opens before me a depth that attracts me and is familiar to me" (22). That depth is repeatedly filled with what he termed "the poetic fallacy of animality" (22), a fallacy which Flint arguably repeats in her assumption of anger and passion. It is a discourse which has little rational justification, but is best regarded as an inherited and confused metaphor; as Keith Tester convincingly phrases it, animality is "not actually some trace of a common mammalian ancestry" but "simply that which the creators of morality did not do" (95-96). I want to explore the way in which Woolf and one of her contemporaries used the Zoo to explore and perhaps dispute this poetic fallacy.

The institution has always been inextricably entangled in this cultural confusion over the animal; alongside the "real" scientific Zoological Gardens, there is a "metaphorical" Zoo that is a seething hotbed of animality. Several writers used this latter image uncritically, but perhaps most notably David Garnett in his 1924 novel *A Man in the Zoo*. This text's major characters, John and Josephine, visit the Zoo as a courting couple, but soon argue about their relationship. Josephine angrily insists that from love of her family, she is "not going to live with you, or do anything they would mind if they found out" (5). She accuses him of being a "wild beast" (7), and in response he surrenders himself to the Zoological Society, which accepts him as an extremely popular exhibit. After a series of tense interviews through the bars, Josephine eventually accepts her status as beast as much as John's, and begs entrance to his cage, saying "be damned to everyone else…. Nobody can make me feel ashamed now" (91). This realisation brings about resolution, for the Zoo reveals that John's contract releases him should he ever become engaged to be married, and they pass out into a "crowd…chiefly composed of couples like themselves" (94). There is an obvious subtext here, as with Garnett's earlier novel, *Lady Into Fox* (1922), that human sexuality is somehow inherently animalistic and requires freeing from social repression; Garnett's own expression of the poetic fallacy of animality. However, it is important to recognise that in both instances, it is principally female sexuality which is explored. As Michael L. Ross notes with a shared enthusiasm, Garnett believed that liberation could come through female characters "hearkening to the call of the wild" (229). However, Garnett also fears the full animal force that he detects in woman. This is clearest in the figure of the orang-utan which occupies the cage next to John's, and which is repeatedly, and uniquely among the Zoo creatures, emphasised as female. In a fit of jealous rage, it embraces John in a symbolically emasculating sexual attack, "slowly grinding his fingers to a mere pulp" (69). Female sexuality, therefore, must hearken to the call of the wild, but, for the good of Man, not surrender to it.

I am using Garnett here as a representative of an ancient and resistant tradition of women as the embodiment of the transgressive power of the poetic fallacy of animality. As Carol Adams and Josephine Donovan remark in a historical review of the feminine and the animal, since classical times "the ideological justification for women's alleged inferiority has been made by appropriating them to animals" (1). It is Woolf's reaction to this metaphor, and to the patriarchal claim to own and manipulate it, which lies at the heart of her consideration of the Zoo. Woolf unconvincingly assured Garnett that she preferred *A Man in the Zoo* to his earlier work "though its [*sic*] clumsier and less accomplished." She also told him that "Your humans are a little stiff I think" (*L3* 99-100), a damning criticism of a novel where, despite its setting, there are only two minor animal "characters." However, Woolf understood all too well the fallacies which underpin Garnett's plot before she had read his novel, for she had depicted the significatory dangers of London Zoo five years previously, in *Night and Day*. The novel's heroine, Katharine, her secretly estranged fiancé William, her potential lover Denham, and her cousin Cassandra, all make an unsuccessful trip to the Zoo. At first, there appears to be no hint of animality as, alone with Denham, Katharine gazes at the bears and sees seeming humans. She asks, "I wonder if these animals are happy," and then buys buns, and is seen happily "breaking the bun into parts and tossing them down the bears' throats" (386-87). However, the Zoo as locus of murky atavistic desire is soon evident, but only through male eyes. Denham sees his beloved "against a background of pale grottos and sleek hides; camels slanted their heavy-lidded eyes at her" (387), and easily appreciates her as the bestial woman, in communion with the non-human. He later "saw her bending over pythons coiled upon the sand" and gazing at "slim green snakes stabbing the wall again and again with their flickering cleft tongues" (387-88). The snake as clichéd image of disruptive female eroticism hardly requires comment. Katharine becomes increasingly under his gaze a sexual force of nature, so that in the aquarium, "squadrons of silvery fish...ogled her...quivering their tails straight out" (387).

Thus, Woolf almost depicts two Zoos herself, one where the infantilised bears are for Katharine a cause for concern, and one where the male sexual gaze finds the animals both a fitting backdrop and an enlivening stimulus to the fetishisation of inhuman woman. From a writer who would barbedly describe women as "the most discussed animal in the universe" (*AROO* 34), we might expect an overt backlash against this male use of animal imagery to limit women. Indeed, the patriarchal restriction of Katharine is later explicitly envisaged as that of a Zoo animal, when, under an attack from her father about her decision not to marry William, she is described as looking "for a moment like a wild animal caged in a civilized dwelling-place" (501). In the Zoo scene itself, although the exact extent of the narrator's sympathy is ambiguous, there is undeniable irony in the presentation of Denham's steamy poetic fallacy. Furthermore, when we see William "tempting some small reluctant animal to descend from an upper perch to partake of half an apple" (388), a retaliatory inversion of the Eve myth is striking. However, the image here is still of man controlling the woman/animal. Moreover, it engenders a peculiar exchange in which Katharine remarks that "William isn't kind to animals.... He doesn't know what they like and what they don't like." William snaps at his rival, "I take it you're well versed in these matters, Denham," gathering the reply, "It's mainly a question of knowing how to stroke them" (388). These two men are quite clearly not disputing their ability to charm and caress the animal in the cage, but the woman who stands between them. The indelicacy of this situation is underlined by the embarrassment of Cassandra, who, "in obedience to her new-found feminine susceptibility" (388), asks for directions to the reptile house. However, the metaphor comes from Katharine; there is clearly something in William's inability to know what she likes which frustrates her. She defends it when he challenges her about the propriety of her remarks, replying, "it's true. You never see what anyone feels" (390), where the jump from ape to human self is complete. Woolf is thus detecting and mocking the repressive discourse of animality in relation to women, but is also toying with retaining it in order to explore Katharine's desires.

However, this complexity of engagement with the Zoo appears to be abandoned by Woolf in the years after this novel. Increasingly, the image of the Zoo animal becomes essentially asexual, in a way which threatens to more clearly etch the often drawn caricature of Woolf in terrified flight from sexuality. In effect, it is rather as if Woolf notes only *Night and Day*'s bun-eating bears. Indeed, in her 1921 address to the Bloomsbury Memoir Club, she spoke of an elderly visitor to Hyde Park Gate for tea and buns who, when suddenly roused, was liable to spout "two columns of tea not unmixed with sultanas through his nostrils; after which he would relapse into a drowsy ursine stupor" (*MOB* 142). What renders this old man ursine, the drowsy consumption of tea and buns, is evidently a quintessentially human activity. However, the passive, bun-stuffed Zoo bear, reassuringly stripped of all hint of animality, is such an attractive image for Woolf that it threatens to become her only truth about bears. Characterising David Garnett in a letter as a "surly devil," she describes herself rebuking him, after which he weakly "rolled over like a sulky bear" (*L3* 120).

The effective eradication of all hints of "animality" in such images is shared by her characters. In *The Voyage Out*, for example, Rachel does not attempt to "defend her belief that human beings were as various as the beasts at the zoo, which had stripes and manes, and horns and humps" (376-77). There is no suggestion of threat attached to these beasts, their variety is all that is of significance. In *Mrs. Dalloway*, Septimus Smith sits in Regents Park with his wife, and "dun-coloured animals stretched long necks over the Zoo palings, barking, howling" (21). Recalling the doctor's advice to make him "notice real things," Rezia looks around, despairingly deciding, "what was there to look at? A few sheep. That was all" (22). The noisy, intrusive animals described are clearly not sheep, but they are literally eradicated from Rezia's view, as if they become imaginary. Woolf increasingly treats Zoo animals in her writings as empty similes, so that the statues outside parliament are described in *The London Scene* as being "black and sleek and shiny as sea lions that have just risen from the water" (37). Such images carry no weight of animality, and the Gardens in fact become for Woolf a place that aids contemplation upon things quite unconnected to them:

> And the truth is, one can't write directly about the soul. Looked at it vanishes: but look at the ceiling, look…at the cheaper beasts in the zoo which are exposed to walkers in Regents Park, & the soul slips in. It slipped in this afternoon. I will write that I said, staring at the bison. (*D3* 62)

Here, this large hairy quadruped is inciting in the author consideration of an entity that is perhaps the antithesis of animality, and routinely produced as the primary uniquely human characteristic, the soul.

Arranged here in chronological order, these very selective instances might suggest Woolf as only overcoming the hesitancy of *Night and Day* by gradually withdrawing to a position of carefully maintained distance from the Zoo animal. It is as if the actuality of the bison has had to be all but written out along with its association with metaphorical animality. So does Woolf's exploration of the Zoo fail to tackle and overcome the sexist discourse suspected in *Night and Day* because of authorial frigidity? Where Craig Smith suggests that Woolf's "inhibitions in writing about the body limit her art" (355), perhaps her appreciation of the Zoo creature is similarly limited.

However, Woolf does come to re-examine and to forcefully re-evaluate the Zoo animal, notably in her 1928 article, "The Sun and the Fish." Ostensibly describing a solar eclipse, Woolf's mind in this piece is soon transported to the Zoo. We are introduced not to another empty simile, but rather "the complete and perfect effigy of two lizards" (*E4* 523). These animals are having sex but, as Jane Goldman observes, "this is not the celebration of the flesh we might expect" (101). Animal sexuality rather emerges as ascetically superior:

> one lizard is mounted immobile on the back of another, with only the twinkle of a gold eyelid or the suction of a green flank to show that they are living flesh, and not made of bronze. All human passion seems furtive and feverish beside this still rapture. Time seems to have stopped and we are in the presence of immortality. (*E4* 523)

Rather than merely retreating from images of animal sexuality, Woolf is here casting her own image of the Zoo animal as less metaphorically animalistic than humanity. Moreover, in finding such an image here in the Zoo, she draws attention to the hopelessly partial vision of the Gardens offered in Garnett's heaving animal fallacies. What she ultimately demonstrates is not a psychosexual avoidance of fallacious human animality but a firm corrective response to its distasteful discourse. Moreover, by revealing the intellectual bankruptcy of such ideas, she effectively dismantles any attempted connection between the human and the real animal.¹

However, it is ultimately difficult to declare that Woolf has achieved complete ease with the Gardens and her own manipulation of them, or that she has wholly divorced the animal from animality. A particularly intriguing piece of evidence here is her diary account of a late evening visit to a floodlit Zoo with Mary Hutchinson:

> So to the Zoo: a mist rising; white bears elongated like El Grecos: stinking meat held near my nose: bear bit a boy's arm off; bears dived; white explosion; red & yellow fairy lamps; distant music; the sea lions, rushing like torpedoes, flouncing up the rocks; in silk coats; the blind bear; one swollen white eye; birds flying under the livid green; baby sea lions, like puppies; Mary tipping the man: her sexual response. (*D4* 111)

The prose here is terse and almost telegraphic, and seems to attach no greater emotional impact to the statement that a "bear bit a boy's arm off" than to any other detail. What is most intriguing about this account is that, although Woolf did make this visit, it is demonstrable beyond all reasonable doubt that no boy was attacked. This can be asserted for a variety of reasons, the first being its absence from contemporary newspapers, despite their enthusiastic and thorough coverage of the Zoo, including the glamour of these summer late openings. Neither is an attack mentioned in the Zoo's record of daily occurrences, nor in the minutes of the meeting of the Gardens Committee.² Moreover, Woolf doesn't mention such an incident in any letter, although she does speak of her visit to the Zoo. Lastly, the design of the Mappin Terraces in the Gardens makes such an attack almost impossible.

This falsification must be seen at some level as an evasion of troubling material. Indeed, the scene of hungry bears being fed decaying meat in a dark, overcrowded garden seems manufactured to ooze all of the clichés of animality. One could argue that rather than accepting that such associations press upon her mind as keenly as Garnett's, Woolf distances herself by containing them within an apparently objective record of an incident. Similarly, sexuality is present but held at arm's length, the diary records only Mary Hutchinson's "sexual response" (111).

Clearly, by inventing an incident in her own diary, Woolf is taking an extreme action, she is trying to close her eyes to something. Despite her earlier resistance, it is as if this real Zoo animal has become for her as confused with the cultural image of animality as it was for *Night and Day*'s Denham. However, this incident can be valuably contextualised through a brief consideration of Woolf's naming of the animal other. Her enthusiasm for natural history has been traced by Bonnie Kime Scott to Leslie Stephen, who provided "Woolf's entry into the patriarchal discourse of scientific classification" (2: 36). There is much more to be said on this topic, but I would suggest that this ordered classification is fundamental to Woolf's alternative view of the Zoo. Rather than a carnival of furred embodiments of animality, it has come to represent for her a bastion of order. This is seen even at a trivial level, so that when Woolf laments the chaos of her desk, she says, "I must tidy up…. I shall also go to the…Zoo" (*D5* 50). The precise scientific categorisation of the Gardens debars animality altogether, presenting rather a series of known and classified entities.

On that particular evening, what is most importantly disturbed is this sense of order.

Firstly, there is a "mist rising," casting an image of indeterminacy. This recalls another vision of the Zoo as "a dreary place," from Woolf's diary of 1918, when "mist rolls up over that vast open space" (*D1* 224). The polar bears are moreover described as "elongated like El Grecos," seeming distorted, as if in a mannerist painting. Moreover, after discussion of the sea lions, she comes back unexpectedly to the bears, saying, "the blind bear; one swollen white eye."

The bears are thus triply deformed, imperfect, not according to type. Crucially, Woolf calls them simply "white bears," whereas she is by no means unfamiliar with the accepted term, "polar bears." However, her use of this label is restricted to occasions when they do not appear so resistant to the naturalist's gaze, as in a vision from the essay "Royal Academy," of "polar bears…turning into carriage rugs as we look at them" (*E3* 92). Rather than Woolf's underlying struggle with a natural connection between bears and basic human drives, it is arguably the creatures' resistance to their proper classification which unleashes fears to be displaced in an invented animal attack.

The "animal" in this specific and wholly metaphorical sense, of a being that transgressively defies zoological classification, does occur throughout Woolf's writing as an image of violence or of disorientating sexuality. Perhaps most obviously, Rachel's disturbing sexual dream in *The Voyage Out* features a "little deformed man…. His face was pitted and like the face of an animal" (81). Here we have the same deformity, and the same indeterminacy. Similarly, in 1939, Woolf remembers a dream caused by her abuse by Gerald Duckworth, where she "was looking in a glass when a horrible face—the face of an animal—suddenly showed over my shoulder" (*MOB* 69). However, it is true also in less highly charged situations, where a series of animal insults always stress this indeterminacy. For example, Dorothy Todd, editor of *Vogue*, is described as "like some primeval animal emerging from the swamp, muddy, hirsute" (*D3* 175), where "muddy" can be read as suggesting obscurity or lack of clarity rather than simply being covered in earth. David Garnett's literary father, Edward, is similarly dismissed as a "surly shaggy unkempt old monstrosity" (*D3* 204) and historian R. C. Trevelyan as "some shaggy, surly, unkempt old animal" (*D4* 76). In both of these instances, I would suggest that that surliness which Woolf detects lies in a recalcitrant resistance to classification. It is worthwhile being quite clear that comparison to a non-human being is not itself considered insulting, but only this accusation of having no identifiable species. Thus, Ethel Smyth is damningly described in Woolf's diary as an "unclipped and rather overgrown woodland wild beast, species indeterminate" (*D4*: 68). However, in letters, Woolf is confident that other animal imagery will be received as affectionate, for example a fond description of Smyth as "my old striped tiger cat, with her growl and her claws and her soft fur" (*L6* 301).

What is emerging here is Woolf's own specific vision of the fallacy of animality, as the transgressively unquantifiable. Of course, this gestures towards other discourses, notably Julia Kristeva's definition of the abject as that which "disturbs identity, system, order. What does not respect borders, positions, rules. The in-between, the ambiguous" (4). However, what is important to understand here is that such images have nothing in common with Zoo animals, although those unstable "white bears" uniquely begin to approach them. The two uses of a disturbing "face of an animal" above exactly capture the indeterminacy of a wholly alien and yet simultaneously familiar depth that for Bataille is the foundation of the poetic fallacy of animality.[3] Woolf, in other words, is quite aware of the power of that fallacy, and plunders its vocabulary, but she carefully and intentionally refuses to site it in the "real" or Zoo animal, as Garnett did and by extension other modernists, perhaps most obviously D. H. Lawrence, repeatedly attempted. This is crucially not a restriction on Woolf's discourse; rather her early and close consideration of the real Zoological Gardens, and not an unconsidered apprehension of the metaphorical Zoo, allowed her more squarely to face the animal outside of the cage in later works from *Flush* to *The Waves* and *Between the Acts*. Woolf had learned what Garnett never would, that the boundary between human and animal is more than a Zoo railing or a repressive society, and that whether metaphorical animality is celebrated or repressed, it does not reside in any real (non-human) animal.

## Notes

1. These observations intersect with and ratify Jane Goldman's feeling that we must "rethink our analysis of [Woolf's] engagement with oppositions" (19), contrary to an increasingly received notion of her as a "deconstructor of binary opposites *par excellence*" (16).
2. I would like to acknowledge my gratitude to Michael Palmer, Archivist at the Zoological Society of London, for his assistance in this research.
3. These usages, in their emphasis on the face, also almost anticipate Emmanuel Levinas's ambiguous declaration that "one cannot entirely refuse the face of an animal" (169).

## Works Cited

Adams, Carol J., and Josephine Donovan, ed. *Animals and Women: Feminist Theoretical Explorations*. Durham, NC: Duke UP, 1995.
Bataille, Georges. *Theory of Religion*. Trans. Robert Hurley. New York: Zone, 1989.
Flint, Kate. "Introduction: Woolf and Animals." *Flush*. By Virginia Woolf. Ed. Kate Flint. Oxford: Oxford UP, 1998. Xii-xliv.
Fudge, Erica. *Animal*. London: Reaktion, 2002.
Garnett, David. *A Man in the Zoo*. London: Chatto, 1924.
Goldman, Jane. *The Feminine Aesthetics of Virginia Woolf: Modernism, Post-Impressionism and the Politics of the Visual*. Cambridge: Cambridge UP, 1998.
Kristeva, Julia. *Powers of Horror: An Essay on Abjection*. Trans. Leon S. Roudiez. New York: Columbia UP, 1982.
Levinas, Emmanuel. "The Paradox of Morality: An Interview with Emmanuel Levinas." *The Provocation of Levinas: Rethinking the Other*. Ed. Robert Bernasconi and David Wood. London: Routledge, 1988. 168-80.
Ross, Michael L. "Ladies and Foxes: D. H. Lawrence, David Garnett, and the Female of the Species." *D. H. Lawrence Review* 18 (1985-86): 229-238.
Scott, Bonnie Kime. *Refiguring Modernism: Postmodern Feminist Readings of Woolf, West, and Barnes*. 2 vols. Bloomington: Indiana UP, 1995.
Smith, Craig. "Across the Widest Gulf: Nonhuman Subjectivity in Virginia Woolf's *Flush*." *Twentieth Century Literature* 48 (2002): 348-61.
Tester, Keith. *Animals and Society: The Humanity of Animal Rights*. London: Routledge, 1991.
Woolf, Virginia. *The Diary of Virginia Woolf*. Ed. Anne Olivier Bell with Andrew McNeillie. 5 vols. London: Hogarth, 1977-1984.
——. *The Essays of Virginia Woolf*. Ed. Andrew McNeillie. 4 vols. London: Hogarth, 1986-1994.
——. *The Letters of Virginia Woolf*. Ed. Nigel Nicolson and Joanne Trautmann. 6 vols. London: Hogarth, 1976-1980.
——. *The London Scene: Five Essays by Virginia Woolf*. New York: Hallman, 1975.
——. *Moments of Being: Unpublished Autobiographical Writings*. Ed. Jeanne Schulkind. London: Chatto for Sussex UP, 1976.
——. *Night and Day*. Ed. Suzanne Raitt. Oxford: Oxford UP, 1992.
——. *A Room of One's Own and Three Guineas*. Ed. Morag Shiach. Oxford: Oxford UP, 1992.
——. *The Voyage Out*. Ed. Lorna Sage. Oxford: Oxford UP, 1992.

# PESTS AND PESTICIDES:
## EXPLORING THE BOUNDARIES OF WOOLF'S ENVIRONMENTALISM

### *by Christina Alt*

Woolf enjoys a growing reputation as a "green" author for her attention to the world beyond the human. However, ecocritical interpretations of Woolf can benefit from a grounding in historical specificity. Woolf's biographical sketch of Eleanor Ormerod, a nineteenth-century economic entomologist, provides an opportunity to examine Woolf's view of the science of pest control, to relate this to early twentieth-century valuations of past and emergent disciplines within the life sciences, and to suggest both the limits of Woolf's environmentalism and the knowledge—and lack of knowledge—that determined her outlook.

Eleanor Ormerod (1828-1901) was an early practitioner in the field of applied or economic entomology, specialising in the study of insect pests. Having grown up with a recreational interest in taxonomic entomology, the classification of insects, Ormerod found her calling in 1868 when she encountered in the *Gardeners' Chronicle* a request from the Royal Horticultural Society for contributions to a collection of "insects beneficial or injurious to man" (Wallace 55). This project was innovative in its interest in collecting specimens not purely for the sake of classification, as in the taxonomic tradition of natural history, but in order to study a specific issue relating to insect behaviour and the interaction of insects with their environment.

Taking up the subject in its earliest stages of development, Ormerod soon found her expertise in great demand. In 1877, she began issuing annual reports on insect pests and methods of combating them compiled from responses to circulated questionnaires and correspondence with farmers and market gardeners throughout the country. In 1882, she was appointed the honorary entomological advisor to the Royal Agricultural Society of England (RASE). Ormerod also promoted the institutionalisation of economic entomology, campaigning to have the subject taught in agricultural colleges and universities, and to this end gave lectures, wrote textbooks, and acted as an examiner for the University of Edinburgh. She was the recipient of awards from institutions both in Britain and abroad, culminating in an honorary LL.D from the University of Edinburgh—the first ever bestowed upon a woman.

However, in contrast to the success that she achieved in her own time, recent assessments of Ormerod have criticised her science, condemning her promotion of pesticides and the extermination of pest populations. In "Eleanor Ormerod (1828-1901) as an Economic Entomologist: 'Pioneer of Purity Even More than of Paris Green,'" the environmental historian J. F. McDiarmid Clark accuses Ormerod of encouraging farmers to "drench Nature in a slurry of poison" and of seeking to "attain professional status upon the heads of lifeless sparrows" (447).[1] Clark's criticism of Ormerod takes an ecofeminist form: he regards her environmentally suspect science as evidence of her betrayal of her feminine and feminist self, arguing that Ormerod "allied herself with the 'male' science bent upon the dissection of the passive, feminine bosom of nature" and won a place for herself in the field of economic entomology only through "a denial of her sexuality" (443, 452).

Clark focuses his criticism on two of Ormerod's campaigns: her promotion of the use of pesticides and her support for the extermination of house sparrows. Clark notes that Ormerod "played a pivotal role in the promotion of the large-scale use of Paris green," a copper acetoarsenite compound, as an insecticide (446). There was limited understanding of the dangers of arsenite compounds in the late nineteenth century. Medical doctors and agricultural scientists were aware of arsenic's acute toxicity in large quantities but were less alert to its chronic toxicity when encountered in small amounts over a long period (Clark 446). The compound was widely used as a pigment in green paints (hence its name) and was also used medicinally in preparations such as Fowler's solution. As a result, there was little public objection to the adoption of Paris Green as a pesticide, and Ormerod herself proudly declared that she wished her tombstone to read, "SHE INTRODUCED PARIS GREEN TO ENGLAND" (Wallace 206-7).

Clark cites Woolf's biographical sketch, "Miss Ormerod" (published in the *Dial* in December 1924 and later incorporated into "Lives of the Obscure" in the American edition of *The Common Reader*), in support of his condemnation of Ormerod and her science. He takes Woolf's description of Ormerod as a "pioneer of purity even more than of Paris Green" as confirmation of his contention that Ormerod's success in the masculine field of applied entomology was made possible only by the suppression of her sexuality (*E4* 136, cited in Clark 431). However, Clark's deployment of Woolf as a guarantor of his ecofeminist argument demands examination. Much of Woolf's writing does, without question, support ecocritical interpretation, but Woolf's representation of economic entomology in "Miss Ormerod" complicates this view.

I would argue that, unlike that of Clark, Woolf's portrayal of Ormerod and her science is essentially approving. To what extent, then, did the nature of Ormerod's science figure into Woolf's evaluation of her subject? Did Woolf champion Ormerod simply because she was a woman who achieved success in a male-dominated field, regardless of the focus of her research, or was the nature of Ormerod's science in some way responsible for Woolf's interest in and approval of Ormerod? If the latter, what are the implications of this approval to an understanding of Woolf's views of science and nature? I will argue that Woolf championed Ormerod because Woolf was not primarily concerned with the environmental effects of Ormerod's policies but instead viewed Ormerod and her science in relation to the earlier nineteenth-century tradition of taxonomic natural history and welcomed the overthrow of this quintessentially Victorian scientific tradition by more modern disciplines such as economic entomology.

In his critique of Ormerod, Clark describes economic entomology as part of "the new empirical science, bent upon the dissection of nature's anatomy" (451). In the early twentieth century, this new science was seen as possessing a revolutionary potential. Writers such as H. G. Wells and Marie Carmichael presented the new biology of the laboratory alongside Fabian socialism, feminist activism, and free love as a possible means of social amelioration. Woolf was also susceptible to such optimism. With regards to the study of nature, Woolf appears to have viewed only the established tradition of taxonomic natural history as irredeemably patriarchal. She saw modern sciences, economic entomology included, as potentially transformative, having the capacity to overthrow the dogmatism of not only the old scientific order but also established social conventions and hierarchies.

As Clark correctly notes, Ormerod was not an overt feminist. She was publicly dismissive of the women's movement, responding to Lydia Becker's praise that she was "proof of how much a woman could do without the help of a man" with a declaration of her gratitude to the men who had furthered her career (Clark 435). Woolf likewise observes that Ormerod was conservative in many of her social and political views: she depicts Ormerod toasting the Queen's health, assembling her servants for prayer, lamenting the prospect of Home Rule, and preserving her father's "pigtail...in a box" (*E4* 139). Woolf suggests, however, that where her scientific training came into play, Ormerod was iconoclastic, that she was encouraged by her science to overturn established conventions, whether these took the form of the taxonomic tradition of natural history or restrictive social and gender norms. Woolf presents Ormerod as, almost against her will and certainly against the conditions of her upbringing, challenging received values by means of her science.

In the most general sense, Woolf suggests that, over the course of Ormerod's life, her science gradually emboldened her to challenge masculine authority. As Woolf tells it, Ormerod's first scientific observation, made as a small child while watching a tumbler full of water grubs, sends her running to her father, filled with "eagerness to impart her observations" (*E4* 133); her father dismisses her report that the grubs have eaten one of their companions as "Nonsense" and, on this occasion, she does not protest, accepting that "little girls are not allowed to contradict their fathers" (*E4* 133). During her apprenticeship as a taxonomic entomologist, she continues to appeal to male authority figures, sending a captured specimen to an Oxford professor for classification (*E4* 134). Even once she feels herself a competent judge, she initially conceals her own authority behind that of a man: Woolf causes her to remark that "Dr Ritzema Bos is a great stand-by. For they won't take a woman's word" (*E4* 136). Gradually, however, Ormerod gains the confidence to challenge even her former mentor, offering the pronouncement, "these, though Ritzema Bos is positive to the contrary, are the generative organs of the male. I've proved it" (*E4*: 136). By the end of her career, Woolf suggests, Ormerod has achieved public recognition as an expert, as is demonstrated by her dictated letter to Messrs. Langridge: "Gentlemen, I have examined your sample and find..." (*E4* 138). From being a seeker after the opinions of others, Ormerod has become an authority herself.

Woolf was justified in regarding taxonomic natural history as a conservative influence. As Londa Schiebinger has demonstrated in *Nature's Body*, taxonomy in the Linnaean tradition was socially conservative, importing human gender conventions such as male priority and the domestic, nurturing role of the female wholesale into the classification of nature and thus reinforcing the existing social order by permitting it to appear "natural." Taxonomic natural history was also religiously orthodox. Linnaeus regarded taxonomy as a continuation of Adam's naming of the beasts in the garden and the practice received further religious sanction from the philosophy of natural theology which argued that the variety and complexity of natural forms offered proof of the power and wisdom of their creator and that the study of nature was thus a means of reverencing God. This doctrine continued to serve as the primary justification for the study of nature for much of the nineteenth century, thanks in part to its reiteration in William Paley's *Natural Theology*. As a result, for much of the Victorian period, the study of nature, particularly as a pastime for women, children, and the working classes, was recommended as much on moral grounds as on educational ones, the contemplation of God's creation being regarded as a spiritually edifying activity leading the attention "from the works of Nature up to the God of Nature," to quote F. O. Morris (*History* iv).

Taxonomy in its popular, Victorian form was also rather prim. Although the Linnaean system of classification was a sexual system, distinguishing between species based on the number, form, proportion, and situation of sexual organs, in translations and reformulations of Linnaean taxonomy meant for the general public, this basis was concealed: Patricia Fara highlights in particular William Withering's "bowdlerised botany," which "translated contentious words into harmless but meaningless English equivalents such as 'chives' and 'pointals'" (42).

The moralising of nature was one of the aspects of the Victorian practice of natural history that Woolf disdained, an attitude that placed her in agreement with the emerging class of professional biologists who, in the words of Suzanne Le-May Sheffield, "sought to rid science of its moral, religious and metaphysical associations" (179). Ormerod herself "focussed exclusively upon the practical utility of entomology, completely ignoring any entertainment value or moral or religious worth" (Sheffield 172). Woolf notes that the injurious insects that were Ormerod's chosen specialty were "Not, one would have thought, among God's most triumphant creations" (*E4* 136): the natural theology that had justified the study of nature for much of the nineteenth century played no part in Ormerod's motivation. Though her brother Edward sought to bar her from the unseemly study of anatomy, "never lik[ing] [her] to do more than take sections of teeth," Ormerod persevered, and Woolf has her heroine preface her discussion of her anatomical investigations with the airy remark, "my brother—oh, he's dead now—a very good man" (*E4* 136). The death of this embodiment of Victorian morality released Ormerod to engage with nature on new terms.

Woolf regards this casting off of the moralised view of nature as Ormerod's greatest triumph. Apostrophising Ormerod, Woolf declares:

> Ah, but Eleanor, the Bot and the Hessian have more power over you than Mr Edward Ormerod himself. Under the microscope you clearly perceive that these insects have organs, orifices, excrement; they do, most emphatically, copulate. Escorted on one side by the Bot or Warble, on the other by the Hessian Fly, Miss Ormerod advanced statelily, if slowly, into the open. Never did her features show more sublime than when lit up with the candour of her avowal. "This is excrement; these, though Ritzema Bos is positive to the contrary, are the generative organs of the male. I've proved it." Upon her head the hood of Edinburgh most fitly descended; pioneer of purity even more than of Paris Green. (*E4* 136)

It is Ormerod's frank, scientific treatment of anatomy, sex, and other bodily functions—purifying organs and excrement of taboo—that Woolf celebrates above all her other accomplishments.

Clark takes Woolf's description of Ormerod as "a pioneer of purity" as a demonstration of Woolf's agreement with his own assessment that Ormerod denied her sexuality in order to achieve success in the masculine world of science. Yet Woolf's description seems rather to suggest that Ormerod's science, far from being grounded in a suppression or rejection of sex, was based upon a frank and unashamed treatment of it.

It is this demystification that Woolf highlights as well in her discussion of Ormerod's campaign against the house sparrow. By the 1890s, the systematic destruction of birds of prey by farmers and game keepers had upset the "balance of birds," as E. M Nicholson termed it (25): the numbers of natural predators had declined and as a result adaptable species such as the sparrow had proliferated and, in some areas, become pests. That the young Virginia Stephen was familiar with the sparrow problem is suggested by a diary entry from 6 June 1897: "we planted seed in the back garden. This is to produce grass—but whether the sparrows will have left any is a question. As soon as we had left the garden, the horrid little creatures swooped down twittering & made off with the oats" (*PA* 96). Controversy arose over the best method of addressing the proliferation of sparrows: sparrow clubs dedicated themselves to the extermination of the birds, but the domestic associations of the house sparrow in English culture and the biblical significance of the sparrow suggested in the promise, "one of them shall not fall on the ground without your Father" (Matt. 10.29), meant that the persecution of the sparrow was opposed with particular vehemence by Victorian animal protectionists.

Woolf argues that the momentum of Ormerod's scientific work compelled her, despite her cultivated "disposition" towards tradition, to defy conventional sentiment and in an act of "disloyal[ty] to much that she, and her fathers before her, held dear" set herself against the sparrow, emblem of "the homely virtue of English domestic life" (*E4* 139). As a scientist, Ormerod challenged conventions which as her father's daughter she felt it her duty to protect, for her science accepted nothing as sacred just as it accepted nothing as profane. Through her campaign against the house sparrow, Woolf suggests, Ormerod set herself in opposition to both the traditionally feminine domestic sphere and the paternalism of Christian tradition and Victorian society more broadly.

In her account of the sparrow controversy, Woolf displays no sympathy for Ormerod's opponents, the animal protectionists. She mocks the moralising clergymen and sentimental ladies of the *Animals' Friend* and the Humanitarian League. Woolf was not opposed to the cause of animal protection in principle. In an essay on the Plumage Bill she states that as a child she took a vow never to wear the plumes of wild birds because of the cruelty and destructiveness of the plumage trade (*E3* 241). The source of Woolf's objections to the protectionist movement lay in the religiosity and sentimentality of tone which often characterised the movement's rhetoric and the reinforcement of gender stereotypes which occurred under its banner. The Reverend J. E. Walker's response to Ormerod's campaign against the sparrow, printed in the *Animals' Friend* under the title "God Save the Sparrow" (to which Woolf alludes in her essay), exemplifies the biases of protectionist rhetoric:

> Madam,—It is with infinite regret that I see a lady's name quoted in the *Daily Chronicle* as giving "the sentence of death" to the very bird of which the gentle voice of the Son of God said…"one of them shall not fall on the ground without your Father." Surely as having the compassionate heart of *woman*, unsteeled (I hope) by your scientific studies, you will feel a throb of *agony* whenever you hear those all-sacred words, and know that your verdict has been taken as a wholesale sentence of extermination…upon these birds, which "the Father" cares for. (241)

Woolf's bias against the Victorian protectionist position may be further explained through reference to the views of F. O. Morris, the clergyman-naturalist from whose works of piety-infused taxonomic natural history Virginia and her siblings first learned the art of entomological collection and classification. In *The Sparrow Shooter*, a pamphlet specifically targeting Ormerod, Morris defends the sparrow on biblical grounds and on the grounds of the bird's good character: he opens his defence with the contention:

> The name of the Sparrow, his Latin name, [*Passer domesticus,*] ought to have secured him from...ignorant persecution.... His natural haunt is where men have their home, and if he ever emigrates, it is only to go along with them, whithersoever they may direct their steps. He, as it were, says, like Ruth of old, to Naomi, "Whither thou goest, I will go, and where thou lodgest, I will lodge...his name, as given to him so long ago by Linnaeus, tells us his natural character.... He is a most stay-at-home bird, by no means of a roving turn. (3)

Morris's defence takes the form of an anthropomorphising guarantee of the sparrow's moral character. Morris concludes his response to Ormerod with the assertion that "Miss Ormerod would have employed her time and feminine talents much better if she had confined herself to the use of her needle in working for some charitable object or other" (*Sparrow* 4). There is no evidence that Woolf knew of Morris's attack on Ormerod; nevertheless, the exchange between these two figures illustrates the tendency of Victorian protectionism towards sentimentality, religiosity, and misogyny and suggests why Woolf was reluctant to align herself with the protectionist position against Ormerod's modern science.

The protection movement was one in which women played a large and often public role and it might therefore be expected that it would promote a feminist agenda. However, female protectionists very often justified their participation in this public movement with the argument that animal protection was an extension of women's private role as caregivers. In the first issue of the *Animals' Friend*, Mrs Henry Lee appeals as "A Woman to Women" to take up the work of animal protection, a cause to which "surely no true-hearted woman can be indifferent" (6). This reinforcement of traditional gender identities was a further obstacle for Woolf to sympathy with the protectionist cause.

In praising Ormerod as "the pioneer of purity *even more than* of Paris Green" (emphasis added), Woolf shows herself to be more concerned with the social significance of Ormerod's science than with the practical details and environmental ramifications of pest control. She never identifies Paris Green as an arsenite pesticide and she discusses Ormerod's campaign against the house sparrow in terms of the dismantling of a social myth rather than the extermination of living creatures. Woolf perceived economic entomology primarily in contrast to the moralised, sentimental, and gender-conditioned view of nature that she disdained in the nineteenth-century practice of natural history and on these grounds she gave Ormerod her approval.

One question that remains to be asked is whether Woolf should be regarded as remiss in overlooking the toxicity of Paris Green or whether her failure to address this matter simply reflects contemporary ignorance of the danger of arsenite pesticides. As James C. Whorton states, at least until the end of the nineteenth century, "the medical profession maintained a virtually unbroken silence on the question of arsenical insecticides" and agricultural scientists likewise "failed to appreciate the hazard of chronic arsenicism" (226). However, by December 1924, when "Miss Ormerod" appeared in the *Dial*, there was some awareness of the dangers of chronic arsenic poisoning. In the winter of 1900, an epidemic of peripheral neuritis amongst the poor in Manchester was linked to long-term exposure to arsenic in cheap beer. This contamination was not the result of pesticide use, but it raised concerns about the presence of arsenic in food and drink and led to the appointment of a Royal Commission to investigate the dangers of arsenic contamination and to set an official limit for arsenic levels in foods (1/100th of a grain in the gallon or pound). Yet in spite of this "sensational demonstration of the harmful consequences of long-term exposure to arsenic," well into the early decades of the twentieth century an attitude of "uninformed optimism" towards the potential danger of pesticide residues prevailed (Whorton 230, 232). Then, in late November 1925, less than a year after the publication of "Miss Ormerod" in the *Dial*, four Londoners fell ill after eating imported American apples that were subsequently revealed to be heavily contaminated with arsenic. The British press launched an attack upon American produce and the British Ministry of Health threatened an embargo of American fruit unless British tolerance levels were observed (Whorton 235). This incident resulted in a heightened awareness of the danger of pesticide contamination both in Britain and overseas and protests from medical and consumer critics persisted until the post-World War Two introduction of synthetic pesticides ended the debate over "the old arsenicals" (Whorton 241).

Woolf's light-hearted discussion of Paris Green in "Miss Ormerod" was written only a short time before the public outcry against pesticide contamination began. Even a year later, for her to have written about arsenite insecticides without acknowledging their toxicity or addressing their impact—on public health if not on the environment—would have been far less likely. However, in 1924 it was still conceivable to champion economic entomology on the basis of what it replaced—the sentimentality, religiosity, and social conservatism of both taxonomic natural history and the Victorian protection movement—rather than what it promoted. Woolf's view of nature and the life sciences was very precisely of her time.

## Note

1. Clark is a leading authority on Ormerod and his accounts of her life and work elsewhere, such as in the *Dictionary of National Biography*, offer less polemical descriptions of her science.

## Works Cited

Clark, J. F. McDiarmid. "Eleanor Ormerod (1828-1901) as an Economic Entomologist: 'Pioneer of Purity Even More than of Paris Green.'" *British Journal for the History of Science* 25 (1992): 431-52.
Fara, Patricia. *Sex, Botany and Empire: The Story of Carl Linnaeus and Joseph Banks*. Cambridge: Icon, 2003.
Lee, Mrs. Henry. "A Woman to Women." *Animals' Friend* 1.1 (1894): 6.
Morris, F. O. *A History of British Butterflies*. London: Groombridge and Sons, 1853.
———. *The Sparrow Shooter*. London: S. W. Partridge, 1886.
Nicholson, E. M. *Birds in England: An Account of the State of Our Bird-Life, and a Criticism of Bird Protection*. London: Whitefriars, 1926.
Schiebinger, Londa. *Nature's Body: Gender in the Making of Modern Science*. Boston: Beacon, 1993.
Sheffield, Suzanne Le-May. *Revealing New Worlds: Three Victorian Women Naturalists*. London: Routledge, 2001.
Walker, J. E. "God Save the Sparrow." *Animals' Friend* 3.12 (1897): 241.
Wallace, Robert, ed. *Eleanor Ormerod, LL.D., Economic Entomologist, Autobiography and Correspondence*. London: John Murray, 1904.
Whorton, James C. "Insecticide Spray Residues and Public Health: 1865-1938." *Bulletin of the History of Medicine* 45 (1971): 219-41.
Woolf, Virginia. "Lives of the Obscure." *The Essays of Virginia Woolf*. Ed. Andrew McNeillie. Vol. 4. London: Hogarth, 1994. 118-45.
———. *A Passionate Apprentice: The Early Journals of Virginia Woolf*. Ed. Mitchell A. Leaska. London: Hogarth, 1992.

# "CE CHIEN EST À MOI": VIRGINIA WOOLF AND THE SIGNIFYING DOG

## by Jane Goldman

Woolf's signifying dog belongs to the "companion species" that marks the boundaries between the human and non-human.¹ My concern, however, is not primarily with the modality, or dogginess, of the dog but with its status as signifier. It marks the boundary between literal and figurative. In exploring the dog's metaphorical status, I risk its "erasure," confirming it as "absent referent," according to animal ethicist-feminist, Carol Adams. "Could metaphor itself be the undergarment…of oppression?" she asks, since through the reifying action of metaphor "the object is severed from its ontological meaning," something that also occurs in the discourse of racism and misogyny (209, 213). But what interests me is the behaviour of such metaphors in Woolf's modernist free indirect discourse. Woolf's dog is a sliding signifier representing not least the historic, unequal struggles between men and women over artistic subjectivity and voice. Marking and marked by race, gender, and class, it is a constructed, monstrous, multivalent figure whose referent is certainly not just a dog, but nor, *contra* Adams, does this metaphor cleanly evacuate the dog from its vehicle merely to accommodate "woman" or "slave" (Woolf gestures to both). A few critics note the metaphoricity of Woolf's dogs, but only as simple allegories of sexuality, particularly lesbianism (Dunn, Eberly, Vanita).

My focus is the notorious "fine negress" passage (*AROO* 76), and the performance there of Woolf's slippery canine metaphors in her free indirect discourse. These elude Jane Marcus's attention in her fine scrutiny of the passage. But, hunting with canine and animal ethicists, I will chase Woolf's dog in one crucial sentence back through some of the sentences it has previously frequented in Woolf's and others' writing. My book, *Virginia Woolf and the Signifying Dog* learns a trick or two from Henry Louis Gates's *Signifying Monkey* (except there's no originary feminist trickster-dog). It explores the intersection of feminist theory with philosophical interests in animal ethics: Marjorie Garber's *Dog Love*; Donna Haraway's companion species manifesto; Emmanuel Levinas's essay, "The Name of a Dog." Giorgio Agamben, in *The Open: Man and Animal*, considers the aporia in Western thought's shifting caesurae between man and animal. Woolf's signifying dog may occupy the very "zone" Agamben identifies: the empty interval between man and animal that is neither animal life nor human life (Agamben 38).

The "anthropological machine," Agamben shows, in seeking to identify the evolutionary bridge between animal and man in fact "functions by excluding as not (yet) human an already human being from itself, that is by animalizing the human, by isolating the non-human within the human: *Homo alalus* [significantly, man without speech], or the ape-man," and conversely by the "humanization of an animal: the man-ape [or non-man], the *enfant sauvage* or *Homo ferus*, but also and above all the slave, the barbarian, and the foreigner, as figures of an animal in human form." This model made possible the Nazi identification of the Jew as "the non-man produced within the man, or the *néomort*…the animal separated within the human body itself" (37). Interestingly, a dog-ape is identified as a phase in the evolution of the pre-human. Agamben touches on human sexuality, but is silent on the status of women in the anthropological machine. Presumably a non-speaking pre-human ape-*woman* is posited as giving birth to the non-animal *Homo sapiens*, man, "the animal," according to Linnaeus, "that must recognize [or read] itself as human to be human" (cited Agamben 26). I correlate Agamben's "open" with the shifting caesurae between subject and object in Woolf's metaphors and free indirect discourse, and read Woolf's mobile signifying dogs through Levinas's stray dog.

I invite you to think of Paula Rego's *Dog Woman* (1994) as the opening narrator of *A Room of One's Own*, who, it is not difficult to infer, has been chased *like a dog* from the hallowed ground of patriarchal learning:

> It was thus that I found myself walking with extreme rapidity across a grass plot. Instantly a man's figure rose to intercept me…. His face expressed horror and indignation. Instinct rather than reason came to my help; he was a Beadle; I was a woman. This was the turf; there was the path. Only the Fellows and Scholars are allowed here; the gravel is the place for me. (*AROO* 9)

Haraway makes only a little more explicit this famous Woolfian analogy in recognising: "Woolf understood what happens when the impure stroll over the lawns of the properly registered…when these marked (and marking) beings get credentials and an income" (88). That animals and women are excluded from traditional notions of enlightenment is inferred in the "instinct" rather than "reason" that assists the speaker to realise her ironic identification by the Beadle, himself only one consonant away from the canine, as alien to the institution of education. As patriarchy's dutiful watchdog, he has hardly been secured on the side of "reason" in this sentence. His double designation of the trespasser as both a woman and, implicitly, dog shocks the wandering "I" who finds herself merely "walking," a self-definition by action and process, before she is so rudely hailed. *A Room of One's Own* becomes a lesson in how to resist this interpellation. But what may have slipped our notice is that Woolf's canine trope has *already* been initiated in the previous paragraph, where the narrator refers to the burden of her agreed talk: "That collar I have spoken of, women and fiction…a subject that raises all sorts of prejudices and passions, bowed my head to the ground" (8). The very invitation to speak has already interpellated her as a dog.

Yet this collar metaphor speaks also of the shackles of human *slavery*.[2] "Like a good deal of feminist protest literature," Marcus reminds us, *A Room of One's Own* "uses the tropes of slavery to make the case for women's oppression," "brilliantly link[ing]" scenes of violence against Englishwomen to violence against slaves (48). It would however limit the resonance of Woolf's rhetoric here to confine this convergence of racially marked and gendered tropes of oppression to the prior historical record of the centuries of Atlantic slavery, or indeed to the continuing British imperial context she was writing in. The slave economies of classical Greece, and of Biblical times, are cited too; Woolf also addresses, directly in places, the emergence of fascist and Nazi powers in Europe and their attendant racism and misogyny. Woolf's elusive narrator, who refuses a stable nomenclature or identity, is doubly yoked by the metaphors of "dog" and "slave," but the third yoke is surely "woman." The three terms coalesce at several points in the book, most strikingly in the clinching argument on the prospects for women's writing, which rearranges and amplifies a statement by Sir Arthur Quiller Couch: "Intellectual freedom depends upon material things. Poetry depends upon intellectual freedom. And women have always been poor.... Women have had less intellectual freedom than the sons of Athenian slaves. Women, then, have not had a dog's chance of writing poetry" (162-63).

The troika slave-woman-dog is rooted in the legacy of counter-enlightenment discourse that links slaves and dogs, as well as an equally entrenched patriarchal discourse that links women and dogs. The significance of dogs in the history of slavery is powerful and complicated, not least because of the way certain dogs were bred to discipline and hunt down fugitive slaves. But there is also a connected discourse that figures slaves themselves *as* dogs. Canine slave metaphors are simultaneously engaged and refigured when Woolf interferes with the patriarchal legacy of misogynist canine troping, which, I have shown elsewhere, she sources in Johnson and Carlyle.[3] Woolf's narrator, then, embodies her own predicament: to speak of Women and Fiction, she represents herself as already collared by the fiction "woman" and its implicit synonyms "dog" and "slave."

Marcus's thoroughgoing examination of the "fine negress" passage notes parenthetically the association "of the Negress with the dog [as wild creatures to be tamed and domesticated]," linked to Woolf's earlier citation of Johnson's canine analogy for a woman preaching (Marcus 49), but she does not address the more complicated canine troping at play in this passage (indeed, in the same sentence), nor the complexities of its racial marking. She does, however, judge Woolf's conjunction of "Negress" with "woman" and "Englishwoman" that the embedded citation of Johnson's dog makes available as "unfortunate" (Marcus 50). Can Woolf's text, and Woolf herself, slip the collar of "racist" that Marcus's persuasive argument seems inevitably to secure? She finds Woolf "has robbed her 'very fine negress' of subjectivity in much the same way as men appropriated hers"(52). She is persuasive on the alarming sense of appropriation in Woolf's text. After all, ownership is overtly in the tract's title. "Is she not saying," Marcus asks, "we have rooms of our own because they don't—our sisters in the former colonies on whose labor the 'first' world largely functions?" (42). A "room" of one's own discloses in mirror form the "moor" of one's own, then, standing for the black dispossessed who make white freedom possible.

Marcus's concern for the subjectivity of the "fine negress" is reasonable especially considering the slippery metaphoric, and free indirect discourse of the sentence and the larger tract that she inhabits. In such a multi-vocal text, one that is at pains to explore the connected politics of voice and subjectivity, *why*, we must ask, is there no clear and direct citation of a black woman's words? A more difficult, and radical, concern to voice would be over the subjectivity of the dog. Is it possible that the mutable speaker of this book, who famously acknowledges a destabilised subjectivity by declaring "'I' is only a convenient term for somebody who has no real being…(call me Mary Beton, Mary Seton, Mary Carmichael or by any name you please)" (7), does herself inhabit a canine morphology? In one version of the cited "Four Maries" Ballad, Mary Hamilton, whom Woolf pointedly elides and leaves unnamed, sings from the gallows of "This dog's death I'm to die."[4]

In the controversial "fine negress" passage, women are distinguished from men by their historical, inured, "anonymity":

> They are not even now as concerned about the health of their fame as men are, and, speaking generally, will pass a tombstone or a signpost without feeling an

irresistible desire to cut their names on it, as Alf, Bert or Chas. must do in obedience to their instinct, which murmurs if it sees a fine woman go by, or even a dog, Ce chien est à moi. (76)

Here Woolf prefigures patriarchal colonialism and inscription as a dog marking its territory: women, unlike men, then, do not mark out territory as a matter of "irresistible desire" and "obedience" to "instinct." The act of writing is expressed as "a reflex reaction ingrained in any European male" to appropriate and colonise (Phillips 73). But even as she reproachfully figures men writing as colonial patriarchs, which are in turn figured as dogs pissing on signposts and monuments to the dead (themselves figures of signification), she is also aligning—in the same sentence—the object of this very process, the "fine woman" with dogs: "Ce chien est à moi." Marcus recognises this crucially presents women's signature as erasure, but while she connects "ce chien" to Woolf's earlier citation of Johnson's canine trope, she ignores the dogginess of Alf, Bert and Chas. The double-gendered dog is both subject and object of colonialism. The repeated "even" ("*even* a dog;" "*even* a very fine negress," herself reprising the "fine" of "fine woman") strengthens the analogy between dog and negress, amplified in the next sentence, to show the dog as interchangeable with "a piece of land or a man with curly black hair." The dog as usual performs a number of vehicular tasks: its tenors are both men and women, English and African, coloniser and colonised.

But who is speaking in this sentence? It is not a simple matter of plumping for either Woolf or her narrator: there are too many voices, citations, and ventriloquised citations compressed here. It begins by "speaking generally" of canine men provisionally called "Alf, Bert or Chas." who are then the murmurers of "Ce chien est à moi" ("this dog is mine"), itself a citation of Blaise Pascal (Pascal 295), but which comes to Woolf, as Phillips points out, via her husband's book, *Empire and Commerce in Africa* (1920) (Phillips 73). Already, deictic functioning is in crisis: the "ce" of "ce chien," the this-ness of "this dog," is receding just as "Alf, Bert or Chas." recede. The proposition "Ce chien est à moi," in keeping with Woolf's free indirect mode, has no speech marks to collar it as the direct speech of "Alf, Bert or Chas.," nor as the verbatim citation of Pascal, albeit a citation of Leonard Woolf's citation of Pascal in the epigraph to his book on Africa: "'This dog is mine,' said those poor children; 'that is my place in the sun.' Here is the beginning and the image of the usurpation of all the earth."

Virginia Woolf has omitted from the epigraph Pascal's amplification of the claim "Ce chien est à moi" as the originating cause but also the *image* of all colonial appropriation. "Ce chien est à moi" has, then, a self-consciously figurative pedigree. But Woolf also elides the information that these words constitute the directly quoted speech of "ces pauvres enfants" (Pascal 295). Pascal has "poor children" as the origin of the primary utterance of appropriation, the universal image. Pascal universalises an instinct to appropriate by making the most innocent and the least wealthy his image of possessiveness. But Woolf sheds Pascal's "pauvres enfants," and the didactic "voilà" that Leonard Woolf retains. In her analysis, the poor are themselves the objects of appropriation, and the prospects of the poor to become poets is the basis of her argument, something she presses at the close of her book in her adapted citation from Quiller-Couch that embraces the images of the poor, women, slaves, and a dog.

The sentence that comes between those of "ce chien" and the "fine negress" is also slippery: "And, of course, it may not be a dog, I thought, remembering Parliament Square, the Sieges Allee and other avenues; it may be a piece of land or a man with curly black hair" (*AROO* 76). Without quotation marks, a full stop is all that comes between "Ce chien est à moi" and the sentence presented, also unadorned by quotation marks, as the thought of the narrator. Is "Ce chien est à moi" therefore also the thought of the narrator? Does "of course" indicate a moment of recognition, the dawning of a new thought, or is it merely the confirmation of a commonplace? As if in Socratic dialogue with the citation clipped from Pascal's dictum, it implicitly seizes on an absent "voilà," and offers an interpretation of the "chien": "And, of course, it may not be a dog...." This suggests firstly that any other object may come into the sights of the colonisers, but it also confirms Pascal's sense of the figurative work that the dog performs here: the dog is the very *image* of the appropriated object, yet it is at the same time a moveable signifier whose signified is something *not* a dog. The switch from French to English is interesting: the act of translation may suggest the signified (or referent) remains untouched by the change of signifier from "chien" to "dog." But it occurs in a proposition that states that the signifier and signified "may not be a dog" after all! Aside from raising linguistic questions concerning translations and questions of the national identity of the dog (is it French or English?), it also confirms the status of the dog (or "chien") as metaphoric vehicle for other tenors. This thought is prompted (or accompanied) by the speaker's "remembering Parliament Square, the Sieges Allee and other avenues," places which are "favoured sites of memorial statues" (Shiach 417-18).

"Sieges Allees" seems to continue the French slant of Pascal, but it is German in location and culture: it is "The Avenue of Victory" in Berlin. What "other avenues," what other sentences has Woolf's Signifying Dog run in before finding itself in this one? The allusion to the site of Berlin's imperial monuments returns us again to Leonard Woolf's book, which, marked by Pascal's "chien," addresses the Final Act of the historic Congo Conference in Berlin, and turns a canine simile to describe the rapacious actions of imperial colonial powers unleashed after the conference: "the nations of Europe...[fell] upon Africa like a pack of snarling, tearing, quarrelling jackals." The simile allows agency and choice, rather than instinct. "And when Africa in a few years had been completely divided up amid a yapping and yelping of mutual recrimination, it saw the same pack take itself off to Asia" (44). The turn to metaphor, itself an act of violence, returns the violence of the oppressors' own impositions of metaphorical discourse. The status and subjectivity of African people occupies Leonard Woolf, turning on European marauders their own dogs (racist, canine figurations).

The thought of the appropriated, marked dog, in Virginia Woolf's sentence, where previously a canine trope has the dog appropriating and marking tombstones and signposts, prompts thoughts on two locations of imperial monuments, which themselves represent the acts of colonial appropriation figured as dogs pissing on tombstones and signposts, but which simultaneously present themselves (as monuments) as the very targets for this canine practice. This heady metanarrative arabesque, which has tombstones, monuments, and signposts figured as both the subject and object of canine marking, mediates the thought "it may not be a dog" with the corresponding thought on the figurative burden of the dog: "it may be a piece of land or a man with curly black hair." If the dog is both a marked and marking being, this contradictory double status is also conferred to its tenors, "land or a man with curly black hair." It is difficult to read her "Ce chien est à moi," then, as merely parroting Pascal on colonial appropriation (Shiach 417), or parroting her husband's citation of Pascal (Phillips 73), although this latter also marks her citation with further anti-imperialist discourse that brings canine resonance to the allusion to Berlin's Sieges Allees. Woolf clearly leaves her own passing canine mark on Pascal's *Pensée*, a rhetorical feat she performs in tandem with her resignification of Dr. Johnson's dog.

The canine signifying on canine signifiers, in the two sentences that precede the sentence in which the "very fine negress" finds herself, strain the collar on the gender and racial and national markers of both the subjects and objects of the act of colonial inscription and appropriation explored here. But Woolf has already marked similar territory in *Jacob's Room*, where Clara's dog "Troy" marks the statue of "Achilles," monument to colonial imperialism (273), and where Jacob himself furnishes the familiar Johnsonian analogy for his account of the reviled presence of women in King's College Chapel: "No one would think of bringing a dog into church. For though a dog is all very well on a gravel path... the way he wanders down an aisle...approaching a pillar with a purpose...a dog destroys the service completely. So do these women" (50). Likewise the gravel path here returns in *A Room of One's Own*, as does the sacred architecture of Cambridge University. But in the "fine negress" passage, the canine trope is also doubly *racially* marked, while similarly mobile between subject and object status. Furthermore, following the scent of the Johnsonian dog trope in *The Voyage Out*, I have shown Woolf to smuggle in a semitically marked and marking dog to the already unsettling "fine negress" passage (Goldman 2001). "Fine woman" and "fine negress" recall Mary Datchet's epithet for "Sailor," the pet dog of the suffragist leader Miss Markham, in *Night and Day*: "A very fine dog, too" (*ND* 70). The suffragist dog, Sailor is also an allegory of lesbianism, according to Dunn (177).

Marcus exposes the colliding historical, aesthetic, and colonial discourses that inform the term "fine negress." She also scrutinises the term "pass": "The narrator's gaze is raced as well as gendered and powerfully erotic.... Was Woolf aware of the racial meaning of the word *pass*?" (44). Woolf certainly seems aware of the *canine* qualities of passing (Levinas's stray dog becomes relevant here). The narrator's gaze reifies the "very fine negress" as "art object" and "sexual object" for Marcus, who posits "a polished figurine the viewer conflates with the African woman it resembles" (55, 57). And why not a statue, too? The slippery canine turns of Woolf's preceding sentences certainly encourage this reading of the negress as a co-sign of the tombstone, signpost, and monument that the canine Alf, Bert, or Chas. mark when they pass, but that women do not mark when they pass, *and* as a cosign of the "fine woman" who when passed by Alf, Bert, or Chas. causes them to murmur, "Ce chien est à moi." Again, the subject and object of passing perform an intricate dance.

Just how firmly is the "narrator" collared by the term "woman"? Not a unified subject, famously, she speaks in many personae, but, I suggest, she is always and already speaking through a canine morphology. Her citation of the primary utterance of appropriation "Ce chien est à moi" is thus complicated by her own demonstrable canine morphology, hailed (interpellated) as she has been all through *A Room of One's Own* as woman, slave, and dog. Momentarily accepting the collar of "woman," she reflects on "one of the great advantages of being a woman." But how far is she speaking as a woman at all (she is pointedly not a self-designated "*English*woman"), and as a woman in the first person, when she admits "one can pass even a very fine negress without wishing to make an Englishwoman of her"? "One" can mean both "I" (nominative) and "a woman" (accusative), but it has a certain distance from both. The canine instinct of "Alf, Bert or Chas." is aligned through

Woolf's citation of Pascal to the "pack of snarling, tearing, quarrelling jackals" in her husband's simile for Europe's rabid colonisation of Africa, the jackals whose choice is to subordinate African peoples to national, imperial order. The speaker of Woolf's sentence is aligned with the canine objects, not subjects, of canine "instinct": the "woman," the "fine woman," the "very fine negress," and the "dog," all of whom are aligned with "ce chien." And the very notion of "instinct" itself has already been undermined by the "dog woman" narrator's encounter with the Beadle.

It would be a grotesque misreading to conclude that Woolf herself runs with the jackals and not the dogs in this sentence, or even that she has clumsily but unintentionally aligned herself with the jackals in using the terms "Englishwoman," "fine woman," and "very fine negress." Woolf as jackal or as dog aside, we must attend to how her sentence has been engineered to interpellate its readers as canine. Nor is it simply a matter of her reader running either with the jackals, or with the dogs, or of realising, as Woolf's slippery syntax and sliding canine signifiers encourage us to realise, that the potential for jackal and dog, for "reason" and "instinct," is there in us all. It is also the way her slippery, rhythmical repetitive syntax and her sliding canine signifiers have the reader reading and re-reading, returning to images and figures, marking and re-marking their significance, digging up her half-buried allusions, and chasing them down. Marked and marking beings, we readers (by choice, reason, or instinct?) leave our own traces on her tombstones and signposts. Meanwhile Woolf declares herself a different animal: "I'm the hare," she records in her diary of 1931, "a long way ahead of the hounds my critics" (*D4* 45).

## Notes

1. A significantly different and much expanded version of this paper is forthcoming in *Woolf Studies Annual*. See Jane Goldman, "'Ce chien est à moi': Virginia Woolf and the Signifying Dog," *Woolf Studies Annual* 13 (2007): 49-86.
2. As if to confirm that "the train of thought" is canine, a dog's view of the terrain is offered: "To the right and left bushes of some sort, golden and crimson, glowed with the colour, even it seemed burnt with the heat, of fire. On the further bank the willows wept in perpetual lamentation, their hair about their shoulders" (*AROO* 8). And again, the Biblical allusions to lamentation and to the burning bush (from where God spoke to Moses of delivery to the promised land) speak of slavery and the prospect of emancipation.
3. Woolf makes explicit her engagement with misogynist canine troping, in *A Room of One's Own*, when she invokes Dr. Johnson's infamous analogy for women preachers (*AROO* 72, 82-83); I've shown (Goldman 2006) how Woolf also derives, in her London Scene essays, a racially marked canine trope from Thomas Carlyle's pamphlet, "The Nigger Question."
4. "I charge ye all, ye mariners, /That sail upon the sea, /Let neither my father nor mother get wit, /This dog's death I'm to die." Made up version from Scott's edition of 1833.

## Works Cited

Adams, Carol J. "The Rape of Animals, the Butchering of Women." *Sexual Politics of Meat: A Feminist-Vegetarian Critical Theory* (London: Continuum, 1990). Rpt. *The Animal Ethics Reader*. Ed. Susan J. Armstrong and Richard G. Botzler. London: Routledge, 2003. 209-15

Agamben, Giorgio. *The Open: Man and Animal*. Trans. Kevin Attell. Stanford: Stanford UP, 2004.

Dunn, June. "'Beauty Shines On Two Dogs Doing What Two Women Must Not Do': Puppy Love, Same-Sex Desire and Homosexual Coding in Woolf." *Virginia Woolf: Turning the Centuries*. Ed. Ann L. Ardis and Bonnie Kime Scott. New York: Pace UP, 2000. 176-82

Eberly, David. "Housebroken: The Domesticated Relations of *Flush*." *Virginia Woolf: Texts and Contexts: Selected*

*Papers from the Fifth Annual Conference on Virginia Woolf.* Ed. Beth Rigel Daugherty and Eileen Barrett. New York: Pace UP, 1996. 21-25.

Garber, Marjorie. *Dog Love.* New York: Touchstone, 1997.

Gates, Henry Louis. *The Signifying Monkey: A Theory of African American Literary Criticism.* New York: Oxford UP, 1988.

Goldman, Jane. "Who Let the Dogs Out?: From Dr. Johnson to Horatian Woolf." Unpublished Conference Paper. 11th Annual International Conference on Virginia Woolf. University of Bangor, June 2001.

———. "Who let the dogs out?": Statues, Suffragettes, and Dogs in Woolf's London." Back to Bloomsbury: the 14th Annual International Conference on Virginia Woolf. <http://www.csub.edu/woolf_center>. September, 2006. Forthcoming in *Virginia Woolf's Bloomsbury.* Ed. Lisa Shahriari and Gina Vitello Potts. Basingstoke: Palgrave, 2007.

Haraway, Donna. *The Companion Species Manifesto: Dogs, People and Significant Otherness.* Chicago: Prickly Paradigm Press, 2003.

Levinas, Emmanuel. "The Name of a Dog, or Natural Rights." *Difficult Freedom: Essays on Judaism.* Trans. Seán Hand. Baltimore: Johns Hopkins UP, 1990. 151-53.

Marcus, Jane. *Hearts of Darkness: White Women Write Race.* New Brunswick, NJ: Rutgers UP, 2004.

Pascal, Blaise. *Pensées* (1660). <http://www.gutenberg.org/files/18269/18269-8.txt>.

Phillips, Kathy. *Virginia Woolf Against Empire.* Knoxville: University of Tennessee Press, 1994.

Rego, Paula. *Dog Woman* (oil painting, 1994). <http://library.thinkquest.org/17016/dwoman.jpg>.

Shiach, Morag, ed. *A Room of One's Own* by Virginia Woolf. Oxford: Oxford UP, 1992.

Scott, Walter. "The Queen's Marie." *Minstrelsy of the Scottish Border* (1802-03). <http://www.electricscotland.com/history/other/scott/queens_marie.htm=>.

Steeves, H. Peter. "Lost Dog, or, Levinas Faces the Animal." *Figuring Animals: Essays on Animal Images in Art, Literature, Philosophy, and Popular Culture.* Ed. Mary Sanders Pollock and Catherine Rainwater. Basingstoke: Palgrave, 2005. 21-36.

Vanita, Ruth. "'Love Unspeakable': The Uses of Allusion in *Flush.*" *Virginia Woolf: Themes and Variations.* Ed. Vara Neverow-Turk and Mark Hussey. New York: Pace UP, 1993. 248-57.

Woolf, Leonard. *Empire and Commerce in Africa: A Study in Economic Imperialism.* London: Macmillan, 1920.

Woolf, Virginia. *The Diary of Virginia Woolf.* Ed. Anne Olivier Bell with Andrew McNeillie. Vol. 4. London: Hogarth, 1982.

———. *Jacob's Room.* London: Hogarth, 1922.

———. *Night and Day.* London: Duckworth, 1919.

———. *A Room of One's Own.* London: Hogarth, 1929.

# Virginia Woolf, Ecofeminism, and Breaking Boundaries in Nature

## by Bonnie Kime Scott

As an author and feminist social critic, Virginia Woolf was extraordinarily aware of boundaries of all sorts and of ways that their traversal had psychological, cultural, and political significance. Even in her early diaries, saved in *A Passionate Apprentice*, she made imaginative juxtapositions of scenes and showed interest in the boundaries between indoor and outdoor spaces. Early and late, we find her or her characters positioned near a window, with their thoughts diverted from the cultural tasks of reading or writing by a landscape or a perceived communication from another creature. In this paper and *Virginia Woolf's Uses of Nature*, a book manuscript in progress, I am particularly concerned with boundaries on nature—where the cultivated garden meets the moors or the woods, or is invaded by wild "pests," where exotic plants and animals import echoes of the Empire, where science divides the species, or an artist like Woolf traverses such barriers to think like a moth, take in the perceptions of a snail, or the motion of a flock of birds. I shall be concentrating on Woolf's traversals of such boundaries today, testing her ecofeminist potential in the process.

I was encouraged to discover that, for this conference, two full panels were dedicated to Woolf from the environmental perspective. My original concern that there would be unpredictable overlapping of the six papers proved unnecessary; indeed there was a variety in level of abstraction that ranged from Ian Blyth's appreciation of Woolf's accuracy in describing rooks to the slippery metaphors for the dog captured by Jane Goldman. Both Diana Swanson and I see Woolf as a proto-ecofeminist, based on the relation of the human to the non-human she describes, though we focus on different texts. Relatively little has been written about Woolf's ecofeminist potential, or indeed about her attitude toward the environment. Exceptions to this include Charlotte Zoe Walker, who reads Woolf's nature writing as a conversation with nature, Elizabeth Waller, who develops a Woolfian ecology that goes beyond human language, Reginald Abbott, who has thoroughly researched the background of Woolf's essay on the "Plumage Bill," and Elisa Sparks, who offers detailed research into Woolfian gardens. There is an older tradition of those who find Woolf or her father Wordsworthian or otherwise related to the romantics.[1] I'm eager to find what else may be percolating.

Let me begin with a small dose of the still evolving critical resources afforded by ecofeminism. Environmentalist Aldo Leopold's description of the "biotic community," of which "man is...only a member" (204-05) in his landmark 1949 essay, "The Land Ethic," brought the concepts of holism and an ethical resistance to anthropocentrism to the movement now known as deep ecology. By pointing out the historical connection of anthropocentrism to androcentrism, Val Plumwood makes the turn toward ecofeminism, which critiques the notion that humans (read primarily as men) are the ones to set the boundaries on nature, to exert their power over it and control it (22). In *The Death of Nature: Women, Ecology, and the Scientific Revolution*, Caroline Merchant suggests that, for its world view, modern science reconceptualized "reality as a machine rather than a living organism" and in doing so "sanctioned the domination of both nature and women" (xviii). Harriet Ritvo finds that, during the eighteenth and nineteenth centuries, as part of a more general shift that constructed nature as increasingly vulnerable to human control, "people systematically appropriated power they had previously attributed to animals, and animals became significant primarily as the objects of human manipulation" (2). As Janis Birkeland asserts, what singles out ecofeminism from other environmental theories, and also what allows it to weave them together, is that it targets the basic "power paradigm" that lies beneath exploitation of the environment (16-17), and I take this to be basic to an understanding of both Woolfian and feminist epistemology.

Another line of thinking is offered by environmental holism and is related to the idea of the Gaia, the earth as a sacred female figure or goddess. This is an aspect of the spiritual ecofeminism that arose in the late 1970s, and is questioned by some feminists as insufficiently sensitive to differences among women.[2] It had modernist antecedents—no source more important than Woolf's friend, the classicist anthropologist, Jane Harrison. I should like to suggest here that, in addition to its spiritual roots, holism might be seen as a way to break free of the patrolling and enforcing of geographical, scientific, and environmental boundaries. Indeed it is a thought for today (summer 2006), as triple fencing of the entire southern border of the U.S., and a large presence of the National Guard is proposed in order to keep out alien others. Aside from their inhumanity to related peoples, such barriers would block environmental pathways vital to the survival of various species that circulate in their business of survival on a continuous tectonic plate.

Ecofeminist Josephine Donovan notes that first wave feminists (with whom we would include Woolf) "articulated a critique of the atomistic individualism and rationalism of the liberal tradition. They did so by proposing a vision that emphasized collectivity, emotional bonding, and an organic (or holistic) concept of life" (173). Woolf's nature writing is very much a part of her coping with the authorial egotism which arose as an issue particularly as she struggled with the critics and her male modernist counterparts.[3] Her nature writing also invites the emotions that, in *A Room of One's Own,* she theorized as vital to the construction of the novel. Woolf's introduction of emotion as a foundation for creativity anticipates the arguments of ecofeminist ethicists. Donovan explores such work, focusing upon the concept of "sympathy." She finds that "the dominant strain in contemporary ethics reflects a male bias toward rationality, defined as the construction of abstract universals that elide not just the personal, the contextual, and the emotional, but also the political components of an ethical issue" (147). Donovan locates in phenomenology an approach to sympathy that involves complex imaginative constructions and analysis of nature's own expressive language (150-52). The fit with Woolf is a fine one. It has been suggested that in Woolf "phenomenology found its novelist" (Wilde 198).

Current discussions of the importance of enlightenment thought to Woolf are of relevance here. Elizabeth Flynn traces both enlightenment (seen as modernist) and romantic (seen as anti-modernist) strains in Woolf, drawing attention to the importance of emotion in Woolf's reading process, in support of the latter strain. Christine Froula's recent work directs Woolf toward Kantian enlightenment, though her attention to the Garden of Eden and the female chrysalis formation in *The Voyage Out* demonstrate her sensitivity to the power of nature in female construction. Froula quotes Kant on the artist's uses of nature: "By creating 'another nature…out of the material that actual nature gives it,' endowed with a 'completeness' nowhere found in nature, the artist throws a bridge from nature's realm to the realm of freedom" (13). This stands closer to the male modernist mastery of "make it new" than I can comfortably accept. Still, we might ask what sort of freedom comes from various readings of Woolf, and what boundaries we may still wish to traverse or impose on new readings, including ones enabled by an ecofeminist approach.

Though its exclusivity has now been successfully challenged, the modernism framed by the "Men of 1914" had little room for expression of the emotions or respect for observed, as opposed to "made," nature. In his famous quarrel with Roger Fry over the Omega Workshop, which extended into an attack on Woolf in *Men Without Art,* Wyndham Lewis found Bloomsbury too close to nature. His short-lived but influential journal, *Blast* (1914-15), relegated nature to an inferior, feminine position in the hierarchy of creativity and control—a tradition reaching back to Aristotle. Lewis's typical landscape of the period was an urban, technologically-inspired grid-work (see Corbett 106).

I actually think there is a lot of room for a greening of modernism, in both male as well as female writers of the period, and would place T. S. Eliot, D. H. Lawrence, H. D., and Katherine Mansfield high on the list of those susceptible to such rereading. Leonard Woolf, interestingly, has his own place in this project. Of particular interest today is his reaction to Lytton Strachey, who accused him of being sentimental in relation to animals: "There grows up between you affection of a purity and simplicity which seems to me peculiarly satisfactory. There is also a cosmic strangeness about animals which always fascinates me and gives to my affection for them a mysterious depth or background" (100). This attitude can be seen even in Leonard's accounts of his responsibilities regarding wild animals while he was stationed in Ceylon—an episode that must await a longer airing. The challenge to the species barrier expressed in Leonard's empathetic relation to animals is akin to ecofeminist thinking. In his paper concerning the London Zoo at this conference (published in this volume), Richard Espley noted that Leonard, like Leslie Stephen before him, was a fellow of the Zoo. The zoo was a favorite destination for the Woolfs, both during their courtship and after the marriage of the couple who addressed one another as Mongoose and Mandrill. On another natural front, Leonard as a gardener is worthy of the attention Elisa Sparks has given him. His highly quantitative approach, however, may not immediately speak to ecofeminists. Virginia Woolf had the more holistic view of gardens, as sites for conversation, and (starting in "Kew Gardens") places where human and animal activities, light and dark become blurred, erasing boundaries and hierarchies.

Given that segue, I'd like to move on now to a set of Woolf's artistic relations to "others" of nature, placing the emphasis on the boundaries she perceives and occasionally crosses. I am drawing from various chapters of my book in progress, and widespread Woolfian texts—I hope without creating a dizzying effect. I promised in the abstract to present moths, egrets, porpoises, pumpkins, red hot pokers, tulips, and orchids as central characters—a list that now seems far too ambitious.

Woolf's girlhood diaries give us a first look at her shaping of contact with the "others" of nature. She is assigned by her father and her doctor the task of constructing a back garden at the family home at Hyde Park Gate, and manages to shift much of the labor to her more willing gardener sister, Vanessa, who went on to create the memorable, mixed media gardens of Charleston and to transport them into her paintings and illustrations. I say mixed media because mosaics and pottery combined with a large array of flowers, many of them old-fashioned varieties, some imports from the Empire like the red hot poker, with even the occasional artichoke, and silver foliage, mixed in for texture. At fifteen, Virginia is far from sympathetic with marauding sparrows that move right in on grass seed she has planted. It is notable, however, that for the first time she attributes a language to birds, and may indeed be engaging in mock vituperation: "the horrid little creatures swooped down twittering & made off with the oats" (*PA* 96). As the gardening was supposed to be therapeutic, following Woolf's first psychological crisis after her mother's death, it is fortunate that some of the seed does sprout, proving that "the wretched sparrows did not get it all" (100). Interestingly, Eleanor Ormerod, who would become the subject of one of Woolf's "Lives of the Obscure," dedicated her life to the elimination of similar pests (see Christina Alt's essay in this volume). While she is best known as the agricultural entomologist who helped control the green fly's devastation of crops, she also launched a concerted if controversial campaign against the house sparrow, which she identified as a rat with wings! We cannot extricate Woolf or Ormerod from the effort to control nature.

In her mature writing, Woolf continued to represent invasions of the orderly, cultured garden. Red hot pokers grow in the Ramsays' garden. Brought from the colonial territories of South Africa and Madagascar, the pokers' floral spikes may rise up to four feet; they comprise hundreds of small flowers radiating from a thick stem. Strolling in this place, the couple is divided in their thoughts—Mr. Ramsay thinking of the former freedom he'd experienced on the distant sand hills, before becoming the protector of his brood on a diminishing spit of land; Mrs. Ramsay looking toward the town, where in social work she found purpose, aside from her family.[4] They turn to the "path where the silver-green spear-like plants grew" (*TTL* 70). But here Mrs. Ramsay is concerned that her husband doesn't notice the flowers, that rabbits may be ruining her evening primroses (71), and that she cannot bring up the bill for repairing the greenhouse. She plans flowers for the big bed where dahlias currently grow, suspecting that the bulbs she sends down from London may not get planted. She indicts Kennedy the gardener with "incurable laziness…. If she stood over him all day long with a spade in her hand, he did sometimes do a stroke of work" (67). Here Woolf provides a fine example of Mrs. Ramsay's variable status in relation to privilege and oppression. As a home maker of some means, Mrs. Ramsay can maintain exotic species imported from the Empire, and cultivates fragile plants requiring a greenhouse. As the employer of a gardener, she has the power to be oppressive. As a wife, she is subject to her husband's oppressions, unable to speak on economic matters.

The deaths of Andrew, Prue, and Mrs. Ramsay demonstrate that there are gaps in the protective boundaries of this family that resonate with the vulnerabilities of the garden. It runs wild in the "Time Passes" interval, irrespective of boundaries of class and separation of species, vital and sometimes even beautiful in effect: "In spring the garden urns, casually filled with wind-blown plants, were gay as ever" (*TTL* 138). Mrs. McNab takes home flowers, seeing no harm in this, as the family is unlikely to return (139). Thinking of Mrs. Ramsay bending over her flowers, she regrets, "the garden was a pitiful sight now, all run to riot, and rabbits scuttling at you out of the beds" (139). At the final stage of human neglect,

> Poppies sowed themselves among the dahlias; the lawn waved with long grass; giant artichokes towered among roses; a fringed carnation flowered among the cabbages; while the gentle tapping of a weed at the window had become, on

winters' nights, a drumming from sturdy trees and thorned briars which made the whole room green in summer.... What power could now prevent the fertility, the insensibility of nature? (141-42)

Mrs. McNab and her crew at least scythe the grass. The anonymous, cosmic questioner's idea of "insensibility" maintains the rational edge on the random operations of nature.

*The Waves*, particularly in its intervals, offers more observation than control of what goes on in the garden; indeed the material of the intervals is continuous with the matter of the soliloquies delivered by the characters. Birds are no longer invaders, but comprehensive observers. We find them in the third interlude, as they sing in the trees or move in flight, when *"they swerved, all in one flight, when the black cat moved among the bushes, when the cook threw cinders on the ash heap and startled them"* (*TW* 73). Slightly later they are *"intensely conscious of one thing...perhaps...a snail shell, rising in the grass like a grey cathedral...or perhaps they saw the splendour of the flowers making a light of flowing purple over the beds,"* and still later *"they looked deeper beneath the flowers, down the dark avenues into the unlit world where the leaf rots and the flower has fallen. Then one of them, beautifully darting, accurately alighting, spiked the soft, monstrous body of the defenceless worm"* (74). Here Woolf experiments with thinking as a bird, and creates one of many holistic views accessible in her work, one in which the human order is only part of the great cycle of life and death. A very obvious second example is the consciousness of Mrs. Dalloway, feeling continuous with other entities, linking across people, places and time, as she contemplates the trees of St. James's Park "who lifted her on their branches as she had seen the trees lift the mist, but it spread out ever so far, her life, herself" (*MD* 9).

Woolf's girlhood capacity for satire, including both self-satire and satire of patriarchal power in relation to nature and hunting, finds numerous early expressions. A favorite of mine is in her 1899 "Warboys" diary, which takes us on a memorable moth-hunt in Huntingdonshire, subjecting her elder brother Thoby to the heaviest parody. Scientific methods and the British game tradition are implicated in this satire of "the most scientific way of catching moths" (*PA* 144). The leader of the expedition is identified only as J. T. S., echoing the penchant for initials in British academic publishing, including scientific annals. Thoby is cast as a meticulously costumed great white hunter. There is plenty of mockery in reserve for his bumbling accomplices, down to the dog, and including herself:

> Man, the hunter, starts forth in the following procession. Firstly of course the leader of the expedition, the renowned J. T. S. He wears a large felt hat, & muffled round him is a huge brown plaid, which makes his figure striding in the dark most picturesque & brigand like. In his hand he carries a glass jar—of which more anon. 2ndly appears a female form in evening dress, a shawl over her shoulders, & carrying a large stickless net. 3rdly the lantern bearer (none other than the present writer) who lights the paths fitfully with a Bicycle lamp of brilliant but uncertain powers of illumination...4thly Ad. L. S. a supernumerary amateur of no calling who takes little interest in the proceedings & is proficient in the art of obscuring the lamp at critical moments; 5thly Gurth the dog member, whose services are unrequired & unrewarded; being the first to investigate the sugar & having been convicted of attempts to catch moths for no entomological purpose whatever. (*PA* 144-45)

These aspiring entomologists manage to jar a huge, rare red underwing. Young Virginia knows its name because it was her duty to look up such identities for her siblings. Woolf adds an element of emotion to the outcome: "the whole procession felt some unprofessional regret when, with a last gleam of scarlet eye & scarlet wing, the grand old moth vanished" (145).

There are numerous later critiques of hunting in Woolf. Among the most notable is her indictment of the methods men used to garner egret plumes in her essay, "The Plumage Bill," where she also criticizes environmentalists who place blame on women for demanding such accoutrements. Woolf satirizes England's trophy hunters, as in this case via a bored Lady Orlando:

> The Archduke would bethink him how he had shot an elk in Sweden, and Orlando would ask, was it a very big elk, and the Archduke would say that it was not as big as the reindeer which he had shot in Norway; and Orlando would ask, had he ever shot a tiger, and the Archduke would say he had shot an albatross, and Orlando would say (half hiding her yawn) was an albatross as big as an elephant, and the Archduke would say—something very sensible, no doubt, but Orlando heard it not, for she was looking at her writing table, out of the window, at the door. (*O* 181)

Woolf offers more unusual qualms about fishing. One occurrence comes in the "Plumage Bill" essay, where she wonders why only the purchase of bird plumes by women shopping on Oxford Street is subject to critical scrutiny by environmentalists. Aiming at the male consumer, she muses, "Such an outburst about a fishing-rod would be deemed sentimental in the extreme. *Yet I suppose that salmon have their feelings*" (*E3* 243, emphasis added). Grotesque fishing practices are instanced in *To the Lighthouse*, as McAlister's boy carves bait from a live fish, and when a young Bart Oliver appalls his little sister with baiting a hook. Several women, including Lady Bradshaw in *Mrs. Dalloway* and Isa Oliver in *Between the Acts* once fished, until fishlike they went under, or were tangled by their husbands' lines. A mystical, irrational expression of connection to the world of sea creatures may be apprehended in the sighting of the "fin in the waste of waters" by Virginia Stephen off Cornwall in 1905, an image she passes on to Bernard in *The Waves* (e.g., 189).

In her late essay, "The Death of the Moth," Woolf takes up a typical position between indoors and out, near a window. She is writing, but she is also attentive to a day-flying moth, and she enters into its reality via hers. The initial significance of this creature—a humble, less beautiful form of moth than the class of night-flyers—is that it shared "the same energy which inspired the rooks, the ploughmen, the horses, and even, it seemed, the lean bare-backed downs" on a mild mid-September morning (*DM* 4). Her construct suggests the Gaia concept of the globe as a united, living thing. The essay grows somber as Woolf pities the self-imposed limits of the moth, banging around on a single pane of glass, when the wide expanse of the downs lies outside. Slowly she recognizes that this obscure creature is struggling with death, and it wins her respect by righting itself, achieving what Woolf constructs as a sense of composure. While nature's force of death cannot be dominated, a righted position can be achieved. It was all the more moving when the "hay-colored" moth is seen as a neglected "other:" "when there was nobody to care or to know, this gigantic effort on the part of an insignificant little moth, against a power of such magnitude, to retain what no one else valued or desired to keep, moved one strangely" (6). Showing an early sense of shared energy, and a growing respect for the struggle of an insignificant being against the greater power of death, Woolf constructs solidarity across distant species. At strategic points in her writing, which are allied to her feminism, Woolf questions abuses and controls of living things, even as she allows their differences and seeming invasions. She studies earth's living beings with care. Through her characters and narrators she encourages the dispersal of the self into this collective, and thereby defies spiritual defeat, and death itself.

## Notes

1. See, as a strong example, Ellen Tremper's *"Who Lived at Alfoxton?": Virginia Woolf and English Romanticism* (Lewisburg: Bucknell UP, 1998).
2. Notable examples are the work of Carol Christ, Charlene Spretnak, and Starhawk.
3. See for example her response to Joyce in her "Modern Novels" notebook (643).
4. Maria DiBattista suggests that "one is the genius of the shore, the other of the garden, offering their protest against 'the reign of chaos'" (74).

## Works Cited

Abbott, Reginald. "Birds Don't Sing in Greek: Virginia Woolf and 'The Plumage Bill.'" *Animals and Women*. Ed. Carol Adams and Josephine Donovan. 263-89.
Adams, Carol and Josephine Donovan, ed. *Animals and Women: Feminist Theoretical Explorations*. Durham: Duke UP, 1995.
Birkeland, Janis. "Ecofeminism: Linking Theory and Practice." *Ecofeminism*. Ed Greta Gaard. 13-59.
Cantrell, Carol H. "'The Locus of Compossibility': Virginia Woolf, Modernism, and Place." *The ISLE Reader: Ecocriticism, 1993-2003*. Ed. Michael P. Branch and Scott Slovic. Athens: University of Georgia Press, 2003. 33-46.
Di Battista, Maria. *Virginia Woolf's Major Novels: The Fables of Anon*. New Haven: Yale UP, 1980.
Donovan, Josephine. "Animal Rights and Feminist Theory." *Ecofeminism*. Ed. Greta Gaard. 167-94.
Flynn, Elizabeth A. *Feminism Beyond Modernism*. Carbondale: Southern Illinois UP, 2002.
Froula, Christine. *Virginia Woolf and the Bloomsbury Avant-Garde: War, Civilization, Modernity*. New York: Columbia UP, 2005.
Gaard, Greta, ed. *Ecofeminism: Women, Animals, Nature*. Philadelphia: Temple UP, 1993.
Kheel, Marti. "License to Kill: An Ecofeminist Critique of Hunters' Discourse." *Animals and Women*. Ed. Carol Adams and Josephine Donovan. 85-125.
Leopold, Aldo. "The Land Ethic." *A Sand Country Almanac and Sketches Here and There*. Special Commemorative Edition. 1949. New York: Oxford UP, 1989. 201-26.
Merchant, Carolyn. *The Death of Nature: Women, Ecology, and the Scientific Revolution*. San Francisco: Harper and Row, 1979.
Plumwood, Val. *Feminism and the Mastery of Nature*. London: Routledge, 1993.
Ritvo, Harriet. *The Animal Estate: The English and Other Creatures in the Victorian Age*. Cambridge: Harvard UP, 1987.
Walker, Charlotte Zoe. "The Book 'Laid Upon the Landscape': Virginia Woolf and Nature." *Beyond Nature Writing: Expanding the Boundaries of Ecocriticism*. Ed. Karla Armbruster and Kathleen R. Wallace. Charlottesville: University Press of Virginia, 2001. 143-61.
Wilde, Alan. "Touching Earth: Virginia Woolf and the Prose of the World." *Philosophical Approaches to Literature: New Essays on Nineteenth- and Twentieth-Century Texts*. Ed. William E. Cain. Lewisburg: Bucknell UP, 1984. 140-64.

Woolf, Leonard. *Beginning Again: An Autobiography of the Years 1911 to 1918*. San Diego: Harcourt Brace Jovanovich, 1964.
Woolf, Virginia. *The Death of the Moth and Other Essays*. 1942. San Diego: Harcourt Brace Jovanovich, 1970. 3-6.
——. *The Essays of Virginia Woolf*. Ed. Andrew McNeillie. Vol. 3. London: Hogarth, 1988.
——. "Modern Novels." Ed. Suzette Henke. *The Gender of Modernism*. Ed. Bonnie Kime Scott. Bloomington: Indiana UP, 1990. 642-45.
——. *Mrs. Dalloway*. 1925. Annotated and introd. Bonnie Kime Scott. Orlando: Harcourt, 2005.
——. *Orlando*. 1928. San Diego: Harcourt Brace Jovanovich, 1956.
——. *A Passionate Apprentice: The Early Journals of Virginia Woolf*. Ed. Mitchell A. Leaska. London: Hogarth, 1992.
——. *To the Lighthouse*. 1927. Annotated and introd. Mark Hussey. Orlando: Harcourt, 2005.
——. *The Years*. 1937. San Diego: Harcourt Brace Jovanovich, 1965.

# Woolf's Transformation of Providential Form in *Mrs. Dalloway*

## by Emily Kopley

Woolf's preliminary notes for *Mrs. Dalloway* specify that "The interview with the specialist must be in the middle" (Small *Dalloway* Notebook, 9 November 1922). And indeed, Septimus Smith's appointment with Dr. Bradshaw lies halfway through the novel. The scene begins halfway through the day, as well, at "precisely twelve o'clock" (*MD* 80). The question I would like to address is *why* this scene "must" occur "in the middle." Molly Hoff has suggested abundant mythical sources, such as Ovid, for what she calls "the midday topos" of the novel (449). I would like to add to the sources Hoff suggests one concerning not the classical literary tradition, but the Christian one.

That Septimus is a Christ figure is explicit in *Mrs. Dalloway*. That Bradshaw, an evangelical Christian, condemns this Christ figure, is clearly hypocritical. Clarissa Dalloway's disgust with Bradshaw and with Doris Kilman, another self-righteous Christian, confirms the novel's opposition to hypocritical Christianity. The spiritual stances of the novel's main characters are thus evident from the text. What is more subtle, and what I would like to show, is that Woolf subverts the traditional Providential form to highlight Christian hypocrisy. In particular, the noonday scene of Septimus's condemnation to death finds a complement in Clarissa's midnight vision at the novel's conclusion, in which she affirms her own humanistic faith. By working with the boundaries between morning and afternoon (noon), evening and morning (midnight), Woolf stands on the grander boundary between tradition and innovation.

Septimus's status as Christ figure, and Bradshaw's as hypocritical Christian, merit brief detailing. Early in the book Septimus is described as "lately taken from life to death, the Lord who had come to renew society, who lay like a coverlet, a snow blanket smitten only by the sun, for ever unwasted, suffering for ever, the scapegoat, the eternal sufferer, but he did not want [this identity], he moaned" (22). He is "aged about thirty" (12), senses "the birth of a new religion" (19), clings to "miracles, revelations, agonies" (121), sees proverb-like revelations (21, 58), and has "won crosses" (75). Woolf apostrophizes Septimus as one of the "prophetic Christs" whom Bradshaw counsels (84) and as among "the exalted of mankind," "the criminal before his Judges...the Lord who had gone from life to death" (82). Further, Septimus's feeling that "human nature had condemned him to death" (77, and similar on 82) alludes to the book of Luke, which states of Christ that "the chief priests and our rulers delivered him to be condemned to death" (24.20). Indeed, like Christ, Septimus is not recognized by most people around him as prophetic, and sacrifices himself so that others—in particular, Clarissa—may live happily. And finally, his visions are of promoting "universal love: the meaning of the world" (57, 125), the most basic demand of Christianity.

By contrast to the Christ-figure of Septimus, Bradshaw is a Christian lacking Christian spirit. He, like the priests and rulers who condemned Christ, fails to respect the divinity, or at least the humanity in his midst. Bradshaw is a "priest of science" (80) and "worship[s] proportion" (84), while seeking to convert others to his heartless breed of Christianity and to his faith in proportion. In his effort to convert others, Bradshaw is a force against life: he "forbade childbirth" (84) and "feasts most subtly on the human will" (85). At her party Clarissa thinks that he is "obscurely evil...capable of some indescribable outrage—forcing your soul...they make life intolerable, men like that" (157). The capstone of Bradshaw's role as a force against life is, of course, his condemnation to death of Septimus.

Septimus embodies the spirit, not the letter, of Christianity. He regards himself as a *universal* Messiah, unattached to a specific religion, and desiring not to convert and judge others but simply to share his message of love and peace. And in his respect for trees he is a force for life. Bradshaw embodies the letter of Christianity, the dogmatic perversion of Christ's teachings, demanding that people convert to his religious views and condemning nonconformists to death. By equating Bradshaw, in Septimus's view, with "human nature," Woolf intimates the prevalence of the hypocrisy of Christianity. She sees Christianity as having strayed far from striving towards the love and peace that Christ originally preached and which Septimus too preaches.

The confrontation between Bradshaw and Septimus occurs, as already noted, "in the middle of the novel." Woolf repeatedly stresses that it occurs at the middle of the day, noon: "It was precisely twelve o'clock; twelve by Big Ben.... Twelve was the hour of their appointment" (80). During this appointment, as Septimus is evaluated by Bradshaw for apparent madness, he tells himself, "Once you fall...human nature is on you" (83). Septimus regards Bradshaw as "remorseless" and a "torturer" (83), while Bradshaw patronizingly prescribes "milk in bed" for a patient who to him is one of many deluded "prophetic Christs." While Christianity teaches that once you fall—that is, once you sin—the judgment of Christ is upon you, in this case the role of judger and judged are reversed: human nature here judges the Christ figure.

The structuring of *Mrs. Dalloway* around a noon scene exemplifies what Alastair Fowler discusses as the Christian literary tradition of Providential form. This form involves the structuring of a literary work around what Fowler calls a "numerological centre," one concerning Christ's judgment. Fowler explains that this structure emerged in the Middle Ages, when "the theological tradition of Biblical exegesis...taught the habit of regarding the most serious literature as numerically constructed, and of giving special attention to the centre verses of chapters, in the search for types of Christ" (66). This prioritization of a work's centre was prompted by the biblical book of Malachi, which describes how precisely at noon (the centre of the day) the "sun of righteousness" appears (4.2). Christian readers in the Middle Ages regarded this "sun of righteousness" as an emblem of Christ-come-in-judgment. Fowler observes Providential form throughout Elizabethan and Baroque poetry. He notes, for instance, the presence of angels and a rising sun in the numerically central stanza of Donne's "Nuptial Song," as well as the Messiah's returning ascent to Heaven, after defeating Satan and his band, at the centre of *Paradise Lost* (Fowler 72, 116-17).[1]

Douglas Brooks extends Fowler's observations by observing Providential form in eighteenth-century British novels, including Daniel Defoe's *Robinson Crusoe*. Woolf's diary and *Common Reader* essays demonstrate her deep familiarity with the British literary canon, and convey her particular fondness for the writing of, among others, Donne and Defoe. Her essay "Defoe" in *The Common Reader* predates *Mrs. Dalloway* by several years. *Robinson Crusoe* may have offered Woolf the model for the providential structure of *Mrs. Dalloway*, and certainly she might have observed it in many other British literary works. I suggest that Woolf appropriated the Providential form from writers who used it to advance Christianity. This appropriation allowed Woolf both to assert her place in the same tradition and to break with it, arguing against self-righteous Christianity and rather in favor of the *spirit* of Christianity, Clarissa's "atheist's religion of doing good for the sake of goodness" (66).

Brooks notes that in *Robinson Crusoe*, halfway through the book, Crusoe sees the famous footprint. Crusoe writes that the time is "about noon," and when he is "half Way" between two places, he finds the footprint (Defoe 153). Brooks sees this discovery as "a trial of Crusoe's spiritual strength" (22). Crusoe fails the trial, but then spends the second half of the book repenting and converting to Christianity—and converting others, most notably Friday (see Brooks, 20-26, for a full discussion of the centre of *Robinson Crusoe*).

In *Mrs. Dalloway*, Septimus, like Crusoe, is spiritually tested at noon. But by contrast to Crusoe, Septimus is tested by one who *himself* converts others. Woolf uses the sun as an emblem for the converter, the judger, who is in her appropriation of Providential form not Christ but the hypocritical Christian. In both cases, the intensity of the noonday sun corresponds to the intensity of the judgment. Defoe uses the form to celebrate Crusoe and Christian evangelicalism; Woolf to denigrate Bradshaw and the same. While in traditional providential narratives, the hero is judged by Christ, here the *enemy* is judging Christ.

And like *Robinson Crusoe*, which abounds with concern for seeking a life in the "middle station" and "middle State," *Mrs. Dalloway* abounds with talk of "middle"s. For instance, Woolf relates early on that the story occurs in "the middle of June" (*MD* 4), with June being the middle month of the year. Further, when Peter regards himself as the "solitary traveller," he imagines that Clarissa dies, and that "the final stroke tolled for death that surprised in the midst of life" (43). Clarissa herself echoes Peter when she learns of Septimus's suicide, and thinks, "in the middle of my party, here's death" (156). These passages buttress Septimus's feeling of condemnation to death at the mathematical middle of the novel.

Yet the sun does seem to have multiple meanings. The sun is equated not only with Bradshaw's harsh judgment of Septimus, but also with more positive sentiments. Jean M. Wyatt has masterfully explicated how the sun motif represents life and death, and has also suggested many literary and mythic allusions related to life and death throughout the novel. Building on Wyatt's explication, I suggest that the contrary associations with the sun allow for the possibility of resurrection, life-in-death. The proliferation of sun imagery leading up to the middle scene of *Mrs. Dalloway* anticipates human-nature-come-in-judgment at the clash of Septimus and Bradshaw. Septimus has a horrifying vision, early in the novel, of the sun becoming "extraordinarily hot" (13) at a quarter to noon. And Clarissa repeats over and over to herself the *Cymbeline* line, "Fear no more the heat o' the sun." Septimus too echoes the line (118). The phrase "heat o' the sun" suggests Septimus's apocalyptic vision and his noon feeling of condemnation to death by a representative of "human nature" who "make[s] life intolerable." By reciting the refrain, Clarissa and Septimus tell themselves no more to fear others' fatal judgment. The refrain alludes not only to death, but also to life and rebirth. "The heat o' the sun" suggests life at its peak. Right before Septimus leaps to his death, he thinks, "Life was good. The sun hot" (127), equating the sun with affirmation of life. In *Cymbeline*, the line particularly refers to Imogen's death, which is only temporary, a "locking-up the spirits for a time, / To be more fresh, reviving" (1.5.40-42). So too in *Mrs. Dalloway* does the line embrace life and death—in effect saying, "Fear no more the threat of death," "Fear no more the joys of life." Neither death nor life need be feared if resurrection is possible, as it is for Imogen and for Christ. Likewise, by provoking Clarissa's profound celebration of life at the novel's end, Septimus too endures.

I contend that Clarissa's final vision at the novel's end offers a response to Bradshaw's judgment of Septimus at the novel's middle not only through Clarissa's approval of Septimus's suicide, but also through the scene's setting at midnight. This midnight timing highlights how Clarissa's vision affirms life in answer to Bradshaw's noon condemnation of it. In Providential form, since noon marks the presence of Christ-come-in-judgment, midnight marks the absence of such, and thus potentially the absence of meaning. Just as Woolf subverts the form at noon by exchanging the roles of judger and judged, she subverts it at midnight by granting Clarissa an affirmative vision. While in Providential form, noon marks the coming of Christ, who from a Christian perspective, gives life all its meaning, in *Mrs. Dalloway*, midnight marks Clarissa's triumphant revelation that *people* give life its meaning. What prompts this revelation is Clarissa's seeing that "in the room opposite the old lady stared straight at her" (157). Clarissa has seen this lady earlier in the novel: "Why creeds and prayers and mackintoshes? When, thought Clarissa, that's the miracle, that's the mystery; that old lady" (108). Septimus, right before his suicide, has seen a very similar sight: "He did not want to die. Life was good. The sun hot. Only human beings? Coming down the staircase *opposite an old man stopped and stared at him*. Holmes was at the door. 'I'll give it you!' [Septimus] cried" (127, emphasis added). Septimus then leaps out the window to his death. These passages show the differing spiritualities of Clarissa and Septimus. Septimus's faith is not grounded on normal human interaction. Septimus does not find in the old man the humanistic faith that Clarissa finds upon seeing the old lady. Clarissa, though she bears much affinity with Septimus, is sane. Her faith is grounded on experience interacting with other people. Hers is the faith in humanity Septimus might have had if the war had not distorted it for him, and "human nature"—Holmes, in the passage above, and Bradshaw at noon—confirmed this distortion.

The old lady represents Clarissa's and, I believe, Woolf's own faith in humanity and rejection of faith in a Christian God. So when Clarissa sees the woman again at the novel's end, she again celebrates the miracle and mystery of humanity:

> In the room opposite the old lady stared straight at her! She was going to bed. And the sky.... It was new to her [i.e. Clarissa].... She was going to bed in the room opposite.... She pulled the blind now. The clock began striking. The young man had killed himself; but she did not pity him; with the clock striking the hour, one, two, three, she did not pity him, with all this going on. There! The old lady had put out her light! The whole house was dark now with this going on, she repeated, and the words came to her, Fear no more the heat of the sun. She must go back to them. But what an extraordinary night! She felt somehow very like him—the young man who had killed himself. She felt glad that he had done it; thrown it away. The clock was striking. The leaden circles dissolved in the air. (157)

Although Woolf does not say outright that this vision occurs at midnight, the triple mention of the clock's striking recalls the triple mention of Big Ben striking at noon. Nowhere else in the novel does the clock's striking merit three mentions. Further, the fact that Clarissa exults when "The old lady had put out her light!" and "The whole house was dark" (158) shows that total darkness, often associated with the midnight hour, is complicit in her vision. And in fact *The Hours*, the manuscript version of *Mrs. Dalloway*, *does* set the scene explicitly at midnight. In an early draft in the manuscript, Woolf started this passage with, "Big Ben began with his usual solemnity to strike twelve times." In a later draft, Woolf wrote, "Big Ben began striking. One, Two, Three; & she was extraordinarily happy…to hear Big Ben strike Three, Four, five, six, seven, was profound & tremendous…Never would she submit—never, never! / Eight, Big Ben struck, nine, ten, eleven; & / But Clarissa was gone" (*Hours* f. 3.99). Woolf's removal of the explicit mention of the time is more subtle. The final version of the novel hints at midnight, but invites the reader to make the connection between this passage and the noon passage.

Clarissa's happiness about the suicide responds to Bradshaw's noon attempt to thwart Septimus's will to commit suicide. Clarissa feels "glad" about the suicide, and gains deeper appreciation of life from Septimus's defiant death. Clarissa feels reborn, as suggested by the parallel between "the sky.… It was new to her" and *The Tempest*'s "'O Brave New world / That has such people in't!'/ 'Tis new to thee'" (5.1.1883-84). In Clarissa's sense of rebirth lies Septimus's own rebirth, as a catalyst for others' joy in life. Woolf's subversion of Providential form is complete. At noon, Christ does not come in judgment of man, but man comes in judgment of Christ. At midnight, not despair in Christ but faith in humanity prevails, a faith that inspires a sense of rebirth. Woolf employs a Christian literary tradition to honor a secular, modern philosophy. In so doing, Woolf demonstrates how modernist writers found new uses for old literary forms, and engaged with the past while breaking with it.

### Notes

1   Fowler calculates that the Messiah's ascent in *Paradise Lost* occurs precisely halfway through the 10,550 lines of the poem's first edition. In the second edition, the verses describing the Messiah's ascent are not quite mathematically central according to line number, yet the event still occurs halfway through the poem according to another, more obvious calculation: it concludes the sixth of twelve books. Woolf may have been familiar with both editions of *Paradise Lost*, though the second edition has long been the more popular. The ascent in the second edition reads, "he celebrated rode / Triumphant through mid Heav'n, into the courts / And temple of his mighty Father throned / On high; who into glory him received, / Where now he sits at the right hand of bliss" (6.888-92).

### Works Cited

Brooks, Douglas. *Number and Pattern in the Eighteenth-Century Novel*. London: Routledge & Kegan Paul, 1973.
Carroll, Robert and Stephen Prickett, eds. *Authorized King James Version with Apocrypha Bible*. New York: Oxford UP, 1997.
Defoe, Daniel. *Robinson Crusoe*. Ed. J. Donald Crowley. New York: Oxford UP, 1998.
Fowler, Alastair. *Triumphal Forms: Structural Patterns in Elizabethan Poetry*. Cambridge: Cambridge UP, 1970.
Hoff, Molly. "The Midday Topos in *Mrs. Dalloway*." *Twentieth Century Literature* 36 (1990): 449-63.
Milton, John. *Paradise Lost*. Ed. John Leonard. London: Penguin, 2003.
Shakespeare, William. *The Riverside Shakespeare*. Ed. G. Blakemore Evans et al, 2nd ed. Boston and New York: Houghton Mifflin, 1997.
Woolf, Virginia. *The Hours: the British Museum Manuscript of* Mrs. Dalloway. Ed. Helen M. Wussow. New York: Pace UP, 1996.
———. *Mrs. Dalloway*. Ed. David Bradshaw. Oxford: Oxford UP, 2000.
———. Small *Dalloway* Notebook. Ms. Henry W. and Albert A. Berg Collection, New York Public Library.
Wyatt, Jean M. "*Mrs. Dalloway*: Literary Allusion as Structural Metaphor." *PMLA* 88 (1973): 440-51.

# Pilfering Modernism's Image:
## Woolf and Those Other Londoners

### by Thaine Stearns

In November 1918, Woolf wrote to Roger Fry that they had had "that strange young man Eliot to dinner," with whom they discussed contemporary writers, including Ezra Pound, Wyndham Lewis, and James Joyce (*L2* 295). For the American T. S. Eliot Woolf had already begun to form an attachment: "Eliot I liked on the strength of one visit," she says in a diary entry from about the same time (*D1* 235), but about Pound her expressed view to Fry is quite different: although Eliot thought Pound, Lewis, and Joyce "great geniuses," she thought that he was "stuck in this mud." "Can't his culture carry him through," she wonders about Eliot, "or does culture land one there?" (*L2* 296). I shall return to this question because its ambiguity underlies one of my claims in this essay, that Woolf's engagement with Imagism and Vorticism, the literary and art movements advanced by Pound, are subtly nuanced and complicated by her competition for status with other modernist writers. She finishes this letter to Fry with an assurance about her allegiance to him and to Post-Impressionism, which Pound and especially Lewis had attacked: "not that I've read more than 10 words by Ezra Pound," she avers, "my conviction of his humbug is unalterable." She continues by affirming Fry's significance, closing the letter by saying, "Yes, Roger, the more I think of it—and I often do—the more I am convinced that you are of immense importance in the world" (*L2* 296).

Woolf's assurances to Fry indicate her investment in status and her judgment about Pound, who was already a significant force in literary London. Yet her letter to Fry misrepresents how much of Pound's work she knew, erring perhaps on the side of protecting Fry's trust in her loyalty. A year earlier, in December 1917, she says in a diary entry that she had spent the afternoon reading Pound's memoir of the sculptor Henri Gaudier-Brzeska, who had been killed fighting for the French in June 1915 (*D1* 90). Pound's 1916 book contained, along with thirty-eight photographs of the sculptor's work and of the sculptor, the American poet's introduction, numerous editorial comments on Gaudier-Brzeska's work, and the essay "Vorticism," originally published by Pound in the *Fortnightly Review* in September of 1914. His "memoir" of Gaudier-Brzeska is about Pound as much as it is about the sculptor, and his essay "Vorticism" is particularly significant for what I argue here, that Woolf compared the importance of Pound's work to Fry's and that she reacted to it in order to ground her own poetics. Her literary aesthetic, like the poetic movements for which he was the leading spokesman, were based on visuality and visual culture. This competitive exchange with Pound is largely unstated, and the evidence for it suggestive, rather than conclusive; yet considering the case for Woolf's use of Imagism's image shifts how we understand her work in modernism's larger field. In short, Woolf's investment in the role of the visual in writing, and in visual culture generally, underwrites her interest in influencing modernist aesthetics and in the politics that surrounded those aesthetics.

Pound describes both Imagism and Vorticism in his essay, reiterating the famous "Imagiste" tenets that called for "Direct treatment of the 'thing,'" using "absolutely no word that does not contribute to the presentation," and, "regarding rhythm: to compose in sequence of the musical phrase, not in the sequence of the metronome." In addition, he provides his elliptical definition of the image, "that which presents an intellectual and emotional complex in an instant of time," which he clarifies by asserting, "the Image is the poet's pigment." Then, to argue for the link between Imagism and Vorticism, he tells the story behind composing his poem "In a Station of the Metro," which began after seeing faces in a Paris metro station, he says, as a "thirty-line poem" that he destroyed because it was "work 'of second intensity.'" To reach the two line haiku-like version of the poem, he describes his process of writing an intermediate draft half the length of the original, finally arriving at the pattern that satisfied his vorticist desire to present "vivid consciousness in some primary form" (*Gaudier-Brzeska*, 96-103). This mode of artistic expression is distinct from Impressionism and Post-Impressionism, Pound asserts, because it attempts "to record the precise instant when a thing outward and objective transforms itself, or darts into a thing inward and subjective" (103). Indeed, he says, the advent of cinema has made impressionist art irrelevant, whereas Vorticism and its predecessor Imagism forge the way for "an intensive art," which might occasion great works of sculpture, painting, and poetry. There is more that could be said about this essay and about Pound's book on Gaudier-Brzeska generally, but my argument about Woolf's reading of the book will be restricted to these claims—that she views Imagism and Vorticism as the other modernist avant-garde against which she defined her own literary art, and that she works out her visual aesthetic at least in part as a counterclaim to Pound's proclamations about the image.

In at least two places, Woolf provides evidence that she was aware of Imagism and its importance in shaping modern poetry even before reading Pound's memoir of Gaudier-Brzeska. From 1916-1918 while writing *Night and Day* (1919), she wrote more than twenty reviews that addressed poets, poetry, and poetry criticism, and this writing progressively attempts to grapple with the new poetics and their contrast with what had come before. More and more she became an advocate for modern poetry, beginning with her admiration for Whitman, but also in her subtle attacks on critics like Stephen Coleridge who, in his 1916 book *An Evening in My Library Among the English Poets*, "is a very vigilant guardian of the old," but should not, she says "be allowed to choose our new poets for us" (*E2* 48-49). In her 1917 review of Edgar Lee Masters, Woolf states:

> The difficulty of describing Mr Masters lies precisely in the fact that if he is not a prose writer, still less is he a poet. And for this reason it is not necessary to consider him as a man who is making serious experiments in metre like the Imagists or the Vers Librists. He has none of the sensibility which, whether we think it irritable or perverted or inspired, is now urging them to break up the old rules and devise new ones. (*E2* 107)

This singular mention of the poetic movement with which Pound was associated is noteworthy only because Woolf seems otherwise to disregard other avant-garde efforts in London besides Post-Impressionism, and it is unclear how she knew at this point about the attempts by the Imagists to experiment with meter and form. There had been three anthologies of Imagist poetry published by 1917, but Dora Marsden and Harriet Weaver's journal the *Egoist* was the primary place in which the objectives of the movement had been explained in any detail, especially in its "Special Imagist Number" of May 1915. Woolf indicates that she was well aware of what the *Egoist* represented when Weaver met with her and Leonard in April 1918 to engage their publishing Joyce's *Ulysses,* but we can only infer that she had either read or discussed the journal beforehand; the only other time she mentions it is when, in January 1918, Bob Trevelyan gossips that Clive Bell wished to buy "*The Egoist* & start a Bloomsbury review" (*D1* 115).

Woolf's 1917 essay on Siegfried Sassoon's poems suggests how she might have incorporated Imagist ideas into her thinking about poetry, shifting the terms to make them her own. "His vision comes to him directly," she writes, "he seems almost always, before he began to get his words into order, to have had one of those puzzling shocks of emotion...the moments of vision are interesting enough to make us wish to follow them up very carefully." The "shock of emotion" and the direct response to the thing seen echo the Imagist tenets and the definition given by Pound for the image. Woolf also introduces here what would become her familiar "moments of vision." Later in the review, she articulates more of her emerging poetic philosophy, using it to praise Sassoon as a realist: "The real things are put in not merely because they are real, but because at a certain moment of emotion the poet happened to be struck by them and is not afraid of spoiling his effect by calling them by their right names." While no one, including Woolf, would associate Sassoon with the Imagists, the words she uses to describe his method indicate her employment of those other modernist ideas coming out of Kensington rather than Bloomsbury, not as an appropriation *per se,* but rather to assert her sense of what constituted modern poetics. Coincidentally perhaps, the poem of Sassoon's that Woolf incorporates into this discussion of poetics is "The Morning Express," which has as its subject a wounded soldier looking out of the train window at the English countryside. She suggests a link to what is perhaps the most famous Imagist poem, Pound's "In a Station of the Metro," when she says about Sassoon's poem "With this straight, courageous method Mr Sassoon can produce such a solid and in its way beautiful catalogue of facts as that of the train leaving the station" (*E2* 119-21). Pound's poem is set in a metro station, and it provides a catalogue of objective facts to produce its imagistic effects; the Englishman Sassoon's poem is set in a train leaving a station, with a speaker who sees a catalogue of things that includes "trees, cows, and hedges," all of which succeed, according to Woolf, in giving its audience the moment of vision that the soldier has.

Within about eighteen months during 1917 and 1918, Woolf engaged modernist poetry in earnest as a reviewer for the *Times Literary Supplement.* That engagement also contributed to her own evolving literary sensibility, manifested in her increasingly experimental short fiction and, after the publication of *Night and Day* in November 1919, as she began to write *Jacob's Room* in early 1920. Significantly, her friendship with Eliot and her defense of his work as exemplary modernist poetry start during this period as well. Although he was associated with Lewis and Pound, and he was acting editor for the *Egoist,* she supported him publicly in a 1919 defense against initial poor reviews of his volume entitled *Poems,* published by their fledgling Hogarth Press. Woolf dismisses the poor review in her essay, titled "Is this Poetry?," as the "jeering laugh which is the easy reaction to anything strange, whether it be a 'damned foreigner' or a Post-Impressionist picture. Mr Eliot is certainly damned by newness and strangeness," the essay continues, but it is the care and craft with which he weaves in allusions to old poetry with that which is new that warrants attention in his work (*E3* 55-56). While she knew of his involvement in Pound and Lewis's Vorticist project *Blast,* Woolf subtly elides any mention of either Imagism or Vorticism here, comparing the response to what is experimental in Eliot's poetry to looking at a Post-Impressionist painting. Eliot had no association with Post-Impressionism in England, the Fry-orchestrated avant-garde circle with which Woolf has consistently been linked. Perhaps the most significant sign that she thought Eliot's work important was her active role with Pound and others beginning in 1922 to create a fellowship so that he could quit his job at Lloyd's of London and write full time. She cites Eliot as "one of the Georgians" in her 1924 essay "Character in Fiction," asserting that he had "written some of the loveliest lines in modern poetry" (*E3* 434). And Eliot would remain for her through the 1920s the epitome of the "true poet."

Despite his importance during the teens and 20s in London literary circles, Pound is left out of Woolf's public accounts of modern literature and its aesthetic, perhaps most notably in "Character in Fiction," the essay that cogently articulates what is new about modernism, the literary movement beginning famously "on or about December 1910" (*E3* 421). The twelve years that had elapsed from that date included Pound's call to "make it new" in London's literary circles. Privately, however, she was more forthcoming. In contrast to her advocacy of Eliot's poetry, about Pound's poetry Woolf would say in a 1923 letter to Ottoline Morrell that she had "never seen him; and only hate his works" (*L3* 71). In a contemporaneous letter to Fry she compares the two American poets. First she acknowledges to Fry that she had been in correspondence with Pound regarding the Eliot fund, which had resulted in "a complete muddle, as you may imagine." Eliot's psychology about the efforts on his behalf fascinate her, however; he had been embarrassed about the venture to raise money for him, a set of feelings that Woolf imagines as "Very American." "The more I see of that race the more I thank god for my British blood," she says, "which does at any rate preserve one from wearing 3 waistcoats; enamel buttons on one's overcoat, and keeping one's eyes perpetually shut—like Ezra Pound" (*L2* 572). The inside joke between Woolf and Fry about American clothing fashion notwithstanding, it is her assessment of Pound's self imposed blindness that indicates what she thinks of his poetics. Pound argues that Imagism and Vorticist poetics are primarily visual, based on how a poet perceives the world through his or her eyes, and that the poem presents that fixed image to "record the precise instant when a thing outward and objective transforms itself, or darts into a thing inward and subjective," as he explains in his "Vorticism" essay (*Gaudier-Brzeska* 103). In her letter to Fry then, Woolf expresses a pointed critique of Pound by asserting that his eyes were "perpetually shut," especially since, with *Jacob's Room,* her idea of a "new form for a new novel" (*D2* 13) privileges visuality as one of its primary modes of apperception and expression.

Woolf returned to thinking and writing about poetry, poetics, and status in the late 1920s, especially when she was working out her argument regarding women and the history of poetry for *A Room of One's Own*. A pattern emerges in her diary from this period when we trace her thinking about poetry and about her own status as a writer. The reception of *Orlando*, "which surpassed expectations," was accompanied by Rebecca West's praise of the book, calling it in her review "a poetic masterpiece of the first rank." Woolf's mixed response to the praise and the record sales of her book leave her feeling "sheepish & silly" (*D3* 200), but also very aware of her "famous self tapering about the world." Simultaneously, while she's thinking about her fame, she works on "Women and Fiction" and writes, "as usual, I am bored by narrative." So, finding narrative tedious, she imagines the form of her evolving book as something new, "half talk half soliloquy," a kind of condensed lyric structure that "allows me to get more onto the page than any how else." The form "made itself up & forced itself upon me," she says, a description of the process involved in composing a poem rather than writing an essay (*D3* 221-22).

In addition to its other arguments, *A Room of One's Own* asserts the possibility that women can write poetry, as originators as well as inheritors. It is in this vein that I want to finish, by considering one passage from *A Room of One's Own* in the context of Woolf's engagement with modern poetry and in the context of thinking about herself as a poet—not as one who would be, like Mary Carmichael, "a poet…in another hundred years' time" (*AROO* 94) but like Eliot, whom she affirms as "a true poet" in her diary while writing *A Room*, "what they will call in a hundred years a man of genius" (*D3* 223). The final chapter contains an exemplary lyric soliloquy when the speaker begins,

> at this moment, as so often happens in London, there was a complete lull and suspension of traffic. Nothing came down the street; nobody passed. A single leaf detached itself from the plane tree at the end of the street, and in that pause and suspension fell. Somehow it was a signal falling, a signal pointing to a force in things which one had overlooked. (*AROO* 96)

Much could be said about the way that this passage works as poetry—its figuration, its use of alliteration, repetition, and parallelism, but I want here to call attention to Woolf's use of the imagistic moment to frame her lyric. Yet instead of restricting that singular image in suspended time, a leaf falls and signals the overlooked force that will become, in the lines that follow, the invisible river that embodies life and death and the passage of time. In so many words, Woolf challenges Pound's tenets of Imagism and offers her own modernist poetics. She finishes the passage by subtly calling attention to these poetics: "The sight was ordinary enough," she says, " what was strange was the rhythmical order with which my imagination had invested it" (*AROO* 96). Thus, the scene is transformed by the poet's imagination, given rhythm and form in its expression.

Unlike collaboration between writers, the nature of productive exchange in competition tends to be unspoken and undeclared, which is for the most part the case with Woolf in her competition for literary status. Still there are signs of that unspoken exchange, which I have undertaken to evidence here. That unstated competition for status and originality underwrites one of modernism's general anxieties, exemplified in one of Pound's poems, "Portrait d'une Femme," that "there is…nothing that's quite your own" (*Personæ* 58). It is at this point then, that we can see Woolf fully answering her question in her letter to Fry, whether Eliot's culture would "carry him through or does culture" leave one mired in the mud with Pound, Lewis, and Joyce? Her answer defines her perception of Eliot as a poet and, I would daresay, herself as a poet. I have implicitly argued that the competition for status with Pound produced for Woolf distinct results—she honed her literary sensibility and her visual poetics in part because she undertook to differentiate her work from Pound's modernism, at the same time using what was useful in Imagism. In other words, she could acknowledge Pound's contribution to poetic culture by transforming it conceptually into her own moments of vision.

## Works Cited

Lewis, Wyndham. *The Roaring Queen*. New York: Liveright, 1973.
———. "Virginia Woolf, 'Mind' and Matter' on the Plane of a Literary Controversy." *Men Without Art*. Santa Rosa: Black Sparrow Press, 1987. 131-40.
Pound, Ezra. *Gaudier-Brzeska: A Memoir*. London: John Lane, 1916.
———. "Portrait d'une Femme." *Personæ: The Shorter Poems*. Ed. Lea Baechler and A. Walton Litz. Rev. ed. New York: New Directions, 1990. 57-58.
"Special Imagist Number." *Egoist* 5:2 (May 1915).
Woolf, Virginia. *The Diary of Virginia Woolf*. Ed. Anne Olivier Bell with Andrew McNeillie. Vols. 1 and 3. New York: Harcourt, Brace, Jovanovich, 1977, 1980.
———. *The Essays of Virginia Woolf*. Ed. Andrew McNeillie. Vols. 2 and 3. New York: Harcourt, Brace, Jovanovich, 1987, 1988.
———. *The Letters of Virginia Woolf*. Ed. Nigel Nicolson and Joanne Trautmann. Vols. 2 and 3. New York: Harcourt, Brace, Jovanovich, 1976, 1977.
———. *A Room of One's Own*. New York: Harcourt, Brace, Jovanovich, 1981.

# Borderline Personalities: Woolf Reviews Kapp

## by Ben Harvey

In 1969 the University of Birmingham's art museum purchased over 240 drawings by the caricaturist Edmond X. Kapp. At that time, the Barber Institute of Fine Arts probably didn't realize that by collecting Kapp it was also forging a connection with Virginia Woolf, who, at the very end of her essay "Pictures and Portraits," had once expressed her startling desire to emulate, perhaps even impersonate, Kapp. "Oh to be silent! Oh to be a painter! Oh (in short) to be Mr. Kapp!" (*E3* 166).

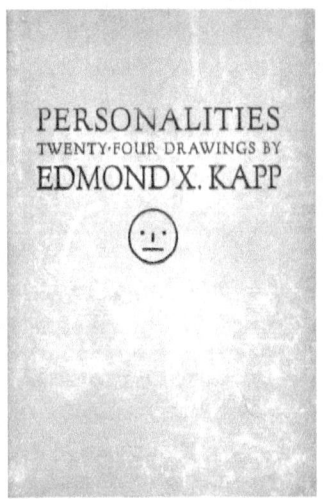

*Figure 1: Kapp's* Personalities *cover and list of subjects*

Published in the book review section of the *Athenaeum* on 9 January 1920, "Pictures and Portraits" is ostensibly a review of Kapp's *Personalities: Twenty-Four Drawings* (see Figure 1). Focusing on six of these personalities, Woolf distinguishes between those subjects of whom she has personal knowledge and those she does not, generally preferring the latter category. Aside from this theme of personal acquaintance, her descriptions are notable largely for their concision and brilliance. In particular, she impresses and amuses us by her ability to tease apt zoological affinities out of Kapp's drawings. While George Bernard Shaw's "fingers are contorted into stamping hooves," the Duke of Devonshire:

> for all the world resembles a seal sleek from the sea, his mouth pursed to a button signifying a desire for mackerel. But the mackerel he is offered is not fresh, and, tossing himself wearily backwards, he flops with a yawn into the depths. (165-66)

As for "'The Politician' (Charles Masterman)," we read that he

> has the long body cut into segments and the round face marked with alarming

black bars of the Oak Eggar caterpillar.... There is something sinister about him; he swarms rapidly across roads; he smudges when crushed; he devours leaf after leaf. (165; see Figure 2)

*Figure 2*

We are left convinced that Woolf might easily claim to be, if not Kapp himself, then certainly a Kapp-of-prose.

Woolf's interest in the brutishness lurking within Kapp's caricatures (and perhaps, by implication, within civilization itself) might be read as a subtle corrective to another reviewer. As a "publisher's note" in Kapp's book makes clear, the twenty-four caricatures were culled from an earlier exhibition of his art, which had taken place in May and June, 1919, at the Little Art Rooms, London. The exhibition was well received and many excerpts from the more positive reviews were reprinted at the back of the subsequent book. "His critics are all agreed," writes Woolf, alluding to this part of the book, "that he combines the gifts of the artist with those of the caricaturist" (164). Among these excerpts was a short review or notice by Jan Gordon, the *Athenaeum*'s regular art critic, which had appeared in that publication on 23 May 1919. "Mr. Kapp's caricatures," wrote Gordon, "are unlike most, without that music-hall bestiality which seems to be the mainspring of so much of our satiric art" (163). The very next section of Gordon's short review was the only part of it not reprinted in Kapp's book: "for," he continues, "it is so easy to remember that man is at root an animal." As we have seen, Woolf will not hesitate to make this "easy" point, nor hesitate to imply that Kapp is encouraging her to make it. Knowing that the *Athenaeum* had recently published a piece on Kapp's art and that her readers might recall this, Woolf would have probably made the effort to track down Gordon's earlier piece.

If this encouraged Woolf to think about the potential bestiality of Kapp's caricatures—and to find in them hooves, seals, and Oak Eggar caterpillars—then another, more prominent, article might also have had a bearing on her review. Appearing in the Contents page of the journal, a space reserved for editorials, and in the very same edition as Gordon's notice, "The Usurpation of the Museums" weighs in on a matter that had been increasingly preoccupying cultural commentators in the months following the armistice of November 1918. The piece is attributed to "C. B.," who, one assumes, must be none other than Clive Bell.[1] "The facts are simple," laments Woolf's brother-in-law:

> Half the National Gallery, the whole of the National Portrait Gallery, the whole of the Tate, a good part of the British Museum and of the Imperial Institute, the whole of Hertford House, and half the Victoria and Albert Museum have been taken

over by the Government and stocked with officials.... Which do you prefer—galleries full of beautiful and interesting objects that cost nothing to keep, or galleries full of dull, ugly and expensive Jacks and Jills in office? (357-58; see Figure 3)

As we shall see, Woolf's review makes reference to this controversy and takes place within (or just outside) two of the institutions Bell mentions.

Opting for a digressive format, Woolf's essay approaches Kapp by way of Trafalgar Square's sisterly sites, the National Gallery (NG) and the National Portrait Gallery (NPG).[2]

*Figure 3:* **Punch, *21 April 1920***

By doing so she implies a homology between book space and gallery space *and* acknowledges that this book had its origins in a gallery. Woolf also uses the essay to explore the physical boundaries and limits of art institutions as she attends to the issue of *which* objects and *which* people make it into an art gallery, or else fail in the attempt. Concerned with how gallery space is qualitatively different from other spaces, Woolf will suggest that a gallery's walls are not impermeable to larger cultural and ideological forces. By helping us to identify these forces, "Pictures and Portraits" provides us with the kind of institutional critique that allows us to imagine the potential emergence of a different kind of art collection.

Despite the fact that the journal clearly designates Woolf's essay to be a review of Kapp's book, she does not write directly about it until her last lengthy paragraph. Rather, she devotes the first three paragraphs of the essay to a discussion of the NG, the NPG, and the "incessant tide" of traffic flowing past these buildings, which are located "on the same promontory of pavement." "In order to enter either [gallery]," she writes, "it is only necessary to pass through a turnstile, and, on some days of the week, to part with a sixpenny bit." Psychologically, Woolf suggests, entering is not so simple. "As easily might a pilchard leap from the shoal and join the free sport of dolphins as a single individual ascend those steps and enter those doors" (163). Although it sounds as though Woolf is talking about both galleries here, only the NG is fronted by an impressive flight of rather steep steps (see Figure 4), and so it is within this building that the second paragraph of the essay seems to take place. Here, Woolf considers the difficulties of ekphrasis, of translating intense visual experiences into adequate language, and pursues these thoughts in relationship to the genre of landscape. The heights of art, and perhaps the stiffest challenges to the would-be art writer, are thus associated with the canonical works found in the NG. But since Kapp combines "the gifts of the artist with those of the caricaturist," and since the latter focuses on the individual human subject, Woolf strides off in the direction of the NPG, so that she might also "approach him from that point of view" (164). She moves, that is, from pictures

*Figure 4: Entrances to the National Gallery and National Portrait Gallery*

to portraits, the essay's title hinting at the sequence of Woolf's essayistic peregrinations.

Woolf predicts that she will be less intimidated by the prospect of entering the NPG, presumably not merely because of its lower threshold but also because of its less stringent aesthetic standards and because of portraiture's focus on the human face (it's more a matter of a pilchard looking, not at dolphins, so much as other, perhaps superior, ancestral pilchards). "It needs an effort," she writes, "but scarcely a great one, to enter the National Portrait Gallery" (164). Her hope is soon dashed. In a scene that anticipates the swooping beadles of *A Room of One's Own* (1929), Woolf finds her approach to the gallery rebuffed by a gate-keeper:

Sometimes…an urgent desire to identify one among the dead sends us post haste to its portals. The case we have in mind is that of Mrs John Stuart Mill. Never was there such a paragon among women. Noble, magnanimous, inspired, thinker, reformer, saint, she possessed every gift and every virtue. One thing alone she lacked, and that, no doubt, the National Portrait Gallery could supply. She had no face. But the National Portrait Gallery, interrogated, wished to be satisfied that the inquirer was dependent upon a soldier; pensions they provided, not portraits. (164)

Woolf, it turns out, was approaching the NPG with more than just Kapp in mind. Hoping to find Harriet Taylor Mill, she was instead met by one of Bell's "Jacks and Jills in office" or, to be more exact, an employee of the Separation Allowance Department of the War Office, which had been occupying the entire building since the early years of the Great War.[3] "Pensions they provided, not portraits." At the time Woolf's essay was published in early 1920, the Army Pay Clerks had in fact recently left the building—"Art Galleries Freed," *The Times* had announced on 1 November 1919 ("Art")[4]—but the gallery was not to reopen to the public until April 1920. "Pictures and Portraits" appeared during a curious interregnum in the NPG's history, a time when it was neither "occupied" nor entirely "free" for business as usual. Woolf's description seems to be based largely on an earlier visit she had made, in July 1918, when, as a letter to Vanessa Bell records, she had found the NPG "shut save to the widows of officers" (*L2* 259). In the essay, having failed in her search, Woolf is "set adrift in Trafalgar Square once more," where she reflects "upon the paramount importance of faces":

Without a face Mrs John Stuart Mill was without a soul. Had her husband spared three lines of eulogy to describe her personal appearance we should hold her in memory. Without eyes or hair, cheeks or lips, her stupendous genius, her consummate virtue, availed her nothing. She is a mist, a wraith, a miasma of anonymous merit. The face is the thing. (164)

There is a certain resonance between the humorously blank facial schema on the cover of Kapp's book (again, see Figure 1) and the idea of anonymity Woolf extracts from her frustrating experience at the NPG. Kapp's cover introduces us to the general idea of a face but, in contrast to those contained inside the book, it is a face devoid of any specific information, any sense of personality; Woolf, on the other hand, has a strong sense of Harriet Taylor Mill's personality, but no idea of what her face looks like and, further, no immediate way of prizing open the NPG's doors to find out. Curiously, even had Woolf stormed past the army clerk blocking her way, even had she searched the NPG's collections high and low, she still would have been disappointed. There was, at least at this time, no portrait of Harriet Taylor Mill in the collection—a fact Woolf might have known from previous visits to the collection or could have discovered simply by consulting a catalog of the collection (see, for example, Holmes). I consider it likely that she did know this, for her failure at the door strongly seems to imply this more fundamental curatorial and institutional shortcoming.[5]

Of all the absent portrait subjects Woolf could have chosen to make her point, why did she opt for the friend, companion, and eventual wife of John Stuart Mill, who, as Woolf notes, devoted much ink to the cause of singing her praises?[6] Perhaps it was to underline an obvious asymmetry in the "field of representation," in both the political and aesthetic senses of this phrase. "Aesthetic" because John's portrait was already in the NPG, and because the gallery repeats John's mistake when it, too, fails to provide a record of Harriet's appearance. "Political" because Harriet and John were crucial figures in the women's suffrage movement: John through his activities as an MP and as the author of *The Subjection of Women* (1869) and Harriet through her essay, "The Enfranchisement of Women" (1851) and through her profound influence on John. So it is notable that in her essay, which was published just a little over one year after women had for the first time voted in Britain, Woolf invokes Harriet as though she is noting a significant lacuna, a gap in the way the struggle for representation is being represented in this repository of national memory. Ultimately, the political and aesthetic senses of representation become thoroughly intertwined in the NPG.

The very London spaces Woolf traverses in "Pictures and Portraits" would have evoked still-fresh memories of the struggle for the vote. Trafalgar Square had been an important location for pro-suffrage speeches and parades, and in 1914 suffragettes had entered the NG to slash Velasquez's *Rokeby Venus* and the NPG to desecrate Millais's *Portrait of Thomas Carlyle*. Notably, the choice of paintings in these acts focused attention to the distinctive rationales underpinning each museum. To attack Venus was to attack beauty itself, while an assault on Thomas Carlyle was also an assault on an early advocate and trustee of the NPG.[7] Carlyle, moreover, had helped to strengthen the ideological grounds for the gallery by stressing the "hero worship" of great *men*—a view Woolf references and undermines in *Jacob's Room* (1922)—as well as portraiture's importance as a means through which these men might be worshipped. Had Woolf cast her eyes upwards when she failed to enter the NPG, she would have discerned that one of the portrait busts carved in stone above the

*Figure 5*

door belonged to Carlyle (see Figure 5).

The subject of the struggle for political representation returns us to Kapp's *Personalities*. In her essay, as she transitions away from the subject of the NPG to that of Kapp's art, Woolf casually (but surely very pointedly) notes the disparity between the number of women and men included in the book, implying continuity between its biases and those of the gallery, which at this time had about one portrait of a woman for every nine of men (Holmes). "Therefore we turn eagerly," she writes, "though we have paused too long about it, to see what faces Mr Kapp provides for the twenty-three gentlemen and the one old lady whom he calls *Personalities*" (164). "There is very little," she continues, "of the anonymous about any of the twenty-four. There is scarcely a personality, from Mr Bernard Shaw to Mrs Grundy, whom we have not seen in the flesh" (164-65). This "scarcely" is an important qualification. Whereas Woolf knew from personal experience what George Bernard Shaw looked like, she certainly could not have laid eyes upon Mrs. Grundy, the book's "one old lady," at least, not in any simple way. Mrs. Grundy was not the stuff of flesh and bone, but a figure of speech, or a type, and she is certainly the most anonymous of the twenty-four (see Figure 6). She is an embodiment of conventional propriety and prudery and, as such, is twice mentioned by John Stuart Mill in *The Subjection of Women*. Mrs. Grundy's insubstantiality was established from the moment of her inception. In Thomas Morton's 1798 play *Speed the Plough* she is invoked as a figure of neighborly opinion, without ever actually appearing on stage. Rather, her opinions are mouthed by others. "What," they fret, "would Mrs Grundy say?"[8]

*Figure 6*

Mrs. Grundy, then, stands apart from the other personalities in Kapp's book. She stands apart because of her gender and as a literary abstraction rather than an actual person. She also stands apart physically, as the last caricature in the book. Depicted as a fragmentary white presence against a black background, she is situated by a vertical line that suggests a doorway or window. She is a borderline personality. An observer rather than a participant, she appears to be attentive, to be contemplating and listening to the life that is taking place around her. Her inclusion is an ingenious touch on the part of Kapp, and in the context of his book, we might understand her on a number of different levels. Firstly, she helps to suggest the range of Kapp's interests and skills, as he goes about giving form to a non-existent figure, rather than distorting an existing one. Bracketing his book with differences of gender and race, Kapp places his last caricature, Mrs. Grundy, in relationship to his first, which depicts his only non-western subject, the Japanese poet, Yone Neguchi. Kapp captions the work "The Seer of Visions," but it is not until his depiction of Mrs. Grundy that he seems to stake an obvious claim on this mystical title for himself. It is only here that he truly catches a phantom personality in his artistic net.

*Figure 7*

Associated with issues of decorum and (self-)censorship, Mrs. Grundy is partly a figure Kapp must fight against, or ignore, as he goes about his business of poking fun at the great, the good, and the powerful. For this reason, her presence draws our attention to questions of taste and to editorial issues, to acts of selection and arrangement. "Art is essentially selection," wrote Henry James in "The Art of Fiction," "but it is a selection whose main care is to be typical, to be inclusive. For many people art means rose-coloured windowpanes, and selection means picking a bouquet for Mrs. Grundy" (58).

How, we might ask, is Mrs. Grundy placed within the bouquet of Kapp's book? We have already noted that she is the last of his personalities, but also of significance is the fact that she is immediately preceded by "The Anti-Suffragist: Mr Reginald McKenna" (see Figure 7). This sequence inevitably brings to mind the pre-war years, when the suffragette campaign of militancy was at its height (Kapp's Mrs. Grundy even bears the date 1914 alongside his signature). Known to be a staunch opponent of women's suffrage, McKenna was Asquith's Home Secretary between 1911 and 1915, and the politician most closely associated with the passing and implementation of the notorious Cat-and-Mouse Act, which allowed for the release from prison and re-arrest of hunger-striking suffragettes.[9] Margaret Gibbs, the suffragette who, in 1914, had attacked the portrait of Thomas Carlyle invoked McKenna's name during her trial. "When she was found guilty," the *Times* reported, she "said she smashed the picture because of Mr. McKenna's refusal to see a deputation" ("Sentence"). An unlikely advocate for women's rights, Mrs. Grundy's presence in the *Personalities* could nevertheless be taken as a sly allusion to this anti-suffragist's ultimate failure; despite all his efforts, she has crept in through the book's back door.

Woolf neither mentions McKenna's presence in Kapp's book nor talks at any greater length about Mrs. Grundy. But the suggestive placement of these two figures, together with Mrs. Grundy's connection to questions of selection and inclusion, may help to account for the logic of her essay's structure, for Woolf's decision to describe herself meandering through the spaces of Trafalgar Square and the NG in order to beat on the door of the NPG in search of one of the founding figures of British feminism. Parts of Woolf's description of Harriet, or the lack of Harriet, might serve double-duty as a description of the rather spectral, and insubstantial, Mrs. Grundy: "a mist, a wraith, a miasma of anonymous merit." "The face is the thing," continues Woolf, alluding to Shakespeare's *Hamlet* and to the "mouse-trap" within that play. With all this ghostliness in the air this is entirely appropriate. A portrait, like a play, might deploy mimesis to resurrect the dead, might add flesh to a specter, so that we can again (or for the first time) hold the dead "in memory."[10]

Certain physical aspects of Kapp's book might, I have been arguing, impact the way we might read "Pictures and Portraits." I want to end by suggesting that Woolf is also using the essay to participate in the debate over the so-called "Usurpation of the Museums." Clive Bell, to return to his 1919 article, summarized two of the major arguments in favor of expediting the return of these spaces to their pre-war uses. That they should be reopened for the edification of those American and colonial soldiers still stationed in Britain; and that reopening them would demonstrate the strength of the government's commitment to "civilization." "During the last five years," Bell points out, "the British Government has left us in no doubt that, if it stands for anything, it stands for civilization" (357). Suspicious of both arguments, Bell implies that they might still be usefully deployed as part of a letter-writing campaign. "Above all," he concludes:

> you write to the papers and persuade your friends to write. If you know anyone who can make use of some vaguely formidable signature such as "Fifty Years a Trade Unionist," so much the better: better still, something vaguely patriotic, as "Demobbed" or "A Lad from Tasmania".... "A Lover of Art" is not much to be recommended. The great public does not love art. But it loves Government officials even less, and therein lies our strength. (358)

In "Pictures and Portraits," Woolf takes up Bell's call for a letter writing campaign but pointedly provides an alternative reason for why the closed museum spaces, or at least the NPG, should be re-opened. She writes as a British woman who wants, in the language of *A Room of One's Own*, to continue the project of thinking back through her intellectual and artistic mothers.

In 1920, this might involve trying to make the historical roots of the suffrage movement visible by retrieving images of its important figures, figures like Harriet Taylor Mill.

Alternatively, it might involve drawing attention to the very obscurity of this visual record.[11] For the process of retrieval could obviously not be satisfied merely by returning the NPG to some kind of pristine, pre-war state. The gallery's traditional shortcomings and lacunae were obvious enough. More to the point, it was an institution in a state of flux. Immediately after the end of the war, its trustees were calling for more than just their museum's reopening; they were also pressing for its physical expansion, so that it could adequately house its existing collection and so that it had room for future acquisitions, including portraits "of persons distinguished for their services to the Empire during the war" ("Gift"). This last reason, one imagines, would have particularly vexed Woolf and her Bloomsbury friends.

Many of the *Athenaeum*'s readers would have been attuned to these issues and would have understood that identifying an obvious weakness in a collection, as Woolf does, is tantamount to pointing out an alternative or additional direction for it to take. So although Woolf is frustrated by her inability to find Harriet Taylor Mill in the NPG, this frustration could also carry the hope that their rendezvous might eventually take place there. Alas, this would never happen—at least, not in the way Woolf seems to have hoped. When, in 1982, a portrait of Harriet Taylor Mill finally entered the NPG, it entered a collection that already contained several likenesses of the writer who had once come looking for it.[12]

## Notes

1. Although this article is not included in Donald Laing's checklist of Clive Bell's publications, Bell became a regular contributor to the *Athenaeum* around this time and the piece is consistent with his opinions and prose style.
2. The relationship between the NG and NPG became even closer in January 1919, when the NG became the temporary home of "some 40 of the choicest historical portraits from its still secluded neighbour, the National Portrait Gallery" ("Famous").
3. This is the explanation that eluded Andrew McNeillie who, in editing the essay, was left perplexed by "the matter of soldiers and pensions" (*E3* 166 n.3).
4. The other art gallery "freed" at this time was the Wallace Collection.
5. Notably, Woolf's letter to Vanessa Bell, where she describes her failure to enter the NPG, gives a different motive for the visit and makes no mention of this search for Harriet Taylor Mill (*L2* 258-61). Of course, just such a search may have motivated her then; it is also conceivable that it occurred on a separate occasion or, indeed, that Woolf invented it solely for the purpose of reviewing Kapp's book.
6. Most notably, see John Stuart Mill's *Autobiography* (1873) and the dedication from *On Liberty* (1859). The question of the exact nature and extent of Harriet's influence on John is famously controversial and Woolf was familiar with the debate about "whether it was Mill or his friends who was mistaken about Mrs. Mill" (*D2* 341). Later in 1920, she brought the topic up in her exchange of letters with Desmond MacCarthy on "The Intellectual Status of Women," which appeared in *The New Statesman*. Elsewhere, in her essay "The Modern Essay," Woolf quotes Richard Hutton's dismissive assessment of Harriet Taylor Mill's influence on her husband, and acidly notes that a "book could take that blow, but it sinks an essay" (*E4* 217).
7. In the statement she issued after slashing the *Rokeby Venus*, Mary Richardson justified her act by arguing for a notion of beauty that went beyond the merely aesthetic: "I have tried to destroy the picture of the most beautiful woman in mythological history as a protest against the government for destroying Mrs. Pankhurst, who is the most beautiful character in modern history. Justice is an element of beauty as much as colour and outline on canvas" ("National"). Of relevance to my argument is Richardson's allusion to the Cat-and-Mouse Act, which at the time was implicated in the public spectacle of Mrs. Pankhurst's physical deterioration.
8. This, and related phrases ("What will Mrs Grundy say? What will Mrs Grundy think"), are sprinkled throughout Morton's play.
9. McKenna's name appears in Woolf's correspondence a couple of times. Most notably in a letter to Lytton Strachey, dated 12 October 1918, she describes attending a speech by Lord Grey on the subject of the League of Nations. Woolf's distaste for McKenna is apparent: "I had the pleasure of sitting exactly behind Mrs. Asquith and Elizabeth. I felt, at that distance, fairly secure against their fascination, and when McK-

enna and Lord Harcourt came in and sat down beside them I felt it would be a very great condescension on my part to drink tea out of the same cup—which I suspect to be one of their domestic habits. However I was impressed and exalted by Lord Grey" (*L2* 281).

10. Woolf's allusions to Shakespeare are also appropriate in the wider context of her discussion. The famous Chandos portrait of Shakespeare was the first work to enter the NPG and thus sports the accession number "NPG 1." If, in this respect, it contrasts sharply with the missing image of Harriet Taylor Mill, it nevertheless participates in the broader issue of the importance, and difficulty, of attaching faces to names. In 1919, as now, there was a nagging doubt about "whether this picture…even represents [Shakespeare] at all" ("Famous").

11. We might compare Woolf's "Pictures and Portraits" with a book by her friend (and her portraitist) Ray Strachey. In *The Cause*, Strachey discusses Harriet Taylor Mill's life in some detail and takes the time to lament those factors that "obscured her image in the records which are to be found in the lives and letters of her day" (68). This might be read, in part, as an oblique apology for her inability to include a portrait of Harriet Taylor Mill in her text; although plate III of *The Cause* shows portraits of four "pioneers," a portrait of John Taylor Mill is left to stand in for his absent wife.

12. Charles Saumarez Smith has discussed the NPG's acquisition of portraits of Woolf and also provides an (incomplete) history of her relationship to the institution. It is worth noting that the portrait of Harriet Taylor Mill is still not on permanent display. It can, however, be seen on the NPG's website <www.npg.org.uk>.

## Works Cited

"Art Galleries Freed." *Times* 1 November 1919: 12d.
Bell, Clive. "The Usurpation of the Museums." *Athenaeum* 23 May 1919: 357-58.
"Famous Portraits. An Hour at the National Gallery." *Times* 10 March 1914: 10a-b.
"Gift of National War Portraits." *Times* 8 Aug. 1919: 13c.
Gordon, Jan. "Exhibitions of the Week." *Athenaeum* 23 May 1919: 372.
Holmes, Charles. *Historical and Descriptive Catalogue of the Pictures, Busts, &c., in the National Portrait Gallery*. 15th ed. London: H. M. Stationery Office, 1914.
James, Henry. "The Art of Fiction." *Henry James: Essays on Literature, American Writers, English Writers*. Ed. Leon Edel. New York: The Library of America, 1984. 44-65.
Kapp, Edmond X. *Personalities: Twenty-Four Drawings*. London: Secker, 1919.
Laing, Donald A. "A Checklist of the Published Writings of Clive Bell." *Clive Bell's Eye*. Ed. William G. Bywater Jr. Detroit: Wayne State UP, 1975. 211-42.
Morton, Thomas. *Speed the Plough: A Comedy in Five Acts*. London: Longman and O. Rees, 1806. *Project Gutenberg*. 26 January 2007 <http://www.gutenberg.org/files/19407/19407-h/19407-h.htm>.
"National Gallery Outrage." *Times* 11 March 1914: 9f.
National Portrait Gallery. Portrait of Harriet Taylor Mill by an Unknown Artist (NPG 5489). 26 January 2007. <http://www.npg.org.uk/live/search/portrait.asp?search=ss&sText=harriet+mill&LinkID=mp05582&rNo=0&role=sit>.
"Sentence for National Portrait Gallery Outrage." *Times* 22 July 1914: 10e.
Smith, Charles Saumarez. "A Question of Fame: Virginia Woolf and the National Portait Gallery." *Charleston Magazine: Charleston, Bloomsbury and the Arts*, 12 (Autumn/Winter 1995): 5-9.
Strachey, Ray. *The Cause: A Short History of the Women's Movement in Great Britain*. London: G. Bell, 1928.
Woolf, Virginia. "Pictures and Portraits." *The Essays of Virginia Woolf*. Ed. Andrew McNeillie. Vol. 3. San Diego: Harcourt, 1986. 163-66.

# Performing the Self: Woolf as Actress and Audience

## by Elizabeth Wright

That Woolf used her friends and acquaintances as templates for the characters in her fiction is no secret, but that this transformative process also translated into life is perhaps more surprising. Out of the lives of her social circle, where Woolf's imagination met reality, dramatized life exploded. Clive Bell, amongst others, notes Woolf's ability to create life-dramas "in which any one of her friends might find him or herself cast, all unawares, for a part" (Noble 70). This assertion is borne out by the letters in which she regularly portrays herself "play[ing] my game of making you up" (*L2* 177) or of "invent[ing] you for myself" (*L3* 78, 204). In 1925 she assures Vita Sackville-West: "if you'll make me up, I'll make you" (*L3* 214), while in 1930 she writes to Ethel Smyth: "I'm building up one of the oddest, most air hung pageants of you and your life" (*L4* 214). The characterisation of real people was often calculated. In a letter to her nephew Quentin Bell she discusses his "new character:"

> Please write again, and let us go at some length into the question of your new character. Quentin was an adorable creature and I'm sorry he's been sloughed (sluffed) like the gold and orange skin of the rare Mexican tsee-tsee snake. Why not be him and Claudian on alternate days? Claudian is a secretive marble-faced steady eyed deliberate villain. (*L4* 25)

Woolf did not exclude herself from this dramatic characterisation. In a letter dated 4 November 1923, she challenges Jacques Raverat to "write Virginia's part, because she is oddly enough, the last woman I have any idea of" (*L3* 78) and in her diary ponders "the fictitious Virginia Woolf whom I carry like a mask about the world" (*D5* 307).

    For Woolf, personality was made up of roles and the ability to play the part of another was a positive, a means of delving into different worlds. In her essay "Street Haunting" (1927) the writer walks the London streets entering, momentarily, the lives of the people she meets. The perambulation leads her to reflect "Into each of these lives one could penetrate a little way, far enough to give oneself the illusion that one is not tethered to a single mind, but can put on briefly for a few minutes the bodies and minds of others" (*DM* 35). The ability to leave the "straight lines of personality" is a trait of the consummate actor. In her essay "From the Scene of the Unconscious to the Scene of History," Hélène Cixous calls this ability *démoïsation* (cited in Cohen 13), Richard Schechner "transportation" (191), meaning the process by which the actor *becomes* the role. To Cixous the successful performer is "someone whose ego is reserved and humble enough for the other to be able to invade and occupy him; he makes room for the other" (cited in Cohen 13). The actor is the platform on which alternate identities are performed. Cixous cries in *L'Incarnation*: "Let the Others in! I have the honour of being the stage of the other" (cited in Dobson 49), a sentiment which Woolf's Orlando might easily express.[1]

    In the letters and papers for the Memoir Club Woolf's role-playing evolved into a series of mini-performances for her reader or listener. Her letters, for example, are often addressed to the alter-egos of the recipients, while her own alter-ego, tailored to that particular individual, is signed off at the bottom. The personae ask the recipient to collude in the creation of the fantasy, bonding Woolf and her reader in closer communion. Woolf's personae found their origin in childhood when Virginia Stephen took on the role of Miss Jan who appears in stories, letters, and diaries. Her double becomes the receptacle for all childish misdemeanours and the means by which she is able to sublimate her social ineptitude. Miss Jan performs a therapeutic function, allowing Virginia Stephen to exorcise her anger, frustration, disinterest, and embarrassment. In an early diary entry, she records how she

> Sat and was talked to by Lisa, till another lady came in. Poor Miss Jan utterly lost her wits dropped her umbrella, answered at random talked nonsense, and grew as red as a turkey cock. Only rescued from this by S. proposing to go away. So we left, I with the conviction that what ever talents Miss Jan may have, she does not possess the one qualifying her to shine in good society. (*PA* 39)

Real-life role-playing, while a rich source of creativity and entertainment, was also a means of survival. Woolf's Miss Jan was one method of dealing with being a young lady in Victorian England and she was by no means alone in requiring such a strategy. The personae adopted by women were made necessary by their powerless position within society. Carolyn Heilbrun describes this process: "Lying with one's body and one's words is, among the oppressed, a dreadful necessity. Outsiders must often lie to survive. Only women, I think, have also consistently lied to themselves" (70). However, in the Stephen sisters' cases they resisted believing the reality of their acts. Woolf recalls proudly how Vanessa eschewed social conditioning while superficially representing the model of it:

> Unfortunately, what was inside Vanessa did not altogether correspond with what was outside. Underneath the necklaces and the enamel butterflies was one passionate desire—for paint and turpentine, for turpentine and paint. But poor George was no psychologist. His perceptions were obtuse. He never saw within. (*MOB* 149)

Role-playing for Vanessa and Virginia was an expediency, a temporary measure until freedom broke through with Leslie Stephen's death.

At its worst, dramatising life through role-play leaves the reader or audience uncertain as to what point role-playing becomes reality and at what point acting becomes being. The danger lies in seeing, according to Wilshire, "the offstage world only [in terms of] passivity, fascination, hypnotic-lie engulfment, or…instinctual cunning and calculation" (xv-xvi). Reading socialised behaviour as a "lie" or "act" can lead to the supposition that, as Erving Goffman warns, "all role playing and nearly all human behaviour [is] defensive or phoney" thus leading to the "doubt that a real self exists" (cited in Wilshire xvi). Brecht's *Verfremdung* effect translated into life if you will. However, Woolf's various personae which she plays out in the letters, or her reflections on the multiplicity of the human character, lead more towards the conclusion that her differing tones do not always imply defence, deceit, or the loss of a unified self, they simply enliven and entertain.

In the process of recreating real individuals as dramatised characters, Woolf organises her actors giving them scripts, stages, and sets, as well as costumes and properties. The tedium of the familiar social script with its rehearsed rituals, daily structure, and stock phrases is anathema to Woolf. She notes that the social scene "doesn't encourage one to say anything more interesting than Thank you & please don't trouble, & other phrases of the kind" (*D1* 245). In response to this turgid tea-table talk Woolf and her circle substituted their own more scintillating repartee. Gerald Brenan recalls "conversation of a brilliance and (in spite of the rehearsals) spontaneity which, I imagine, has rarely been heard in England before…only continual practice by people who share the same general attitude to life and who are as pleased by their friends' performance as by their own can provide anything like it" (Stape 89-90). Frances Marshall corroborates, and remembers Woolf's contributions in particular being "dazzling performances" (Noble 75). The implication that conversations were rehearsed, and the suggestion that the speakers consciously performed for the amusement of an audience, reinforces the sense that life mimicked art as much as art mimicked life. Woolf took this one step further in the letters and diaries by actually writing out scripts of various kinds, designed for a multitude of effects. Many are transcriptions of past conversations, some are of possible future conversations, and others of outrageous imaginary conversations. In 1927, for example, she plays out the imaginary dialogue between Vanessa and Duncan following the publication of *To the Lighthouse*:

> Scene: after dinner: Nessa sewing: Duncan doing absolutely nothing.
> Nessa    (throwing down her work) Christ! There's the Lighthouse! I've only got to page 86 and I see there are 320. Now I cant write to Virginia because she'll expect me to tell her what I think of it.
> Duncan    Well, I should just tell her that you think it a masterpiece.
> Nessa    But she's sure to find out—They always do. She'll want to know why I think it's a masterpiece
> Duncan    Well Nessa, I'm afraid I cant help you, because I've only read 5 pages so far, and really I don't see much prospect of doing much reading this month, or next month, or indeed before Christmas.
> Nessa    Oh its all very well for you. But I shall have to say something: And I don't know who in the name of Jupiter all these people are… (*L3* 375-76)

By creating her own version of events Woolf entertained her reader or listener with a scene that, according to Leonard, "left the ground" to become "almost like a fantasy" (Stape 147). In her essay "On Not Knowing Greek" Woolf describes Aeschylus's ability to translate life into another dimension and in doing so describes her own hyper-real view of the world. Woolf was able to "amplify and give us, not the thing itself, but the reverberation and reflection…close enough to the original to illustrate it, remote enough to heighten, enlarge, and make splendid' (*CR1* 31). Basing her fantasies in reality allowed Woolf not only to entertain, but also to get serious points across whether to edify, argue, flatter, or apologize (*D1* 309; *L2* 508-9). The script format lifts the reader just far enough out of reality to cushion whatever Woolf's message happens to be.

Even structurally, life arranges itself into scenes and acts. Both past and present are reduced to specific moments of action, for example, Ethel Smyth running to catch her train provokes the reflection: "It's odd how little scenes like that suddenly illumine wherever one may be—Waterloo Station. I could swear a ring of light surrounded you me and the guard for one tenth of a second" (*L4* 241). In an account of afternoon tea at the house of Leonard's sister the scene is part of a society play: "Then the servant said 'Mr Sturgeon'; Flora cried 'I will go' dashed from the room; everyone said Oh! Ah! How splendid! as if on the stage, which indeed the whole scene might have been. We went, after the 2$^{nd}$ act" (*D1* 68). While in *Moments of Being* she notes that "Scene making is my natural way of marking the past" (*MOB* 142). This compartmentalisation of past and present into scenes and acts helps Woolf to make the transition between her sentient reality and her written fiction. By structuring the real world dramatically Woolf can live and relive experiences, thus smoothing the transition of life into art and vice versa.

Naturally stage, set, lighting, and costume are vital to both Woolf's "scene making" and characterisation of real people. Indeed, once Bloomsbury became home, interior design became increasingly important and evermore theatrical. Painted murals on walls and furniture formed the ideal backdrop for the life dramas played out within their houses. Some decorations have a consciously theatrical feel, such as the cupboard doors painted in 1918 by Bell and Grant.[2] The murals and decorated furniture were only a step away from stage set design and many of the Bloomsbury artists also provided scene paintings for drama and ballet which suited their talent for interior design, fine art, and dramatic living.[3] In addition to this, the artists also designed costumes for these productions.

Costumes were yet another link between life and art, from the disguises of the Dreadnought Hoax to the numerous fancy dress parties. Woolf was particularly interested in the duplicitous nature of clothing, including everyday attire which could be just as much of a costume as costume. In 1903 she states "Though I hate putting on my fine clothes, I know that when they are on I shall have invested myself at the same time with a certain social demeanour—I shall be ready to talk about the floor & the weather & other frivolities, which I consider platitudes in my nightgown" (*PA* 169). The effect of clothing on the performance of the self is of course an issue explored in her novel *Orlando* as well in her diaries.

Considering Woolf's connections with theatre and drama it is not surprising that she dramatised life in this way. As an avid reader and publisher of drama Woolf was familiar with the whole range of theatrical movements and genres, she also participated in readings with the Play Reading Society and wrote the comedy *Freshwater* (1923, revised 1935).[4] As a consequence, the non-fiction demonstrates a clear awareness of theatrical genres: Restoration farce, Victorian melodrama, Greek and Shakespearian tragedy, the late nineteenth century comedy of manners, and, particularly in *Moments of Being*, a hint of the problem play with herself and her sister appearing as Ibsen's trapped and desperate heroines. Each of these genres possesses its own formula which Woolf fits onto life. Woolf describes how "the scene was often fit for the stage" (*MOB* 35) in the drawing room at Hyde Park Gate and, in a paper for the Memoir Club entitled "22 Hyde Park Gate," the listener was thrown into the midst of a Victorian melodrama or a comedy of manners:

> Suddenly there would be a crisis—a servant dismissed, a lover rejected, pass books opened, or poor Miss Tyndall who had lately poisoned her husband by mistake come for consolation.... Cousin Adeline, Duchess of Bedford, perhaps

would be on her knees—the Duke had died tragically at Woburn; Mrs Dolmetsch would be telling how she had found her husband in bed with the parlour-maid. (*MOB* 142)

In contrast, Bloomsbury, Monk's House, and Charleston became associated with pastoral and Shakespearian comedies, to Vanessa Bell she writes:

> Nessa will come across with holes in her stockings—Quentin will come across with a hole in his trousers. I shall think, "How Shakespeare would have loved us!" for this sort of thing, the gramophone playing Mozart, the stars, the heat, the combination of shabbiness and splendour. (*L3* 416)

The tragic mode was reserved for Woolf's darker wishes. To Edward Sackville-West, she writes: "your aunt's behaviour could only be tolerated in an Elizabethan play. That she may take a dagger to her own throat or drink broken glass is rather my hope, I admit" (*L3* 458). As usual, Woolf is not content to follow the formula of each genre to the letter. Thus, the melodrama at Hyde Park Gate is both amusing and revolting; the comedy of manners is funny, but stifling; the Charleston and servant farces are witty, but irritating; the tragedies are terrible, yet delightful.

Woolf enjoys her vantage point in the audience at these dramas and often takes a comically obscene delight in the unfolding action:

> Bloomsbury is ringing with two great excitements: 1: Julian Morrell is engaged to a son of old Vinogradov: 2: Miss Bulley—the stormy petrel of revolution—is engaged to her Cousin Armitage. You will be delighted to hear that Ottoline and Philip are behaving scandalously…dislike the young man who is penniless; and ignore the whole affair. Julian is behaving with great spirit, and it is said that Garsington presents a scene of unparalleled horror. Needless to say, I am going to stay there. (*L3* 269)

However, Woolf's position as audience member was perfected under duress. Her memories of George Duckworth's socializing when Woolf was in her teens left her feeling

> as a tramp or gypsy must feel who stands at the flap of a tent and sees the circus going on inside. Victorian society was in full swing; George was the acrobat who jumped through hoops, and Vanessa and I beheld the spectacle. We had good seats at the show, but we were not allowed to take part in it. We applauded, we obeyed—that was all. (*MOB* 132)

However, the ability to observe serves a vital function in terms of her literature when an event is translated from first-hand experience to diary entry, to acquaintance via letter, to public via novel. Woolf was as dependent on observation as she was on participation for the creation of her lived reality.

Reading Woolf's life through the framework of theatre presents a writer who was keenly aware of life's dramatic dimensions and of the self as performance; "a life-actor in and for the world…experienc[ing] herself via the 'audience"s experience of her" (Wilshire 203). Clive Bell recalls this ability to amplify reality: "Such was the spell she threw, such the cogency of her imagination, that many a time poor Lady X found herself, not only playing up to the role assigned to her, but positively accepting Virginia in the role she had allotted to herself" (Noble 70-71). Nevertheless, Woolf's dramatisation of the self was neither fake nor false, it was an element of her personality which served a practical function: it allowed her to create a more vivid lived and written world.

## Notes

1. In the final chapter of *Orlando* the eponymous hero/ine calls out repeatedly for one of his/her alternative selves:

    Then she called hesitatingly, as if the person she wanted might not be there, "Orlando?" For if there are (at a venture) seventy-six different times all ticking in the mind at once, how many different people are there not—Heaven help us—all having lodgment at one time or another in the human spirit? Some say two thousand and fifty-two. So that it is the most usual thing in the world for a person to say, directly they are alone, Orlando? (if that is one's name) meaning by that, Come, come! I'm sick to death of this particular self. I want another. Hence, the astonishing changes we see in our friends. (*O* 212)

2. These panels are currently hanging in the Archive Room at King's College, Cambridge.
3. Vanessa Bell, Duncan Grant, and Roger Fry, between them, painted scenery for *Twelfth Night* (1914), *Pelléas et Mélisande (1918)*, *High Yellow* (1932), *Pomona* (1933), *Fête Galante* (1934), *Le Lac des Cygnes* (1932), and *The Enchanted Grove* (1932).
4. The Play Reading Society was formed in December 1907 by Clive Bell and originally consisted of Vanessa Bell, Virginia Stephen, Adrian Stephen, Lytton Strachey, Saxon Sydney-Turner, and Clive Bell.

## Works Cited

Cohen, Ralph, ed. *The Future of Literary Theory*. London: Routledge, 1989.
Dobson, Julia. *Hélène Cixous and the Theatre: The Scene of Writing*. Bern: P. Lang, 2002.
Heilbrun, Carolyn G. *Reinventing Womanhood*. London: Norton, 1993.
Noble, Joan Russell, ed. *Recollections of Virginia Woolf*. London: Peter Owen, 1972.
Reed, Christopher. *Bloomsbury Rooms: Modernism, Subculture, and Domesticity*. New York: Yale UP, 2004.
Schechner, Richard. *Performance Theory*. London: Routledge, 2003.
Stape, J. H., ed. *Virginia Woolf: Interviews and Recollections*. London: Macmillan, 1995.
Wilshire, Bruce. *Role Playing and Identity*. Bloomington: Indiana UP, 1982.
Woolf, Virginia. *The Common Reader*. Ed. Andrew McNeillie. Vols. 1 and 2. London: Vintage, 2003.
———. *The Death of the Moth and Other Essays*. New York: Harcourt Brace, 1970.
———. *The Diary of Virginia Woolf*. Ed. Anne Olivier Bell with Andrew McNeillie. 5 vols. London: Hogarth, 1977-1984.
———. *The Letters of Virginia Woolf*. Ed. Nigel Nicholson and Joanne Trautmann. 6 vols. London: Hogarth, 1975-1980.
———. *Moments of Being: Unpublished Autobiographical Writings*. Ed. Jeanne Schulkind. London: Chatto and Windus for Sussex UP, 1976.
———. *Orlando: A Biography*. London: Penguin, 1993.
———. *A Passionate Apprentice: The Early Journals 1897-1909*. Ed. Mitchell A. Leaska. London: Hogarth, 1990.

# "Whose Face Was It?": Nicole Kidman, Virginia Woolf, and the Boundaries of Feminine Celebrity

## by Wendy Parkins

"Passers-by who, of course, stopped and stared, had just time to see a face of the very greatest importance.... Whose face was it? Nobody knew." (*MD* 15)

In *Mrs. Dalloway*, a car passes down a London street, giving onlookers a glimpse of a face both well-known and yet unfamiliar, allowing Woolf to evoke—in a characteristically elliptical way—the pervasive imbrication of fame and visibility in modernity. In Woolf's novel, the face belongs to a public personage. In Michael Cunningham's novel, *The Hours*, which revisits and reworks *Mrs. Dalloway*, the famous face glimpsed in the city street is a Hollywood star. When Cunningham's novel was adapted for the screen, the central female characters in the three separate (but intertwined) narrative strands were played by three famous Hollywood "faces," any one of whom could have been the star glimpsed by Cunningham's Clarissa: Nicole Kidman, Julianne Moore, and Meryl Streep. While all three were critically acclaimed for their performances—and nominated for awards—media attention tended to centre on Kidman, as a "face of the greatest importance," for her portrayal of Woolf, a focus that only intensified with Kidman's "Oscar triumph." In this paper, I will examine the meanings of Kidman-as-Woolf (as I will refer to the film characterization) which emerged from this media attention and, through this examination, consider the boundaries of celebrity embodiment. Informed by Brenda Silver's analysis of the shifting status of Virginia Woolf as a cultural icon whose definition relies on contested meanings of gender (12; see also Lee 2005), I will argue that the significations of Kidman are played off against those of Woolf in a binary of more and less successful femininity. Genius, madness, and childlessness (in the form of Woolf) are represented as ugliness, while by implication, on the other side of the feminine binary, beauty is associated with celebrity, success, and motherhood (Kidman). Within this binary, moreover, the two figures are positioned in relation to differing understandings of (feminine) suffering. With particular attention to the media fetishization of Woolf's nose, I will argue that such reportage constructed Kidman as a contemporary embodiment of both female heroism—one who has triumphed over suffering—and the "star-as-performer" (Geraghty 191), while Woolf was constituted as an image of feminine failure through the visual representation of her embodiment in the movie.

As Christine Geraghty has argued, any examination of a film star needs to be located in "the broader context of star within mass popular culture" (184). An analysis of Kidman's performance as Virginia Woolf, then, needs to bear in mind the range of significations already associated with the actress in the public domain, as the star's performance as a famous historical personage is always a two-way construction based on the interplay of meanings of the star and the figure they portray. The critical attention Kidman received for *The Hours* implicitly relied on a cultural stereotype of Woolf that associates the author with qualities such as unconventionality, genius, and madness. These significations of

Woolf were embodied by the actor not only in gesture and expression but by dress, hair, and, of course, *that* nose. Such signs, with their connotations of unsuccessful femininity (or ugliness), served to highlight the performance of Kidman and stress the distance between the character and the celebrity persona Kidman embodies off-screen. While media reportage of Kidman's performance often focused on the actress's "bravery" in attempting such an "unglamorous" role, however, Woolf was of course much-photographed and frequently described as a beauty in her lifetime. Perhaps the most commonly reproduced image of Woolf is the photograph taken when Virginia Stephen was 20 in 1902 which, as Hermione Lee has noted, was a crucial image in the legend of Virginia, with her large eyes, full lips and lacy dress (1996 246). Twenty years after this photograph, Woolf was included in British *Vogue*'s 1924 "Hall of Fame" and in 1930, she featured in Cecil Beaton's *Book of Beauty* (Silver 91-93).

So how is it, we may ask, that when Virginia Woolf was brought to the screen in 2002 she was represented as dishevelled, peevish, and unfashionable?[1] Kidman's distracted and dowdy appearance, together with her affected chain-smoking, is meant to convey writer's block, the difficulty of genius, and incipient mental illness. This image of Woolf as a composite of clichés about women is of course both a historical simplification and significantly different from that offered in Cunningham's novel, and yet the overwhelming preoccupation in critical discussion of the film has been the physicality of Kidman-as-Woolf. While critics were broadly divided between those who couldn't see past the nose, as it were, and those who praised Kidman's total transformation into Woolf, the common currency deployed by both groups of responses served to reiterate a perceived relation between embodiment and an authentic femininity. Hiscock and Turan, for instance, concurred that Kidman was unrecognisable thanks to the prosthetic nose, while Holden praised Kidman's "uncanny physical resemblance" to Woolf. Critics dismissive of Kidman's performance, by contrast, were not only scathing about the "putty" (Griffin) nose but deplored Kidman's failure to *embody* Woolf: "She seems bloodless, a series of stiff poses in a flicker book," wrote Sandhu, while Iannone described "a one-note, zombie-like" performance (51). Both sides of the debate, then, privilege embodiment in the evaluation of performance, differing only in their respective judgments of the actress's achievements.

The favourable critical reception of Kidman-as-Woolf was also bolstered by interviews with the filmmakers who praised Kidman's embodied performance by recounting production anecdotes to illustrate the way Kidman "fleshed out" her characterization. For example, Cunningham reported that Kidman turned down the use of a hand double for the writing scenes, instead learning to reproduce Woolf's handwriting (for the scene where she writes the suicide note), which also required her to write with her right-hand when Kidman is herself left-handed ("Kidman" 92). In an interview with Cunningham and screenwriter David Hare, Kidman's corporeal inhabitance of the role of Woolf is offered as proof of the authenticity of her performance—"Her whole body is acting" (Blackwelder). Again referring to Kidman writing as Woolf, Hare sees this not only as evidence of Kidman's dedication but as establishing the accuracy of her embodied performance: "She had a writing board, and she had a scratchy pen, and the physicalization of how Virginia Woolf actually wrote is now totally authentic" (Blackwelder). The filmmakers, however, reserved their highest praise for Kidman's physicalization of Woolf during the suicide scene. No body double was used here either, and Kidman waded into the river and stayed submerged for a full minute, drifting with the current. As director Stephen Daldry stated, "When you see those shots in the film, it is Nicole Kidman" (2). *"When you see those shots in the film, it is Nicole Kidman"* may seem like a laughably obvious statement for the director to make (is this not the *sine qua non* of an actor performing a role?), but the comments of Daldry, Hare, and Cunningham seem to be trying to describe what they see as a qualitatively different screen performance. Here, acting is distinguished from imitation, not merely a copying of voice, posture, or action but instead a more authentic kind of transformation through bodily performance, as demonstrated by the bodily discipline required to enact this transformation. Of course, critical acclaim for cinematic performances is often based on the perception of verisimilitude, the capacity to bring the character to life. What makes this instance interesting is the combination of the insistently artificial (the latex nose) with the emphasis on actual embodiment (teaching oneself to write with the other hand) in these positive appraisals of Kidman so that the prosthetic and the "natural" body together seem to create a kind of authenticity without contradiction.

At the same time, however, the supposedly enhanced authenticity of Kidman's performance co-exists with an insistence on the presence of the star. It requires the boundary between star and character to be firmly demarcated. Far from "disappear[ing] so completely on screen," as one critic (Scott) enthused, both pro and anti-Kidman camps in fact never lose sight of Kidman in her impersonation of Woolf.[2] When Hare contends that in this role Kidman was "liberated from her own prettiness" and Cunningham asks rhetorically "wouldn't Virginia Woolf love being played by someone so beautiful?" (Blackwelder), viewers are being asked to remember that Kidman is a beauty in order to appreciate her performance. If we were to see only Woolf, we would no longer be appreciating the performance *of* Woolf. And as both Hare and Cunningham imply, the key signifier here is beauty, with its always-already implied opposite, ugliness. The meanings of Kidman-as-Woolf, then, rely on the cultural connotations of both Kidman and Woolf to create a complex homonym in which the perceived clashes between movie-star beauty and female literary genius operate to ensure Kidman-as-Woolf remains an object of appeal/fascination.

The positive reception of Kidman's performance, moreover, is not unusual due to the all too predictable admiration for a beautiful woman who is prepared to be grotesquely transformed on screen (witness similar acclaim—and Oscar success—for Charlize Theron as Aileen Wuornos in *Monster* or Hilary Swank as Brandon Teena in *Boys Don't Cry* in recent years). A significant part of this acclaim comes from an actress's willingness to be ugly *in public*. The cultural obsession with beautiful women is perhaps only surpassed by a fascination with beautiful women transformed into ugly women because there is something unresolvable about the nature of female beauty at stake here: is it a given, a natural quality, only embodied by rare, exceptional women (stars)? Or is such beauty inherently inauthentic, a quality manufactured by stars, as a means of becoming exceptional?

Criticism of the perceived "ugliness" of Kidman-as-Woolf is not, however, simply due to a preference for the glamorous Kidman rather than the serious actress but rather derives from a critical objection to the distortion of the historical figure of Woolf that results. The acclaimed cinematic transformations of Theron, Swank, and Kidman, after all, were each cases where actresses put aside their image of celebrity glamour in order to impersonate women who were perceived as monstrous in some way, their physical ugliness signifying some kind of failed femininity. This conflation of ugliness with failed femininity is apparently so unshakeable that, in the case of Kidman-as-Woolf, it requires first re-figuring Woolf as ugly, despite the significant visual archive of Woolf that exists and continues to circulate in both high and popular culture. The latex nose, then, is not simply to enable Kidman to physically resemble the suffering, literary genius that was Woolf as clearly she does not. Rather, I would argue that the latex nose becomes indexical of feminine suffering *per se*, in a chain of associations that conflates Woolf's suffering (for her art, for her sanity) with Kidman's (also for her art, through sacrificing her beauty).

Within the visual economy of cinema, in which the interior must be exteriorised to signify, the prosthetic nose becomes overdetermined, as it were, as ostensibly a means of constructing a physical resemblance between author and actress but in fact connecting what would otherwise seem un-articulable: the Hollywood star and the tragic genius. A screen beauty who is prepared to suffer for her art is, it would seem, one of the few ways contemporary culture can embody feminine achievement in the impoverished terms of our gendered visual economy. As one journalist wryly observed of Hollywood's incapacity to visually represent plain or ordinary-looking women, "In Hollywood, the best way to suggest a woman with an intellect is to cast an actor who doesn't have a deep suntan" (Griffin).

Making suffering visible in *The Hours*, then, involves a process of disavowal; the corporeality of suffering is acknowledged and yet simultaneously denied by the visible artificiality of the prosthetic. In this way, I would argue, the debate about whether Kidman successfully resembles Woolf or not—which is how the nose has figured in public discourse on the film[3]—is almost beside the point. More significant is how the fetishization of the nose offers only a suffering Woolf to public scrutiny: no matter what else transpires in the film narrative, Kidman-as-Woolf's ravaged face is a constant reminder of the inescapability of her failed femininity, embodied in/by suffering.[4] Here the meaning becomes circular: suffering is ugly and to be ugly is to suffer. Kidman's performance of feminine suffering relies on echoes of her own publicized ordeals to "flesh out" her impersonation of a woman whose suffering may be less well-known to contemporary film audiences.[5] Rendered as a series of equations, then, Kidman + nose may equal Kidman minus beauty but it also represents Kidman + award-winning acting (through her portrayal of suffering). Thus, her performance lends a contemporary relevance to Woolf by offering an updated metaphor for suffering: instead of the anguish of the struggle between creativity, social expectation, and mental illness that informs Woolf's biography, *The Hours* starring Kidman offers suffering as being like an actress deprived of her beauty.

One might have hoped that an early twenty-first century representation of Woolf could have better captured some of the complexities of both the historical figure herself and the cultural positionings of femininity (as Cunningham's novel does so carefully). Instead, in the figure of Kidman-as-Woolf we have a reductive representation of suffering woman in which the signs of failed femininity are taken as marks of authenticity and where such failure can only be measured by a limited aesthetic of female beauty. In her own lifetime, for instance, Woolf's nose would have been seen as a sign of aristocratic bearing, confirmation of the author's privileged class status. Silver has argued that the shifts *and* continuities in representations of Woolf have always had a "performative role in the naming and policing of norms that continue to fix women into particular cultural and social positions" (6). The norms of femininity associated with female beauty are exemplified in Kidman's recent Chanel campaign in which her rather patrician profile, porcelain skin, and sculptural body shape almost literally transform her into a style icon and produce the star as commodity.[6] As Richard Dyer has argued, the embodiment of stars seems to offer us a privileged insight into the nature of the human but instead offers "particular, even rather peculiar, ways of making sense of the body" (12). The rather peculiar embodiment of Nicole Kidman in *The Hours*, then, presents us with a very postmodern paradox: in a culture of cosmetic surgery as supplement to, if not foundation of, celebrity, we have a star with a bad nose job whose performance nonetheless, for many viewers, seems to evoke a reassurance of authenticity linked to her perceived beauty. For this reason, commodity stars like Kidman, even when—*especially* when—disguised or disfigured on screen, remain faces of "the very greatest importance" in contemporary visual culture and demonstrate the clear boundaries that still operate to demarcate women by appearance rather than achievement.

## Notes

1. Other cinematic representations of Woolf in the 1990s, such as in *Carrington* and *Tom and Viv*, while also unflattering in terms of Woolf's character, noticeably depicted the author as fashionably dressed, although perhaps overly so (see Silver 179-82, 185-86).
2. It is worth noting that elsewhere, Kidman has been capable of transforming her appearance beyond recognition. One of the best examples of this would be the *Vogue* image of Kidman parodying a MGM musical which John Hartley used as a cover image for his book, *Popular Reality* (1996).
3. Perhaps best encapsulated in an episode of the Australian satire *Kath and Kim* depicting a local theatre production of a musical version of *The Hours*. This innovative production includes a "dancing noses" sequence in which the performers' bodies are entirely obscured by enormous papier-maché noses from which only their tap-dancing feet are visible.
4. For a comparable discussion of the articulation of beauty, celebrity, suffering, and tragedy, see Scott Wilson's analysis of the death of Princess Diana, "The Indestructible Beauty of Suffering: Diana and the Metaphor of Global Consumption," in which he argues that the beauty of Diana "functions to support, that is maintain, sustain and even provoke, the spectacle of suffering," at the same time as her suffering "also guarantees the truth of her virtue" (3). Without her beauty, the suffering-virtue nexus would be broken; leaving only the ugliness of suffering.
5. See Dyer (passim) on the inter-relation between public discourse on the lives of celebrities and their film characterizations to construct the meaning of stars. See also Spohrer on the significance of "Kidman's extratextual stardom" in informing the public's perception of her role in *The Hours* (117).
6. For further discussion of Kidman as a commodity star, see Conor.

## Works Cited:

Blackwelder, Rob. "Half an Hour About *The Hours*." <http://www.splicedonline.com/02features/cunningham-hare.html>. 2002. Accessed 8/4/05.
*Boys Don't Cry*. Dir. Kimberly Peirce. Twentieth Century Fox, 1999.
*Carrington*. Dir. Christopher Hampton. Polygram, 1995.
Conor, Liz. "Nicole Kidman and the Commodity Star." *Metro Magazine*, no. 127/128, 2001: 98-99.
Cunningham, Michael. *The Hours*. London: Fourth Estate, 1998.
———. "Nicole Kidman." *Interview*, 32 (1), February 2002: 92.
Daldry, Stephen. "The Heroics of Everyday Lives." *Film Education* online, <http://www.filmeducation.org/secondary/TheHours/thehours-2.pdf>. 2003. Accessed 8/4/05.
Dyer, Richard. *Heavenly Bodies: Film Stars and Society*. 2nd ed. London: Routledge, 2004.
Geraghty, Christine. "Re-examining Stardom: Questions of Texts, Bodies and Performance." *Reinventing Film Studies*. Ed. Christine Gledhill and Linda Williams. London: Arnold, 2000: 183-202.
Griffin, Michelle. "The Power of Plain." *The Age* online, <http://www.theage.com.au/news/books/the-power-of-plain/2005/08/19/1123958222302.html>. 2005. Accessed 21/11/05.

Hartley, John. *Popular Reality: Journalism, Modernity, Popular Culture*. London: Arnold, 1996.
Hiscock, John. "Nicole Kidman as Never Seen Before." *The Telegraph* online. <http://www.telegraph.co.uk/arts/main.jhtml?xml=/arts/2002/11/02/bfkid.xml>. 2002 Accessed 8 April 2005.
Holden, Stephen. "Who's Afraid Like Virginia Woolf?" *New York Times*, 27 December 2002. E.1.
Iannone, Carol. "Woolf, Women and *The Hours*." *Commentary*, April 2003: 50-53.
*Kath and Kim*. "Kicking Up a Stink." Dir. Ted Emery. Riley Turner Productions, 2003.
Lee, Hermione. *Virginia Woolf*. London: Chatto & Windus, 1996.
———. "Virginia Woolf's Nose." *Body Parts: Essays in Life-Writing*. London: Chatto & Windus, 2005. 28-44.
*Monster*. Dir. Patty Jenkins. Columbia Pictures, 2003.
Sandhu, Sukhdev. "Masterpiece of Miscasting." *The Telegraph* online. <http://www.telegraph.co.uk/arts/main.jhtml?xml=/arts/2003/02/14/bfhours14>. 2003. Accessed 8 April 2005.
Scott, A. O. "A Unified Theory of Nicole Kidman." *New York Times*, 2 November 2003. 2A.1.
Silver, Brenda R. *Virginia Woolf Icon*. Chicago: University of Chicago Press, 1999.
Spohrer, Erika. "Seeing Stars: Commodity Stardom in Michael Cunningham's *The Hours* and Virginia Woolf's *Mrs Dalloway*." *Arizona Quarterly* 61 (2005): 113-32.
*Tom and Viv*. Dir. Brian Gilbert. Miramax, 1994.
Turan, Kenneth. "Movie Review: *The Hours*." *Los Angeles Times* online. <http://www.calendarlive.com/movies/reviews/cl-et-turan27dec27,0,7478042.story>. 2002. Accessed 23/11/05.
Wilson, Scott. "The Indestructible Beauty of Suffering: Diana and the Metaphor of Global Consumption." *Theory & Event*, vol 1 no 4, 1997. <http://muse.jhu.edu/journals/theory_and_event/>.
Woolf, Virginia. *Mrs. Dalloway*. Ed. Elaine Showalter. London: Penguin, 1992.

## "Memory Holes" or "Heterotopias"?: The Bloomsbury Photographs

## by Maggie Humm

"Isnt it odd how much more one sees in a photograph than in real life?" (*L5* 455)

Photographs of Virginia Woolf, from youth and beauty as one of the famous Stephen sisters, to maturity, are inseparable from her status as a writer and her public image. She was photographed by Man Ray, Lenare, and Gisele Freund, as well as by her sister, family, and circle of Bloomsbury friends and artists. But it is the domestic photographs which were important to both Virginia and Vanessa, who included very few professional photographs in their albums.

Certainly Vanessa Bell and the Woolfs took photography very seriously. Leonard's diaries record a regular expenditure showing their addiction to photography, and the amounts are as revealing about British class divisions as about technologies. In April 1922, according to his dairy, Leonard spent ten shillings on photography (approximately nineteen pounds at today's prices) but paid their servant Lottie only two shillings. In 1923 the Woolfs spent one pound two shillings (or twenty-two shillings) on photography, and a year later on 30 May 1924 one pound and one shilling, but gave Nellie only five shillings. This was a period in which the income from Virginia's capital "had shrunk to less than half its original sum by 1918-19" and was even lower in the 1920s at a time when their joint earnings were often in deficit (Spater and Parsons 90). Yet the Woolfs' photographic costs remained fairly constant, with expenditure, in August 1929, of one pound and ten shillings (sixty-one pounds at today's prices).

Photographs in photo albums were crucial to their sense of identity because they expose issues of memory and representation. Although it is again fashionable to read an artist's aesthetics through the small lens of subjective experience, and everyday experiences were very important to Bell and the Woolfs, reading their photo albums is not easy. All albums have their own syntax, their own codes and indices, and are hybrid entities. Albums are not only objects of perceptions, they also structure perceptions. They are archives of a sort. Foucault thought of the archive as a system of functioning and certainly Leonard Woolf, as you know, was an obsessive archivist. He kept daily lists including the total number of words he wrote on each day of his life, car mileages, dates of cacti flowering, and even the times/days of switching on and off his central heating. But the photo albums of the Woolfs lack this obsessive quality. They are much more associative in organisation. I think we need to look at them more topographically as spatial objects. But to date there is no "theory" of amateur photography. Although John Szarkowski established a snapshot aesthetic at the Museum of Modern Art, New York, as long ago as 1966, with the exhibition "Toward a Social Landscape," amateur photographers are thought to lack picture awareness. Szarkowski's aim was to appropriate and formalize a snapshot photographic vocabulary *detached* from its vernacular tradition, and this aim carries through into more recent exhibitions such as "Cruel and Tender" at Tate Modern, London, in 2003.

Histories of photography frequently endorse this formalism by creating a canon of "great" photographers of the everyday (for example, Paul Strand, Garry Winogrand, Martin Parr). Even cultural studies of vernacular photography allow the snapshot only a limited number of features such as "legibility" and "social function." Sociological analyses of camera clubs and ethnographic accounts of colonial photography see photography in terms of class/occupational groups or in terms of constructions of race and the gaze (Bourdieu, Clifford). Feminist artists and critics have examined the relationship between women's lack of economic and social status and depictions of femininities and masculinities in the family album—most famously in Jo Spence's 1979 exhibition at the Hayward Gallery "Beyond the Family Album." But Spence and others often aim to "fix" family photographs in a new feminist framework by means of detailed textual captions. Trauma studies are devoted to amateur photography but necessarily serve as a recovering of a historical project.

Family and memory studies of amateur photography go much further in decoding possible psychic and familial pressures shaping forms of composition (Hirsch, Spence, and Holland). Notions of loss, photographic mnemonics, and gender constructions are crucial themes that impact on amateur selections and on the Bloomsbury snapshots. But family studies are sometimes content-driven at the expense of technical and economic variables. It does matter where and with what cameras photographs are taken. For example, even the National Portrait Gallery, London does not list the place of Man Ray's iconic photograph of Virginia Woolf. Where did Man Ray take the photograph since Man Ray had no London studio? It was Curtis Moffat who invited Man Ray to London and hence his studio is probably the venue. The fact that Moffat was a *Vogue* photographer impacts on the technical quality of the photograph.

My own approach to these photographs is necessarily hybrid—drawing on cultural history, discourse analysis, Bloomsbury biographies and criticism, and photographic and psychoanalytic studies. Constructions of visual identity always involve questions of memory and speculations about how to record the thickness and malleability of personal lives (Lury). In what would now be termed a form of "life caching" or "memory prosthesis," Woolf and Bell used photo albums extensively as autobiographical narrative. Domestic photographs mounted in albums also invite viewer participation in constructing pictorial narratives from these domestic *aides-mémoires*.

As Susan Sontag argues, photographs are "both objective record and personal testimony," simultaneously recording and interpreting reality (23). Photo albums are also a safe space from which to view past presences. Both the Woolfs and Bell used domestic photography, as they used their arts, throughout their lives, to capture both conscious and unconscious responses to family, friendships, and themselves. Importantly, the Woolfs and Bell's constant photographic documentation suggests a need to critically relate to the past by working through representations of the present.

### The Woolfs' Albums and Vanessa Bell's Albums

The Woolfs' seven photo albums, called the Monk's House Albums, together with four boxes containing over two hundred additional loose photographs, are housed in the Frederick Koch Collection, the Harvard Theatre Library, and are un-catalogued, hence I undertook to catalogue these in *Snapshots of Bloomsbury* (Humm 2006). The main features of the albums are firstly the large number of Victorian photographs, pre-dating the Woolfs' lives, and carefully captioned. This panorama suggests, perhaps, a longing for a confirmed familial world.

A second feature is the albums' lack of chronological logic which might match Woolf's refusal of narrative realism in her fiction and illustrates the intertextuality of past and present in her work and life. In Monk's House Album 3 the past vividly "narrates" the present. The album is dated 1930 yet the framing frontispiece is a large six by seven-and-a-half photograph of Julia Stephen taken probably in 1863-65 because it resembles one in the Mia Album given to Maria (Mia) by her sister, the photographer Julia Margaret Cameron, and the Stephen sisters' great aunt (Ovenden plate 113).

A third feature is that there is no closed, hierarchical system, for example, photographs of servants are not separated from family photographs. A fourth feature is the repetition of monumental portraits. The camera is inscriptive, not transcriptive, in its visibility, for example the portraits of Ethel Smyth and the Keynes's in the 1930s. The psychological consistency of composition in these photographs suggests a subtle relationship between photographers and subjects.

Vanessa Bell's ten albums in the Tate archive are a unique record of her family, friendships, and aesthetic interests. The layout of each album is more chronological than the albums of the Woolfs. Bell's mode of collection and organization mimics her family and domestic roles. For example, Bell welcomes into her collection many photographs taken by others just as she warmly welcomed visitors to stay in Charleston and Cassis.

As a genre, photo albums are conventionally read as documents of "real" family life. Indeed snapshot photography is frequently assessed by its ability to document indices of the real. And "Kodaking" is often seen as a mundane cultural practice. Yet although the scenes and people recorded by the Woolfs and Bell are snapshots of everyday Bloomsbury, the camera viewpoints and framing look attentively beyond the snapshot moment into the sisters' past and outward into moments of modernity. The seemingly trivial detail and events in the photographs such as household objects and pursuits are elements of the everyday but can be cognitively viewed from different angles.

## Reading Albums

A major problematic, alongside the issue of evaluating marginalia, is how to know, except by indexical, cultural, and biographical analysis, the photographs' likely "readership" and Bell and the Woolfs' reasons for shooting and selection, since this is not always evident in the many diaries or letters. To purloin Alex Zwerdling's very pertinent questions about the Bloomsbury memoirs: for whom are the photo albums constructed—"for the nuclear family, for an inner circle" or the anticipation of a wider circle? "And for what purpose: to honor the dead?… To make the past cohere? To produce the official record? To amuse and entertain? To illustrate a representative way of life? To confess? To understand oneself?" (Zwerdling 168-69). Zwerdling concludes, in relation to writing, that the "multigenerational Stephen internal tradition of memoir writing illustrated all these options" (169). The Bloomsbury photo albums equally illustrate all these options.

How then to read this marginal minutae of modernism? It is both tautological because self-evident, and yet not enough to argue that the portraits represent the sisters' intense desire for a supportive social/cultural group of like-minded friends and family. There are questions of appropriate femininities and masculinities that remain unspoken as well as questions of class and generational rebellions and visual inheritances. In many ways photo albums resemble Foucault's concept of "heterotopology" which Foucault coined to define marginal sites of modernity, virtual sites such as Parisian arcades, whose "role is to create a space that is other, another real space, as perfect...as ours is messy" (Foucault 27). Foucault's idea has been very influential on contemporary architectural studies. Charles Jencks usefully applies the term "heterotopolis" to Los Angeles's combination of modernism with sites of difference.

By applying Foucault's concept to photo albums I do not intend to imply that photography is purely spatial, nor only a collection of measurable representations. This illusion of clarity would over-substantiate the snapshot world. But focusing on spatial arrangements in album photographs is potentially fruitful not least because it allays a common belief that all amateur photographers are unable to aesthetically manage spatial dimensions. Space is socially produced and actively shapes our subjectivity whether in visual sites such as photographs or in urban geographies. Where everyday representations are often below the threshold of art history, "heterotopology," on the contrary, illuminates the psychodynamics of snapshots. Spaces of representation in snapshots embody complex emotions, the multiple perceived and unconscious spaces of the camera operator, the photographed figures and viewers. These complex symbolisms are sometimes coded, for example by learned artistic conventions, and sometimes not. In third space, or heterotopology, physical, measurable space is interdependent with symbolic and imaginative spaces. For example, in the iconography of nineteenth-century *cartes-de-visite*, the 1892 photograph of Woolf's parents reading at St. Ives suggests simply an intimate family space. But heterotopologically, Virginia's look to Vanessa behind the camera suggests an explicit sorority projected in the sisters' symbolic space of the primal scene.

One good example of a heterotopological "method" is Bell and the Woolfs' use of photo album captions. Their frequent use of nomenclature, with Virginia captioning her own images "VW" and giving full names to friends—for example, "Roger Fry"—and Vanessa using initials for each individual (including her children) is unusual. The sisters clearly did not need to remind themselves of Fry's identity and certainly not of their own. At first glance, Bell and the Woolfs' "objectivity" might seem the antithesis of heterotopology because the function of titles is didactic, even mechanistic. Recording titles is a way of collating information, like a catalogue or dictionary does, into predetermined spaces. But what distinguishes this form of captioning from John Tagg's regulatory archive or from Walter Benjamin's view that captioning "literalises the relationships of life," is precisely Bell and the Woolfs' heterotopology (Tagg, Benjamin 25).

The role of photo albums in their lives more resembles Foucault's account of the role of a mirror in heterotopology "that enables me to see myself there where I am absent" (24). The album captions suggest that Bell and the Woolfs were motivated by several of the possibilities that Zwerdling outlines: to honour the dead, to make the past coherent, to understand themselves (Zwerdling 168). The album captions suggest the sisters' deep desire for a visual remembrance of life and friendships, reinforcing close-up portraits with verbal stress, and matching Bell's domestic aesthetic and the Woolfs' daily diaries and letter writing. The albums become *mementoes mori* in the very act of construction. Foucault likens heterotopologies to slices of time, or heterochronies, precarious spaces of time that are both temporary and permanent. The albums similarly picture present moments shaped by a past that is never permanently past. Objects and places in Bell and the Woolfs' snapshot photographs stand in for the irretrievably lost childhood home St. Ives.

Bell's frequent use of enlargements, and her love of repetitive photographs, especially of her children Julian, Quentin, and Angelica, are also a material celebration of the domestic sphere. Bell enlarged her familial worlds into epic "spaces" with a sure sense of scale and frame. Photographs taken by Bell in 1912 illustrate this issue of framing and relationships. The portrait of Duncan Grant and John Maynard Keynes taken at Asheham in 1912, measuring eight inches by six, is striking. Both figures are in profile in a carefully structured design. The camera is in marked close-up to each figure. The framing and enlargement of figures might reflect Vanessa's nascent regard for Duncan in 1912 when she shared Christmas Day "reading passages aloud from her father's *Mausoleum Book*" and painting alongside Duncan at Asheham (Spalding 119). Keynes's relaxed pose also hints at a residue of his former sexual relationship with Duncan.

In addition, while Bell and the Woolfs' multiple portraits in this period are documents of friends and family visits and events, they also contain the opposing register of the psychic in vivid personal presences. The earlier portrait of Leonard and Virginia taken by Gerald Duckworth during their visit to Dalingridge Place in 1912 is a good example of the pressure of the psychic. The photograph's low angle (which might derive from Duckworth's use of a Frena rather than a more up to date Kodak) renders the couple with great presence. In July 1912 the Woolfs were engaged and yet the pose is one of two separate "unengaged" people. It is unusual in Britain to wear wedding clothes before the wedding day itself. A common superstition is the belief that a fiancé's sight of the wedding dress will bring bad luck to the marriage. Yet Virginia unconventionally wore the same clothes here and again on her wedding day.

It would be anachronistic to read the photograph through a contemporary lens by expecting the couple to fondly touch or look to the camera with smiles or mutual gazes. Studio portraits of couples in this period usually depict separate figures with sitting males and standing females or vice-versa. But physical contact is often centred in these studio photographs with one figure's right hand resting lovingly on the other's left shoulder. The scene of the Woolfs' engagement is mournful, as taut as Leonard's buttoned-up jacket and Virginia's glove clutching. Both gaze into a distant future rather than at each other or toward camera.

As Virginia had written very honestly to Leonard the month before, "I don't know what the future will bring. I'm half afraid of myself…I go from being half in love with you…to the extreme of wildness and aloofness…. As I told you brutally the other day, I feel no physical attraction in you" (*L1* 496). And, knowing that "Leonard and I shall be alone" over Bank Holiday, Virginia wrote pleadingly to Ka Cox "will you come to Asheham this week, Saturday, and spend Bank Holiday" (*L1* 506). The photograph carries Virginia's corporeal resistance in its intense haptic quality. Engagements are public events often involving a whirl of social engagements, a social technology of public relationships. The photograph, with its poses, incorporates into that sociality Woolf's more private fears. Perhaps Woolf's photographic refusal of affiliative looking at the body of Leonard might parallel her attention to the limits of the body in her fiction writing at this time.

The Woolfs' preference for paired self-portraits of themselves and their friends make this issue of identity part of the portrait and constitute a veritable repetitive visual autobiography. In their 1930s photographs the Woolfs assent to each other's camera gaze.

Each is a very central presence in the frame as if each is making a lengthy visual analysis of the other's distinctive image. Such close-up figuration creates embodiment disrupting the normal separation of camera and subject. These repetitive paired sequences go beyond the conventions of candid or instant photography. In their use of repetition the photographs are dialogic, encouraging dialogue between the sitters and between husband and wife as camera operators. Similarly, Virginia's use of a dialogic form in her essays "constitutes Woolf's greatest separation" from conventional academia in the 1920s (Cuddy-Keane 79).

The constant pairing of husband and wife and of friends over decades is a dialogic practice in which relationships are staged in the photographic encounter. The portraits are not static but use space as an "other space," Foucault's synonym for heterotopologies. "The space in which we live, which draws us out of ourselves, in which the erosion of our lives, our time and our history occurs, the space that claws and gnaws at us, is also, in itself a heterogeneous space" (Foucault 23). Taken as a whole the Woolfs and Bell's albums are transactional, containing performances of intimate exchange within the genre of formal portraiture, going beyond what we normally find in family albums.

I have written before about the photographs of Clive Bell together with Virginia taken by Vanessa at Studland Beach in 1910 (Humm 2002). But I now wish to contrast these with the painting *Studland Beach* by Vanessa. In the photographs Clive and Virginia are cooperative models but their gazes are not fully direct. In both photographs there is deliberate repetition. The two figures are in complementary positions with arms and legs in synchronic patterns. The visual ordering and spacing of their relationship are compounded by the inclusion of paired shoes and beach huts within the frame. In one photograph the raised seams of Virginia's gloves parallel the swollen veins of Clive's downward pointing hands. The persistence of any photographic motif, for example a pattern of pictorial relations, confirms its importance and accrues excess through repetition. Any choice, whether conscious or unconscious, of organisational pattern necessarily involves a latent language. It is as if the echoing patterns of Clive's and Virginia's positions are a corporeal allusion to other correspondences in their lives.

After the birth of Vanessa's first child, Julian, in February 1908, Clive and Vanessa interrupted their sex life and Clive began to flirt with Virginia. Hermione Lee suggests that "from this time—May of 1908—they began to play a game of intimacy and intrigue which lasted for perhaps two years," that is until the Studland photographs of 1910 (249). The Studland photographs carry this hidden hint of sororial absorption in the repetitions and patterning of each image. In contrast, in Bell's painting *Studland Beach* the figures, with their backs to the viewer, have no gazes. The painting's subjects are all women and children and presented in clear, spatially distinct forms. Lisa Tickner rightly suggests that *Studland Beach* may have evoked, for Bell, memories of St. Ives and her mother Julia (138). Bell's sororial photographic tensions are resolved in her painting's maternal phantasmagoric space. The artist is in full control using confident abstractions and a careful colour palette. *Studland Beach* consciously distils experience while the photographs reproduce unconscious experience.

The use of spatial patterning and objects in Bell and the Woolfs' photographs seem to represent this unconscious experience materially. As the contemporary photographer Wright Morris pinpointed in his equivalent use of a chair motif, they are "saturated with the quality of life that I find both poignant and inexhaustible. I don't want to sit on them; I want to look at them" (Dow Adams 201). Bell and the Woolfs' photographic use of objects such as chairs should be read much more in terms of Adorno's idea that the enigmatic quality of art objects is linked to suffering, rather than Benjamin's view of objects and the bourgeoisie in which "a dwelling place becomes a kind of casing" enabling the bourgeoisie to "remove objects from the profane eyes of non-owners" (Adorno 62; Benjamin, *Baudelaire* 46-47).

At a general level, Bell and the Woolfs' photographs engage in a process that psychologists, active in photo-analysis, describe as a "conversational remembering with photographs" (Edwards and Middleton 9). The photos are not some Orwellian "memory holes" into which the past, like the paper in *1984*, disappears. Photography, even if improvised and provisional, was another way of telling their life stories in which the albums become a fully expressive "heterotopatic" space, a thickly dense "imagined community," and collective and unique snapshots of Bloomsbury.

## Note

All the photographs described above are reproduced in Maggie Humm, *Snapshots of Bloomsbury: the Private Lives of Virginia Woolf and Vanessa Bell* (New Brunswick: Rutgers and London: Tate, 2006).

## Works Cited

Adorno, Theodor. *Aesthetic Theory*. Trans.C. Lenheued. London: Routledge and Kegan Paul, 1984.
Benjamin, Walter. *Charles Baudelaire*. Trans. H. Zohn. London: Verso, 1983.
———. "A Short History of Photography." *Screen* 13.1 (Spring 1972): 5-27.
Bourdieu, Pierre. *Photography a Middle-Brow Art*. Cambridge: Polity, 1990.
Clifford, James. "On Collecting Art and Culture." *Out There: Marginalisation and Contemporary Cultures*. Ed. R. Ferguson, M. Gever, T. T. Minha-ha, and C. West. Cambridge, MA: MIT Press, 1990. 141-69.
Cuddy-Keane, Melba. *Virginia Woolf, the Intellectual, and the Public Sphere*. Cambridge: Cambridge UP, 2003.
Dow Addams, Timothy. *Light Writing and Life Writing: Photography in Autobiography*. Chapel Hill: University of North Carolina Press, 2000.
Edwards, Derek and David Middleton. "Conversational Remembering and Family Relationships." *Journal of Social and Personal Relationships* 5 (1988): 3-25.
Foucault, Michel. "Of Other Spaces." *Diacritics* 16 (1986): 22-27.
Hirsch, Marianne. *Family Frames: Photography, Narrative and Post-Memory*. Cambridge, MA: Harvard UP, 1997.
Humm, Maggie. *Modernist Women and Visual Cultures: Virginia Woolf, Vanessa Bell, Photography and Cinema*. Edinburgh: Edinburgh UP, 2002.
Jencks, Charles. *Heterotopolis: Los Angeles: The Riots and the Strange Beauty of Hetero-Architecture*. New York: John Wiley and Son, 1993.
Lee, Hermione. *Virginia Woolf*. London: Chatto and Windus, 1996.
Lury, Celia. *Prosthetic Culture: Photography, Memory and Identity*. London: Routledge, 1998.
Ovenden, Graham, ed. *A Victorian Album*. London: Secker and Warburg, 1975.
Sontag, Susan. *Regarding the Pain of Others*. Harmondsworth: Penguin, 2003.
Spalding, Frances. *Vanessa Bell*. London: Macmillan, 1983.
Spater, George and Ian Parsons. *A Marriage of True Minds: An Intimate Portrait of Leonard and Virginia Woolf*. New York: Harcourt Brace Jovanovich, 1977.
Spence, Jo and Pat Holland, ed. *Family Snaps: the Meaning of Domestic Photographs*. London: Virago, 1991.
Tagg, John. *The Burden of Representation: Essays on Photographics and Histories*. London: Macmillan, 1988.
Tickner, Lisa. *Modern Life and Modern Subjects: British Art in the Early Twentieth Century*. New Haven: Yale UP, 2000.
Woolf, Leonard. Diaries and related notebooks (1922-1969). The Leonard Woolf Archive, University of Sussex.
Zwerdling, Alex. "Mastering the Memoir: Woolf and the Family Legacy." *Modernism/Modernity* 10, 1 (2003): 165-88.

# "Over the Boundary": Virginia Woolf as Common Seer

## *by Tara Surry*

Virginia Woolf's writing on art explores the relationship between the verbal and visual arts: there are strong parallels between Woolf and Vanessa Bell's experiments with new ways of looking and new forms of expression. Woolf engaged with different models as she looked at and wrote about art, entering into debate with, among others, Vanessa Bell, Clive Bell, and Roger Fry. She argued with, built upon, and combined different elements, fusing together her surveying and questioning methodologies and her fascination with "the astonishing loveliness of the visible world" (*RF* 45). The art criticism sought a "language that wound itself into the heart of the sensation," and both celebrated and interrogated visual experience "in streets, in galleries and also in front of the bookcase" (*RF* 106, 172). Woolf emphasizes the dialogue between painting and other forms of art and the conversation between the work of art and the self, examining her own spectatorship and exploring questions about ways of representing female experience. She moves toward a new, more inclusive form of modernism: based on new understandings of perception and cognition, responding to and articulated by the gallery, the street, and domestic space, and depicting new forms of subjectivity.

Let us pause for a moment, however, to consider thresholds, spaces hovering between the gallery and the street: "On first entering a picture gallery;" "let us dally for a little on the verge" (*CE2* 234, 241); "pausing upon the threshold," "shillyshallying on the threshold" ("Foreword" 97, 98); "on the paving stone at the doorway" (*E3* 163). Woolf's in-between positioning, which Jane Goldman calls her "doorstep model" (153), signifies, I suggest, at least three interconnected things. Firstly, a strategic drawing of attention to a moment of hesitation, stemming in part from a desire to draw attention to a socially produced sense of insecurity about a woman entering a "masculine" realm which positions women as objects of the gaze rather than subjects.[1] Secondly, the threshold as a space of liminality and marginality, and thus of abjection and haunting: "we are outsiders, condemned for ever to haunt the borders and margins of this great art" (*CE2* 236). Woolf presents herself as doubly excluded from the "silent kingdom of paint" as a woman and as a writer (*CE2* 237), and furthermore one who is "trespassing" by writing about art ("Foreword" 99). Thirdly, however, the threshold is a transitional space. Like the repetition of "But" as a rhetorical and spatial shift in *A Room of One's Own,* it signals a conjunction or hinge, of which the "doorway" is a literal manifestation. It marks a space of contemplation and potential transformation, of contiguity and exchange: a "sunny margin where the arts flirt and joke" (*CE2* 234). It also, therefore, offers the possibility of the emergence of new forms.

The "pause for a moment on the threshold" which begins *Roger Fry,* for example (*RF* 11), is a strategic deployment of uncertainty as what de Certeau calls a tactic (37). Woolf takes up an interstitial position: what Deleuze and Guattari describe as the "*intermezzo*" (27), and Teresa de Lauretis the "space-off" (25), from which to challenge the boundaries themselves. These in-between spaces offer a vantage point from which to look in multiple directions, a temporary imagined space between hierarchized binary oppositions in which to examine and critique the position of women as viewers and producers of art. Woolf asserts the right to look and discuss, and challenges the convention of woman in relation to the gallery space as either the, often nude, subject of the painting or, occasionally, a "feminine," inferior painter. Rather than the Victorian aunt painting "flower pieces," who is literally a skeleton in the closet ("Foreword" 97) or Lady Waterford with "her angel's wings, scandalously unfinished" whilst she tries to "shore...up" "her father's house" (*E4* 327), she substitutes the image of Vanessa Bell, who "looked upon nakedness with a brush in her hand" ("Foreword" 98), taking up the masculine (and phallic) instrument as Woolf took up a pen, and using it to disrupt and to re-represent.

Rooms, doors, and the movement through the spaces between them are significant in both sisters' work: for example, Bell's painting *The Open Door*.[2] Both also used mirrors to present different angles, perspectives, and refractions of the world around them. Compare for example Woolf's mirrors in "odd corners" in "The Art of Biography" and "On Not Knowing Greek," and on doors in "The Captain's Death Bed" (*CE4* 226; *CE1* 7; *CE1* 173), to Bell's use of mirrors in the drawing room she created at Penns in the Rocks (Reed 256). Both sisters could be seen as drawing on their mother's suggestion of bringing a looking-glass into the sick room and thus expanding the boundaries of the space (Stephen 231), and as using literal or metaphorical mirrors as a method of multiplying meanings and refusing to impose an authoritative, unitary perspective. Woolf's writing on art emphasizes diversity and mutability and thus the fluidity of identity.

Her approach is in part a challenge to Clive Bell's doctrine of "significant form," in which the work of art is detached, and seen from the point of view of a generalized viewer, assumed to be male (Bell 8, 25): thus denying that the spectator brings specific, situated experiences, and removing art from the world of human interactions. Woolf disputes the possibility of a "complete theory of visual art," held to be universally true (Bell v-vi). Her attitude is closer to that of Fry, who although he also believed that "All art depends upon cutting off the practical responses to sensations of ordinary life" (*Vision* 192), nonetheless adopted a more speculative, heuristic approach which acknowledged its own provisionality. Woolf stressed these qualities in her biography of Fry, which can be seen as a meditation upon her own methodology: viewing as a circumambulatory "voyage of discovery," in which we "reach the particular picture laden with ideas gathered in other places" (*RF* 107), continually looking "from another angle" ("Foreword" 99), and engaging with art as part of an active process of dialogue and inquiry.

Like Fry, who suggested that "in looking at a work of art, we are continually asking *why*" (*Last Lectures* 29), Woolf extends her principle of interrogating public structures into the art gallery,[3] and asks questions of works of art. By refusing to declare to have found an all-encompassing "truth" about art and substituting an aesthetics of uncertainty, Woolf opens up to argument what Griselda Pollock calls the patriarchal myths and "masculinist discourse" of art (56, 11). Consider for example Clive Bell's mountaineering metaphors, in which the observer is a conqueror of "the superb peaks of aesthetic exaltation...the cold, white peaks of art" (*Art* 32-33).[4] Woolf disputes this oracular and omniscient model of the spectator. The "common seer" invoked in *Roger Fry* (105, 106, 227) offers a different, more inclusive image. Rather than pictures as "treasure houses with locked doors in front of which learned people...would lecture" (*CE4* 88), she argues for throwing open the doors and exposing to debate not only the pictures themselves but also the process of viewing and the responses of the viewer.

The Fry that Woolf depicts is a construct, and not an ideal model: there is ambiguity, for example, in the comment that under his tutelage "no one was allowed to remain an outsider for long.... It was then not so easy to stand aside and laugh" ("Impressions" 11). Woolf values her own "outsider," dual perspective on art, but employs and expands upon Fry as a figure for interrogation and debate. Her narrative strategies foreground exploration, digression, and refusal of closure. "Walter Sickert," for example, presents a meditation on colour, perception, and the connections between writing and painting as a form of life-writing, but in a way that stresses its own "mobility and idiosyncrasy" (*CE2* 240). Paradoxically, it builds upon "the sound of the human voice" (240) by structuring the essay as a symposium on the "silent" art. The essay (originally subtitled "A Conversation about Art") opens up a discussion of perception obliquely, by way of the new electric coloured traffic light system—itself a symbol of modernity. The interchanging voices move rapidly to insects: portrayed as heterogeneous creatures existing solely in their response to colour and changing with what they perceive. In "Pictures," writers themselves are depicted as "irresponsible dragonflies" flitting from picture to picture and topic and to topic (*E4*: 246). Insects' multi-faceted eyes could be seen as tropes for Woolf's essayistic practice: from numerous perspectives they synthesize a point of view, which is, however, continually in movement.

Similarly, Fry gazing at a picture is described as both a "snailhorn" and "a humming-bird hawkmoth hanging over a flower, quivering yet still" (*RF* 121, 152). Woolf uses tropes of combination that collide even with each other, presenting the arts fused together synaesthetically: "Character is colour, and colour is china, and china is music" ("Foreword" [1934]). The transmutation into insects is significant in terms of hybridity and the dissolution of boundaries: "the mixing and marrying of words," as a painter mixes paint, the conjugal union of disparate elements (*CE2* 241). Sickert is a hybrid of different nationalities, and even his name is unstable (*CE2* 244); women also occupy an interstitial cultural space, as "queer, composite being[s]" (*AROO* 40). Woolf valorizes the collapse of categories: "trespassing," "pilferings" ("Foreword" 99; *E4* 246). She associates herself with Sickert and Fry's "raids across the boundaries" and "raids into the lands of others" (*RF* 239-40, *CE2* 243), as a metaphor for her own narrative manoeuvres and transgressing of generic lines of demarcation.

In Woolf's version of the gallery showing her sister's work, "A meaning is given to familiar things that makes them strange.... People's minds have split out of their bodies and become part of their surroundings." Through moving "over the boundary," disrupting categories, and defamiliarizing familiar sites/sights (a technique the Russian formalists called *ostranenie*), she suggests new ways of viewing them ("Foreword" [1934]). The "common seer" is deliberately analogous to the "common reader." In her writing on London, the reader is told to look again at the city: similarly, she encourages new ways of looking at pictures, of using our eyes not as passive "spheres of jelly" ("A Review" 382) but as an active means of thinking and reflecting on what we see, and thus perhaps of envisaging alternative ways of seeing and acting.

Woolf's writings on art are richly complex and ambiguous, exploiting the silence of the topic: "words begin to raise their feeble limbs in the pale border land of no man's language, to sink down again in despair. We fling them like nets upon a rocky and inhospitable shore; they fade and disappear" (*E4* 245). Like Bell's portraits which occlude the facial details of the sitters, which Frances Spalding has argued are thus opened up to dialogue with the spectator, they continually enact a movement between silence and language.[5] They explore the interconnections between the visual and the verbal, and insist on a sense of communication: "painting and writing have much to tell each other: they have much in common. The novelist after all wants to make us see" (*CE2* 241). The essays focus above all on the transformative power of "the eye" (*E4* 244). Yet they also flaunt their verbal facility by submerging the reader in overwhelmingly rich language:

> Under the solemn stare we fade and dwindle and dissolve.... We rise, purged and purified...canvases taciturn and congealed like emerald and aquamarine....
> Let us wash the roofs of our eyes in colour; let us dive till the deep seas close above our heads. (*E3* 164)

This sensual language of rapture signals not only an imaginary abandonment of the self to fluidity through an eroticized aesthetic response to colour, but also bears witness to creative elements beyond language. It is also, I suggest, evocative of Walter Pater: the "once famous" description of the Mona Lisa as a "diver in deep seas" (*E4* 218; Pater 80) seems echoed in "dive till the deep seas," while the description of Vanessa Bell as "silent as the grave" in the 1930 "Foreword" is reminiscent of Pater's "learned the secrets of the grave" (80). Perry Meisel has argued for Pater as a repressed influence on Woolf, but she could also be seen as strategically turning these outmoded "ornaments" of language (*E4* 218) to her own purposes. She inserts her sister into the frame, additionally and ambivalently, as the painter rather than the idealized, enigmatic subject of the painting. Her vocabulary in relation to colour and painting often highlights shades of blue and green, and "blue madonnas."[6] The overall effect blurs boundaries again and sets up a series of visual and verbal resonances, creating an echo chamber in the gallery. It also suggests the necessity of a complex set of interchanges—between different arts and artists, the work of art and its social context, the observer and the picture, and finally the gallery and the street: "Modern art needs the sound of traffic outside to authenticate it" (O'Doherty 44). Various forms of art criticism combine in new ways: "from the collision of many converging ideas a theory forms" (*RF* 227-28).

Woolf apparently praises the silence in Bell's paintings, yet nevertheless wants to maintain, as Jane Goldman points out, a feminist voice (163). The essays engage with silence, but are negotiating the terrain between silence as a form of speech and the fear of a permanent exile from language (this is also in part a question of political engagement[7]). Woolf is interested in the sublime, but also in material and historical realities. The essays move back and forth between the street and the gallery, and recognize that both are complex spaces in which voices of power and of dissent circulate. In "The Royal Academy" for example, the gallery is pervaded by "intolerable vociferations" crying aloud their "patriotism...position, patronage, power" (*E3* 93), but the gallery in the 1934 "Foreword" ushers in "the birth of other sensibilities."

Woolf is concerned with webs and connections, and with the power of interconnections between and within the arts. Writers "pilfer" from painting, she argued (*E4* 246) and for the sisters, this was an ongoing and reciprocal theft (as Jane Dunn and Diane Gillespie among others have discussed). They sometimes collaborated directly, but their letters also show both thinking through analogies between their work.[8] Metaphorical and literal conversations intermesh and reverberate: for example Bell's *The Conversation*, which her sister wanted to experiment with writing "in prose" (*L3* 498). Woolf commented on Fry's ambition to publish a cheap, easily accessible broadsheet with art on one side of the page and literature on the other (*RF* 172), and experimented with a book in which fact and art appeared on facing pages: literally bringing the two into contact with each other.[9] Woolf and Bell also discussed a collaborative work to be called "Faces and Voices" (*D5* 57-58) which would have further embodied what Maggie Humm calls in the context of Bell's photographs "a different picture of modernism...as a feminine, multi-generic space" (290). Woolf is formulating a Post-Impressionist, feminist modernism, in part by applying Post-Impressionist techniques to her writing: "Cézanne and Picasso had shown the way; writers should fling representation to the winds and follow suit" (*RF* 172). In her gallery, "Not a word sounds and yet the room is full of conversations" ("Foreword" [1934]). Rather than the rarefied aesthetic realm of "significant form," the gallery space is a "room full of intimate relationships" ("Foreword" [1934]); the focus is shifted from the dominating male gaze to that of a network of relationships. A conversation continues beyond the frame of the essay and beyond the canvas: "talk is a common habit" (*CE2* 233), and Woolf is staking a claim to the gallery as an expanded cultural space of polylogic voices, a "common ground" (*CE2* 181).

Vanessa Bell's "Lecture Given at Leighton Park School" also demonstrates these shared concerns. Her approach is conversational, and pictures her audience speaking back; it rejects "any show of authority," and claims different values (160, 149). She weaves "Mr Bennett and Mrs Brown" into her speech but refuses to dictate its meaning to her listeners (151-56), and her lecture moves through very Woolfian metaphors, such as a "walk through Reading some winter evening" (159) (Woolf of course often takes such a "walk through reading" and through the city). Bell's paintings move between interior and exterior space, incorporate everyday life, and engage with female experience: "that women are naked, and bring nakedness to birth" ("Foreword" 97).

Both Woolf and Bell are seeking connections, and are experimenting with different ways to represent quotidian experience and "the thing itself" (*MOB* 81) through their own particular forms of Post-Impressionism. Christopher Reed has suggested that Bloomsbury's decorative art was a manifesto for a new, alternative form of living which valued a different kind of modernity and domesticity. It could be argued that even Clive Bell's dogmatic assertions about art allow a challenge to his assumptions. In "Art and War," for example, he contends that "the state of mind which art provokes...is one in which nationality has ceased to exist" and "patriotism has become meaningless" (*Potboilers* 239, 240), thus leaving a potential space for re-imagining boundaries as points of contiguity rather than as impermeable divisions, and creating an area in which the artist and the viewer can engage in conversation. Fry, meanwhile, actively invited debate, and thoroughly explored opposing arguments: it was crucial to him to "have another pair of eyes to see with, another brain to argue with" (*RF* 121). For Woolf, viewing art, like reading, is a dialogic process. This process of exploration and discovery, coupled with a willingness to be wrong and to start again, is an integral part of Bloomsbury's spirit of experimentation and reform, and its valuing of both the enduring work of art and the "easily combustible" (*TG* 155).

In gazing at a picture, Woolf, as her sister recognized, was interested primarily not in "the looks but only the impression the looks made upon you" (*Selected Letters* 87). She was concerned with the viewer rather than, or as well as, the painting; and this places her in an argument with "significant form" as formulated by Clive Bell.[10] Woolf does not reject significant form, but rather than declaring that "Only one answer seems possible" (*Art* 8), she emphasizes instead multiplicity and the process of observation and interrogation, the importance of what Fry called "putting…many question marks into the text of our subject" (*Last Lectures* 48). Typically, her essays deny closure, pivot and turn on themselves. The 1930 introduction to her sister's exhibition, for example, begins by voicing (and parodying) moral concerns about women moving out of their roles as "mother, wife or mistress" (97) by taking up painting in their own right, and ends by infinitely deferring any possibility of a conclusion: "That was the very question I was asking myself as I came in" ("Foreword" 100).

## Notes

1. Compare Lily Briscoe's ambivalence as she begins to paint: "a curious physical sensation, as if she were urged forward and at the same time must hold herself back": *To the Lighthouse* (London: Penguin, 1964 ), p. 179.
2. "The Open Door" was also a title Woolf considered for *Three Guineas* (*D4* 6n).
3. See for example *Three Guineas*, p. 187.
4. In contrast, in her own mountaineering metaphors in "The Value of Laughter," rather than positioning herself on the "heights" Woolf claims the "highways": the space of everyday experience and of laughter, which observes, mocks, and refashions the world around it—including Bell's insistence on positioning himself on the "pinnacle whence the whole of life can be viewed as in a panorama" (*E1* 59) rather than in what Bell dismisses as "the snug foothills of warm humanity" (*Art* 32).
5. Spalding, *The Bloomsbury Group* (London: National Portrait Gallery, 2006), pp. 15-16; "Vanessa Bell's Portrait of Virginia Woolf at Smith College," *Woolf in the Real World: Selected Papers from the Thirteenth Annual Conference on Virginia Woolf* (Clemson: Clemson University Digital Press, 2005), pp. 130-31.
6. See *The Complete Shorter Fiction of Virginia Woolf*, ed. Susan Dick (San Diego: Harvest-HBJ, 1989), p. 142; *The Waves* (London: Penguin, 1992), p.118.
7. As Woolf complains in a letter about Vanessa and Duncan Grant in the 1930s: "There they sit looking at pinks and yellows, and when Europe blazes all they do is screw up their eyes and complain of a temporary glare in the foreground." *Modern Fiction Studies*, 30, 2 (Summer 1984): 189-90, cited by Dunn, p. 151.
8. See for example Vanessa Bell, *Selected Letters*, 367-68.
9. As Andrew McNeillie has noted: *The Common Reader: Second Series* (San Diego, New York, London: Harvest-Harcourt Brace, 1986), p. 4.
10. Vanessa Bell herself held firmly to significant form, feeling that colour and relationships, rather than content, were central to her work: see *Selected Letters* 133-34.

## Works Cited

Bell, Clive. *Art*. 1914. London: Chatto and Windus, 1949.

———. *Potboilers*. London: Chatto and Windus, 1918.

Bell, Vanessa. "Lecture Given at Leighton Park School."1925. *Sketches in Pen and Ink*. Ed. Lia Giachero. London: Pimlico, 1998. 149-65.

———. *Selected Letters*. Ed. Regina Marler. London: Bloomsbury, 1994.

de Certeau, Michel. *The Practice of Everyday Life*. Berkeley: University of California Press, 1984.

de Lauretis, Teresa. *Technologies of Gender: Essays on Theory, Film and Fiction*. Bloomington: Indiana UP, 1987.

Deleuze, Gilles, and Felix Guattari. *A Thousand Plateaus: Capitalism and Schizophrenia*. 1987. London: Con-

tinuum, 2004.
Dunn, Jane. *A Very Close Conspiracy: Vanessa Bell and Virginia Woolf.* Boston: Little, Brown, 1990.
Fry, Roger. *Vision and Design.* 1920. London: Pelican, 1961.
———. *Last Lectures.* 1939. Boston: Beacon, 1962.
Gillespie, Diane. *The Sisters' Arts: The Writing and Painting of Virginia Woolf and Vanessa Bell.* Syracuse: Syracuse UP, 1988.
Goldman, Jane. *The Feminist Aesthetics of Virginia Woolf: Modernism, Post-Impressionism and the Politics of the Visual.* Cambridge: Cambridge UP, 1998.
Humm, Maggie. *Modernist Women and Visual Cultures: Virginia Woolf, Vanessa Bell, Photography and Cinema.* New Brunswick: Rutgers UP, 2003.
Meisel, Perry. *The Absent Father: Virginia Woolf and Walter Pater.* New Haven: Yale UP, 1980.
O'Doherty, Brian. *Inside the White Cube: The Ideology of the Gallery Space.* Berkeley: University of California Press, 1999.
Pater, Walter. *The Renaissance.* 1873. Oxford: Oxford UP, 1986.
Pollock, Griselda. *Vision and Difference.* London: Routledge, 1988.
Reed, Christopher. *Bloomsbury Rooms: Modernism, Subculture and Domesticity.* New Haven: Yale UP, 2004.
Stephen, Julia. *Notes from Sick Rooms.* 1883. *Julia Duckworth Stephen: Stories for Children, Essays for Adults.* Ed. Diane F. Gillespie and Elizabeth Steele. Syracuse: Syracuse UP, 1987.
Woolf, Virginia. *Collected Essays.* Ed. Leonard Woolf. 4 vols. London: Hogarth, 1966-1967.
———. *The Diary of Virginia Woolf.* Ed. Anne Olivier Bell with Andrew McNeillie. 5 vols. London: Hogarth, 1977-1984.
———. *The Essays of Virginia Woolf.* Ed. Andrew McNeillie. 4 vols. London: Hogarth, 1986-1994.
———. "Foreword." *Catalogue of Recent Paintings by Vanessa Bell.* London: Lefevre Galleries, 1934. N. pag.
———. "Foreword to *Recent Paintings by Vanessa Bell.*" 1930. *The Crowded Dance of Modern Life.* Ed. Rachel Bowlby. London: Penguin, 1993. 97-100.
———. *The Letters of Virginia Woolf.* Ed. Nigel Nicolson and Joanne Trautmann. 6 vols. New York: Harcourt Brace Jovanovich, 1975-1980.
———. *Moments of Being.* Ed. Jeanne Schulkind. 2nd ed. London: Grafton, 1989.
———. "A Review by Virginia Woolf of Roger Fry's *Vision and Design.*" 1921. *Roger Fry.* Ed. Diane F. Gillespie. Oxford: Shakespeare Head, 1995. 381-83.
———. *Roger Fry.* 1940. New York: Harcourt Brace Jovanovich, 1976.
———. "Roger Fry: A Series of Impressions." Ed. Diane Gillespie. London: Cecil Woolf, 1994.
———. *A Room of One's Own* and *Three Guineas.* 1928; 1938. Ed. Michèle Barrett. London: Penguin, 1993.
———. *The Years.* 1937. Ed. Hermione Lee. Oxford: Oxford UP, 1992.

# "THE EVENING UNDER LAMPLIGHT...WITH THE PHOTOGRAPH ALBUM": *TO THE LIGHTHOUSE* AS FAMILY SCRAPBOOK

## by Elisa Kay Sparks

Ever since Diane Gillespie's germinal essay "'Her Kodak Pointed at His Head': Virginia Woolf and Photography" (1993), scholarship on, theorizing about, and availability of photographs from the Stephen family archives have continued to increase in quantity and quality.[1] Maggie Humm's recent books, *Modernist Women and Visual Cultures* and *Snapshots of Bloomsbury*, Vanessa Curtis's detailed documentation of *The Hidden Houses of Virginia Woolf and Vanessa Bell*, Marion Bell and Marion Whybrow's account of Virginia and Vanessa's memories of St. Ives, as well as Karen Kukil's helpful curatorship of Leslie Stephen's photo album, now posted on the Smith College Library's web site, represent the latest and best of this tradition. As Humm and Kukil and a number of other scholars have noted, *To the Lighthouse* draws heavily on the collection of family photographs Woolf reviewed during its composition, including not only those selected by her father while he was writing *The Mausoleum Book*, but also those of her great aunt, Julia Margaret Cameron, which she was then sorting for her Introduction to *Victorian Photographs of Famous Men & Fair Women* (published by the Hogarth Press in1926). Recent scholarship has also explored the role public photographs play in the novel; see for example the work of Alexandra Neel and Leslie Hankins on the photography and films of Antarctic expeditions.

In creating an altered book on *To the Lighthouse*, I recently had cause to re-think the role that photography plays in the novel in a seldom used visual register. As I

*Figure 1: Altered book* **Anyone Can Draw** *by Elisa Kay Sparks, pp. 1-2.*

searched for images to incorporate into my own composition, I began to see the work from a wholly fresh perspective. For one thing, the beginning of the novel made a new kind of sense: I realized that James Ramsay, "cutting out pictures from the illustrated catalogue of the Army and Navy Stores" (*TTL* 3), was probably collecting pictures to glue into a scrapbook, and his actions—endowing certain images "with heavenly bliss," "fring[ing] them with joy" (*TTL* 3)—are a "private code," a "secret language" (*TTL* 4) for what Woolf is doing in the novel: creating a family scrap/photo album (see Figure1).

Let me contextualize this discussion with a brief history of scrapbooking. The *OED* lists the earliest print appearance of the word "scrap-book" as 1825: "Scrap Book, or a selection of …anecdotes," implicitly placing the origin of scrapbooks in the seventeenth-century popularity of commonplace books in which "passages important for reference were collected, usually under general headings" (*OED*). While commonplace books generally gathered bits of text, the eighteenth century saw the appearance of "extra illustrated" books, such as William Granger's 1769 history of England which was published with added pages of illustrations, including blank pages where readers could paste in their own pictures (Slatten). In his recent history of commonplace books, Earle Havens notes that by the beginning of Victoria's reign the habit of collecting printed matter such as "pasted-down scraps from newspapers and literary magazines, as well as carefully cut out and hand-coloured images" (90) had become widespread, fostered by the sale of "large blank folio albums…with thick, stiff pages to hold print, sketches, photographs, and so forth" (90-93). And in their *History of Printed Scraps*, Allistair Allen and Joan Hoverstadt date the first appearance of color scraps—"small paper images lithographically printed and often embossed"—and the albums displaying them to the invention of chromolithography in 1837 (8-9).

By the middle of the nineteenth century, a wide range of uses for albums had emerged. Friendship albums, kept mainly by women, contained autographs, favorite poems, quotations, calling cards, drawings, and even hair weavings. Other albums of collectibles included advertising trade cards and *carte-de-visite* photographs (postcards). The John W. Hartman Center for the Study of Marketing and Advertising History at Duke University contends that "Creating scrapbooks became a popular pastime, especially for women and children," noting that "Scrapbooks were used as a way of teaching children to organize and classify information and to develop an artistic sense." Allen and Hoverstadt similarly chronicle the many uses of scraps in entertaining and educating Victorian children such as using the scraps to play various card games, to tell nursery rhymes and fables, and to teach children their alphabet (12). However, scrapbooking was not entirely coded female. Thomas Jefferson for instance, kept newspaper clippings in blank albums. And Mark Twain was such an enthusiast of scrapbooking that in 1872 he patented the designs for and made a good deal of money from a series of scrapbooks sold by Brentano's and Montgomery Ward's (Slatten).[2] Of course the evolution of scrapbooks into photo albums really began in 1888 when the Kodak camera and rolled film were first marketed (Hartman Center; also mentioned by Humm, *Snapshots* 4).

Virginia Stephen's acquaintance with every aspect of the emerging world of Victorian and modernist photography is well known. That acquaintance included the realm of scrapbooks as well. Allen and Hoverstadt call the years 1880-1900—a period bracketing Virginia's childhood—the "Golden Era of the printed relief" (25). Gill Lowe points out how important *Tit-Bits* (which grew out of editor George Newnes's interest in scraps) was as a model for *The Hyde Park Gate News* (xxi).³ Humm's *Snapshots of Bloomsbury* shows us that the first pages of Woolf's own photo album displayed the traditional Victorian collection of *cartes-de-visite* in a format Humm elsewhere describes as having an "almost childlike scrapbook appearance" (*Snapshots*, pl. 1 and 2, pp. 40-41; *Modernist Women* 57). And through Merry Pawlowski and Vara Neverow's eminently useful website, we also have access to the scrapbooks of newspaper clippings (both pictures and text) Woolf herself kept for the writing of *Three Guineas*. Some of Woolf's family members and friends also kept scrapbooks, including her great aunt's sister, Mia Cameron, and her sister's longtime companion, Duncan Grant.⁴ As Susan Stanford Freedman documents in her book on H. D., other modernists also adapted scrapbooking into collage as a means of visual expression (see collages and notes, 430-31). It does not, therefore, seem a great leap to look at *To the Lighthouse* as one of Woolf's experiments in transforming visual methodologies to writing, another form of what Humm calls the "technologies of memory" (*Snapshots* 11). As Allen and Hoverstadt note, "early scrapbooks often seem an extension of the vogue for recording personal memories and thoughts which was popular at the time. A great deal of personal writing was included" (16). In this view, *To the Lighthouse* becomes a copious family album, filled with photographs, personal writing, quotations from favorite poems, and bright colored scraps commemorating famous people and events—all decorating the domestic life of a Victorian childhood.⁵

Woolf's attitude towards scraps and scrapbooks like her attitude towards photography was ironic and ambivalent, veering between seeing them as over-literal and falsely objective and using them subtly to evoke the unconscious shimmer of cathected memory. Woolf was quite capable of using photographs literally and autobiographically. As Humm points out, often "there are close parallels between details in the [family] photographs and descriptive details in Woolf's autobiographies" such that "Woolf seems to be describing not an actual memory but...a photograph in front of her" (*Snapshots* ix). This literalness is what Woolf refers to in the two occasions I have found so far where she mentions scrapbooks. In note 29 to chapter 1 of *Three Guineas*, for instance, she quotes Dr. Alington, former Head Master of Eton, when he refers to his own scrapbook as documenting a particular sum of money given to support scholarships for boys (183); this refers to a scrapbook simply as a collection of notes or facts. Her essay on "Miss Mitford," published in *The Common Reader* in 1925, demonstrates a more complicated view. Here she describes "certain books which can be read without the mind and without the heart, but still with considerable enjoyment" as "scrapbooks rather than biographies" (*CR1* 183). Interestingly, the very limitations of such literal scrapbooks prove to be a paradoxical benefit, for as Woolf points out, such lack of synthesis and analysis "license[s] mendacity. One cannot believe what Miss Hill [the author of the scrapbook biography] says about Miss Mitford, and thus one is free to invent Miss Mitford for oneself" (*CR1* 183).

In *To the Lighthouse*, Woolf invents her own non-literal scrapbook, a collection of private photographs and public illustrations, autobiographical musings, favorite bits of poetry, comments on contemporary philosophical arguments and political events, to be read with not only the heart and mind, but also the eyes. The most obvious series of private photographs collaged into *To the Lighthouse* are, of course, the many pictures of Julia Stephen. A central image of Section 1, "The Window"—the part of the novel I concentrate on in this paper—is the triangular purple shadow Mrs. Ramsay casts while sitting on the steps of the drawing room window at Talland House in St. Ives. Karen Kukil has identified one particular photograph of Julia sitting on these steps with Virginia and Adrian in the background as foundational to the triangle motif in the book (Kukil pl. 37d), along with one of Julia holding Vanessa, which imitates the monumental triangularity of Renaissance Madonnas (pl. 36j). But the tradition of shooting Julia in triangular formats seems to have quite a long history: from an image of Julia as a child wrapped in a cloak rendered by her Aunt, Julia Margaret Cameron (pl. 31a), to the portrait of Julia with her first husband, Herbert Duckworth, also included in Leslie Stephen's album (pl. 33a), to what Kukil designates as Vanessa's favorite photograph of her mother, the image of Julia looking out a triangularly-draped window, haloed by an aura of radiant light (pl. 39c). Clearly, Woolf, like her artist heroine Lily Briscoe, is here synthesizing a whole series of detailed and literal observations into the abstraction of significant form.[6]

We can also find a number of other less abstracted images of Julia in the book. One of the most striking is Mr. Tansley's mythification of Mrs. Ramsay as a kind of earth goddess, standing in front of a picture of Queen Victoria. The lyrical vision of her "With stars in her eyes and veils in her hair, with cyclamen and wild violets" (*TTL* 14) corresponds almost exactly to one of Cameron's photographs of Julia Duckworth, included by Leslie Stephen in *The Mausoleum Book* (facing p. 58). Her pose in Cameron's picture also echoes a common image of Queen Victoria "wearing the blue ribbon of the garter" (*TTL* 14), seen here in a souvenir postcard which I incorporated into my altered book (see Figure 2), and also available as a scrap (Allen and Hoverstadt pl. 91 [111]).

*Figure 2: Altered book* **Anyone Can Draw** *by Elisa Kay Sparks, pp. 5-6.*

Similarly literal though more diffuse and elaborated is the reference to another photograph from *The Mausoleum Book*, the famous one of the young Virginia observing Leslie and Julia reading at Talland House which Leslie Stephen specifically cites as one that makes him "see as with my bodily eyes" Julia's "holy and tender love" (Stephen 58-59).

Humm's research comparing various family albums marks this as a key image in family history, for all three sisters—Stella, Vanessa, and Virginia—also had copies of it in their albums (Humm *Snapshots* 7, pl. 10 [46]; Kukil pl. 38h). The photo seems to provide the setting for the last chapter of Section 1, where Mr. and Mrs. Ramsay read together in the drawing room after the children have gone to bed. Visible in the background of the photo is the wallpaper with a rose motif that is mentioned as fading from the walls of the drawing room early in the novel (*TTL* 27), but nonetheless seems to inspire the references to poems about roses which embody the culmination of the couple's conjugal joy: the "China rose...all abloom" conjuring up "all the lives we ever lived" from Charles Elton's "Luriana Lurilee," and the "deep vermilion in the rose" from Shakespeare's sonnet 98 (*TTL* 98). Close inspection of the photograph reveals that cut-out trellises from the wallpaper had been decoratively glued into the door panels, which seem to metonymically inspire Mrs. Ramsay's mental ascension: "She was climbing up those branches, this way and that, laying hands on one flower and then another" (*TTL* 121).[7] (Figure 3).

*Figure 3: Detail from photo 38h in Leslie Stephen's Photograph Album, courtesy of Mortimer Rare Bookroom, Smith College.*

Photographs associated with Leslie Stephen and Mr. Ramsay do not seem either as literally memorial or as allusively synthetic as those associated with Julia and Mrs. Ramsay, and instead partake of more of the irony commonly seen in Woolf's treatment of public photography associated with patriarchy, such as that included in *Three Guineas*. Frequently associated with "fidelity to facts," Mr. Ramsay, as Alexandra Neel recognizes, "epitomizes a positivist photography associated with biography and the travel genre" (203), and so photographs evoked in his appearances in the novel come as much from the popular press as family albums. Mr. Ramsay's perambulations on the terrace, in particular, bring up a series of references to heroic (and often catastrophic) imperial or colonial expedi-

*Figure 4: A. F. Mummery climbing on the Grépon, 1893. Photo by Miss Lily Barstow. Courtesy of The Alpine Club Photo Library, London.*

tions, starting with the charge of the Light Brigade, "Some one had blundered" (*TTL* 30), moving to an imagined shipwreck, "exposed on a broiling sea" and a "desolate expedition across the icy solitudes of the Polar region" (34), ending up with the leader of a climbing expedition, "who, now that the snow has begun to fall and the mountain top is covered in mist, knows he must lay himself down and die before morning comes" (35).[8] Of all these heroic roles, it is only the last, mountain climber, that Leslie Stephen, the model for Mr. Ramsay, actually enacted (see photo of Leslie

Stephen and his alpine guide in Kukil pl. 35b).

And here I cannot resist inserting a brief but fascinating digression. While researching information and photographs of Leslie Stephen's climbing career, Helen Southworth and I came across a very interesting character, a woman mountaineer named Lily Bristow, who climbed the Alps with A. F. Mummery, snapping a picture of him scaling the Grépon, in 1893, only four years after Leslie and Julia's last visit to the Alps (see *Alpine Club Photo Album*, 13th image) (Figure 4).[9] There is more research to be done on this, but isn't it fun to imagine that the young Virginia Stephen might have learned of this Victorian lady's accomplishments (Virginia would have been eleven in 1893) and later named her artist heroine Lily Briscoe after her? Lily Bristow certainly knew of Leslie Stephen; she entitled her epistolary account of climbing with A. F. Mummery in 1893 "An Easy Day for a Lady"; according to Rebecca Brown, a reference to Stephen's alleged comment that mountains to be climbed pass through three stages: "An inaccessible peak—The most difficult ascent in the Alps—An easy day for a lady" (Brown 113). What a delicious irony to think that Woolf intended the secret comparison of Mr. Ramsay, who cannot get to R, to Lily Bristow, a woman who reached the highest peaks of the Alps (see Alpine Club Photo Album, photograph 5: "Ladies & Guides on the Mer de

*Figure 5: Ladies & Guides on the Mer de Glace, c. 1886. Photo by F & G Charnaux. Courtesy of The Alpine Club Photo Library, London.*

Glace c. 1886"). Women can climb! (Figure 5).

I know I have only begun the long process of identifying possible familial and public sources for the "scraps and fragments" of memory with which Virginia Woolf collaged her vision of life at Talland House (*TTL* 90),[10] but I want to end with another example of visual technology: a print I made while doing the research for this paper. I've named it "Talland House Ghosts," and I mean it to embody the layered richness, the emerging palimpsest of the unconscious, which our growing knowledge of photography can give to our vision of Virginia Woolf's life and work (Figure 6, below).

*Figure 6: Talland House Ghosts, digital print by Elisa Kay Sparks*

## Notes

1. Other important essays on Woolf and photography which I found particularly helpful include those by Helen Wussow, Vara Neverow, and Alex Zwerdling.
2. Jefferson's commonplace books can be perused on-line at the Library of Congress web site. The importance of Twain's contribution to scrap-booking is shown in the *OED* entry on the word which contains several exemplary citations from Twain's letters and autobiographical writings.
3. I learned of Newnes's interest in scraps from Gill Lowe at the Birmingham conference.
4. After I delivered this paper in Birmingham, several fellow researchers were kind enough to inform me about these other scrapbooks. In addition to Gill Lowe, mentioned above, Marion Dell knew about the Cameron scrapbook, and Chris Reed told me that Grant's scrapbooks are housed in the Tate Gallery Archives.
5. Allen and Hoverstadt note that many different kinds of cut-out paper material were commonly pasted into scrapbooks, including clippings about topical events from the *Illustrated London News* and *Punch* (20). Several pages of scraps illustrating children's stories (96-99) suggest a possible scrap connection for the tale of "The Fisherman's Wife." They also comment on the great popularity of scrap prints of fruit clusters (25). See plates 82-85 (pp.102-6) for examples of fruit scraps, many of which feature luscious arrangements of grapes and pears similar to that on the Ramsays' dinner table. Plate 15 features beautifully lustrous sea shells (47).
6. In her article on the uses of photography in *To the Lighthouse*, Alexandra Neel identifies Mrs. Ramsay with a kind of constructivist photography, an ability to combine images into collages (209).
7. As this review of pictures of Julia Stephen suggests, photographs also provided a vivid reminder and specific mapping of the spaces in Talland House itself. Photographs are available which document many aspects of the Stephens' summer home: the tall double glass doors opening out from the sitting room, the pots full of geraniums on the terrace (Kukil pl. 37c), the escalonia hedge (pl. 37f), the view from terrace (Dell and Whybrow, 31, 38), the cricket ground (Humm, *Snapshots*, pl. 6 [44]).
8. Scraps were also available to commemorate various heroic and military expeditions. Allen and Hoverstadt include a "Gigantic Relief" of the Transvaal Campaign designed to be stood up as a diorama, complete with cut-out bullets and shells (pl. 51 [73]) as well as a set of Jubilee scraps commemorating notable events in

Victoria's reign, including the Queen bidding farewell to the troops going out to the Crimea (pl. 93; p. 11).
9. For more information on Lily Bristow, see Brown (111-15). The climb of the Grépon, a granite needle near Chamonix, was quite strenuous and dangerous; the expedition went without a guide, and Bristow took significant risks in making her photographs, sometimes unhooking from the safety line to get a better angle (112). One assumes such a trek could not be made without much previous experience, so it is not a stretch to think Lily Bristow was already climbing when Julia and Leslie Stephen were visiting Switzerland in 1889.
10. This phrase becomes a leitmotiv in *Between the Acts*, appearing no less than eight times in that novel.

## Works Cited

Allen, Alistari and Joan Hoverstadt. *The History of Printed Scraps*. London: New Cavendish Books, 1983.
*Alpine Club Photo Album*. <http://www.alpine-club.org.uk/photolibrary/album.html>. Accessed 3 June 2006.
Bristow, Lily. "An Easy Day for a Lady." *Alpine Journal* 53 (1941-42): 370-74.
Brown, Rebecca. *Women on High: Pioneers of Mountaineering*. Boston, MA: Appalachian Mountain Club Books, 2002.
Curtis, Vanessa. *The Hidden Houses of Virginia Woolf and Vanessa Bell*. London: Robert Hale, 2005
Dell, Marion and Marion Whybrow. *Virginia Woolf and Vanessa Bell: Remembering St. Ives*. Padstow, Cornwall: Tabb House, 2004.
Friedman, Susan Stanford. *Penelope's Web: Gender, Modernity, and H. D.'s Fiction*. Cambridge: Cambridge UP, 1990.
Gillespie, Diane F. "'Her Kodak Pointed at His Head': Virginia Woolf and Photography." *The Multiple Muses of Virginia Woolf*. Ed. Diane F. Gillespie. Columbia: University of Missouri Press, 1993. 113-47.
John W. Hartman Center for Sales, Advertising & Marketing History. "Emergence of Advertising in America." <http://scriptorium.lib.Duke.edu/eaa/scrapbooks.html>. Accessed 28 May 2006.
Humm, Maggie. *Modernist Women and Visual Cultures: Virginia Woolf, Vanessa Bell, Photography, and Cinema*. New Brunswick, NJ: Rutgers UP, 2003.
———. *Snapshots of Bloomsbury: The Private Lives of Virginia Woolf and Vanessa Bell*. New Brunswick, NJ: Rutgers UP, 2005.
Kukil, Karen, curator. "Leslie Stephen's Photograph Album." *Smith College Libraries*. <http://www.smith.edu/libraries/libs/rarebook/exhibitions/Stephen>. Accessed 16 June 2006.
Hankins, Leslie. "Doomed Expeditions in Film & Fiction: Early Antarctic Films in Woolf's *To the Lighthouse*." Paper delivered at the 15th Annual Conference on Virginia Woolf. Lewis and Clark University, 9-12 June 2005.
Havens, Earle. *Commonplace Books: A History of Manuscripts and Printed Books from Antiquity to the Twentieth Century*. The Beinecke Rare Books and Manuscript Library, Yale University. University Press of New England, 2001.
Lowe, Gill, ed. *Hyde Park Gate News: The Stephen Family Newspaper*. London: Hesperus, 2005.
Neel, Alexandra. "The Photography of Antarctica: Virginia Woolf's Letters of Discovery. *Virginia Woolf and the Art of Exploration: Selected Papers from the Fifteenth Annual Conference on Virginia Woolf*. Ed. Helen Southworth and Elisa Kay Sparks. Clemson University Digital Press, 2006. 203-11.
Neverow, Vara. "Thinking Back through Our Mothers, Thinking in Common: Virginia Woolf's Photographic Imagination and the Community of Narrators in *Jacob's Room, A Room of One's Own*, and *Three Guineas*." *Virginia Woolf and Communities: Selected Papers from the Eighth Annual Conference on Virginia Woolf*. Ed. Jeanette McVicker and Laura Davis. New York: Pace UP, 1999. 65-87.
Pawlowski, Merry M. and Vara Neverow, ed. "The Reading Notes for Three Guineas." *The Center for Virginia Woolf Studies*. <http://www.csub.edu/woolf_center/>. Accessed 12 May 2006.
Slatten, Lee Andra. "A Brief History of Scrapbooking." 7 December 2004. <http://www.pagesoftheheart.net/artman/publish/article_727.shtml>. Accessed 15 May 2006.
Stephen, Leslie. *Sir Leslie Stephen's Mausoleum Book*. Introd. Alan Bell. Oxford: Clarendon, 1977.
Woolf, Virginia. *The Common Reader: First Series*. New York: Harcourt, 1984.
———. *Three Guineas*. Annotated and introd. Jane Marcus. New York: Harcourt, 2006.
———. *To the Lighthouse*. New York: Harcourt, 1981.
Wussow, Helen. "Virginia Woolf and the Problematic Nature of the Photographic Image." *Twentieth Century Literature* 40.1 (Spring 1994): 1-14.
Zwerdling, Alex. "Mastering the Memoir: Woolf and the Family Legacy." *Modernism/Modernity* 10.1 (2003): 165-88.

# *Afterword*

## Inside and Outside the Covers: Beginnings, Endings, and Woolf's Non-Coercive Ethical Texts

### by Melba Cuddy-Keane

Coming at the end of this volume, my contribution—to use the title of Sybil Oldfield's recent book—assumes something of the role of Afterwords: words, as in those words praising Woolf after her death, standing as a tribute to the many fine words that have come before. My words, however, are certainly not offered as condolence, but as a way of both drawing these proceedings to a close and looking ahead to new beginnings. In this final paper, it seems fitting to dwell on the some of Woolf's most familiar words, the words with which she begins her works, and the words with which she ends. My interest in this subject "began" when I was asked to contribute a chapter on Woolf for a book on Narrative Beginnings, and I responded enthusiastically with a commitment to write about the way Woolf does *not* begin.[1] But what seemed an easy project caused me endless difficulties. I hadn't realized how hard it is for a writer to *avoid* beginning, if not on the opening page, then on a later page, or at some implied point preceding the first words. I also hadn't fully realized the implications of beginnings for our conception of the end, and the importance of endings to the writing of what I will call non-coercive ethical texts. For the problem of the non-authoritarian writer is the problem I think Woolf stages in the playwright La Trobe: how do you communicate an intense ethical vision (which means imposing a way of seeing), in an ethical way (which means leaving the audience free to see for themselves)? The answer has to do, I think, with both the creation and the reception of words—that is, with both beginnings and ends.

As opposed to the straight edge of the page we turn as we open a book, Woolf writes what I have called beginning's ragged edge. Textual energy, in her works, pushes against the clean cut edge of the paper, reconstructing the opening page as if it were a bit of torn cloth. A ragged beginning exposes dangling threads, those on the present cloth and those, by implication, on the larger cloth from which the piece was torn. And the dangling threads encode both a multiplicity of pre-texts and the formation of the present through ruptures and breaks. The truly revolutionary nature of this practice is indicated by the absence of terms to discuss it; narrative theory has always assumed that a fixed beginning point emerges somewhere in the story and that it supplies the motivating force for the action that proceeds; Gerald Prince's *A Dictionary of Narratology*, for example, defines beginning as "The incident initiating the process of change in a PLOT or ACTION" (10). But Woolf's plots break with the Old Testament creationist mythology in which in the beginning was the word; her novels are haunted by the ghostly presence of voices always remaining outside the text, and prior to it, but there is no absolute single point of origin to which the present narrative can be traced. No god-like creationist act informs the narrative as an *a priori* trope; and, *pace* Stephen Dedalus, the artist's creation is not figured in god-like terms. Woolf's ragged beginning is, furthermore, radically transformative of the end. In their rejection of a fixed point of beginning, Woolf's narratives break with the teleologically driven plot that advances to a single, final goal. Feminist criticism has of course dealt extensively with Woolf's revision of the linear and monologic male sentence: to take an early significant example, more than twenty years ago, Rachel Blau DuPlessis's *Writing Beyond the Ending* (1985) demonstrated the way Woolf's texts not only write beyond the outcomes allotted to women in patriarchal plots, but also employ oscillating, dialogic structures to break with sequentially-driven prose. But a closer look at Woolf's beginnings leads us even more deeply into the philosophical implications of her textual pluralism, revealing the integral tie linking beginnings and endings to the modernist ethical text.

Rather than initiating action, beginnings, in Woolf's works, plunge us into actions in process, in three instances with first lines that articulate a response to, or continuation of, something previously written or said: "'So of course,' wrote Betty Flanders" (*JR* 3); "'Yes, of course...But,'" says Mrs. Ramsay (*TTL* 9); and the Fernham speaker opens with "But, you may say" (*AROO* 1). Although readers subsequently gain enough information to hypothesize a generalized situation, the words anterior to the first line are never explicitly revealed. No flashback situates the opening *in medias res*; we do not, as in epic, stand outside a story whose ordered structure we ultimately reconstruct. As a result, beginning is situated not in the narrative but in the process of reading; it is *we* who begin by "listening in" to a story that is well underway. For the opening words effect a slight hesitation in our attentive processes. As parts of speech that are, in the linguistic sentence, grammatically dependent, "but," "so," and "yes," signal an anterior pre-text that we have missed.

Opening to the word "so" in *Jacob's Room*, we find ourselves well advanced in a narrative (with a prior history), written in a letter (with a previously written but not cited salutation), to an addressee (who may or may not have sent correspondence to which the present letter is a response). From Mrs. Flanders's subsequent reference to an "accident," readers can imaginatively sketch in a plausible story: one of her sons (Jacob?) presumably broke something (what?) at a boarding house where they were staying, causing the family to relocate to other lodgings. When we later grasp how Mrs. Flanders, a widow, serves as a flattering looking-glass for Captain Barfoot's grandiose self-portraits, we can guess his reciprocal function as the sympathetic reflector of her own self-dramatization. But the retrospective reading initiated by our opening questions is never so satisfied with its conclusions that it stops. If "so" precipitates, in the letter, the forward momentum of Mrs. Flanders's hand, it initiates, in the reader, the consciousness of a missing antecedent clause. Lacking a frame, we seek it in multiple places, casting our lines further and further back in time. Where in the larger narrative do we locate the beginnings of Mrs. Flanders's distress? In the accident that precipitated the family's move? In the fatality of her being widowed two years before? In the still vaster realm of "the eternal conspiracy of hush and clean bottles" (14), and the ages-old burden of maternal care in a threatening world? Or, in the less anthropocentric, more universal rhythm of the weakly crab (caught by Jacob) climbing and falling back into its bucket, climbing and falling back (16)? And what could fill in the missing exposition for Jacob's own story? In what sentence is the narrative of Jacob's life the clause that follows "so"? In "A Sketch of the Past," Woolf wrote, "I see myself as a fish in a stream; deflected; held in place; but cannot describe the stream" (80). The "beginnings" of Jacob's life cannot be fixed or determined, or it would cease to be a stream. Strategies of anti-beginning insert the individual into life's continuum and define the act of reading as stepping into the flux.

While the "so" of *Jacob's Room* signals a larger trajectory of time and experience flowing before and around the individual life, "But, you may say" and "Yes, of course...But" situate the individual utterance within a conversational stream. Both *A Room of One's Own* and *To the Lighthouse* open in the dialogic mode, and numerous critics have explored the implications for the ensuing text: the undercutting of hegemonic, monologic authority, the initiation of a feminist discourse informed by polyvocality and chiasmic turns and shifts.[2] But the opening words have the further function of giving shape to a narrative "before." While each work opens on a female speaker pitted against and challenging a dominant patriarchal discourse, her actual words are directed to complicit, not oppositional, ears: an audience of women students in the essay-lecture, and Mrs. Ramsay's son James in the novel. And both speakers' words evidently respond to a previous, but unrecorded, utterance: the lecturer anticipates her audience's objection (But, you *may* say) on the basis of their prior (but not textually stated) request (an invitation to talk about women and fiction); the mother responds to her son's similarly unsounded, unwritten question (*will* he be able to go to the lighthouse the next day?). It is not the speaker who interrupts, but the reader, intruding into a conversation in which a certain discursive contract has already been assumed.

In these works, as in *Jacob's Room*, the reader soon has enough information to sketch in the situation, but my interest here is in the rhetorical effect. "Once upon a time" gets us all ready and nicely settled in our chairs. "But" and "Yes" signal our late arrival on the scene, generating a critical uncertainty about our ability ever fully to know the life that has been in process in a hypothesized prior time. In a diary entry written just after the publication of *To the Lighthouse* and before *A Room of One's Own*, Woolf wrote, "What I like, or one of the things I like, about motoring is the sense it gives one of lighting accidentally, like a voyager who touches another planet with the tip of his toe, upon scenes which would have gone on, have always gone on, will go on, unrecorded, save for this chance glimpse" (*D3* 153). Beginning's ragged edge is the ghostly echo of things that "have gone on, have always gone on, will go on, unrecorded"; listening in, like alighting on a foreign planet, situates the life within the book in the larger stream of unrecorded time.

Beginning uncertainties can also be instilled through a pattern of infinite regression, initiated, in the opening of *Mrs. Dalloway*, by the conjunction "for." Of all Woolf's novels, *Mrs. Dalloway* might seem to make the clearest straight-edge start, with its definitive announcement of determination and act: "Mrs. Dalloway said she would buy the flowers herself" (3). Immediately following this sentence, however, the logic of "for" reveals the previously occurring "ground" or "reason" motivating Clarissa's announced intent:[3] "For Lucy had her work cut out for her." In miniature, we have the structure of *in medias res* and flashback. But as the passage continues, repetitions of "for" refer us to various other possible beginnings, each subsequently less definite as narrative scene. After her thoughts about Lucy, Clarissa experiences the first whiff of fresh, early morning air like a plunge into a lake: "For so it had always seemed"; the scene wobbles through a lifetime of memory, before alighting on a moment when Clarissa was eighteen. In the next paragraph, Clarissa's sensations accumulate antecedents in a further, more indeterminate, "before": "For having lived in Westminster—how many years now? over twenty" (4). The single day of Mrs. Dalloway's present acquires density through the ever-expanding traces of the past, as the narrative, in its larger frame, acquires density through the prior, though largely unnarrated and hence uncontainable, experiences of war. And since the pattern of infinite regression here means not receding further and further back, but receding over and over again, it makes untenable any posited resting place of a single beginning, even in hypothetical time.

Perhaps most radically, this indeterminateness of beginning informs Woolf's most extended allusion to the Biblical myth of creation: the echo of Genesis in the first section of *The Waves*. Opening in darkness, in a world of no distinguishable forms, the italicized prelude would appear to narrate a scene of *ex nihilo* creation (the beginning of day imitating the beginning of consciousness and initiating the beginning of form). Yet the informing paradigm wobbles between tropes of creation and tropes of disclosure or discovery, ambiguously mixing metaphors of birth and revelation. If the sun *is* the creative eye, then the movement from dark to light, from undifferentiated mass ("the sea was indistinguishable from the sky") to articulated forms ("the sun sharpened the walls of the house") suggests the separation of matter from chaos as a generative visual act (*TW* 7, 8). If, however, the sun *strikes* the eye, then a slowly emerging landscape is recorded, notated, and doubled in the mind, the refraction of light instilling the retinal image. Perception in this guise merely apprehends what has preceded, in its existence, the sensory act. And the imagery of Woolf's description reaches back to the previously observed: a wrinkled cloth, a breathing sleeper, sediment clearing in wine, or the arm of a woman raising a lamp. Seven times in the first three paragraphs, the words "as if" and "like" signal the dependency of perception on associations that antedate the immediate scene. The implications are doubly transformative. Unlike the sudden creative fiat of Genesis, here the artist, as the partially obscured figure of the woman whose arm raises the lamp, is a creative figure without being a single and authoritative point of origin. And, for the reader, beginning means entering into a process whose very multiplicity prevents any reduction of the ensuing text into a single narrative line.

In various ways, Woolf's opening words thus creep out from their locations between the printed covers to link with prior life. And the implications again reveal the fallacy of earlier assumptions about modernist thought. Far from being ahistorical, autonomous formalism, Woolf's writing is permeated with historical consciousness; and instead of plunging us into subjective individualism, the adumbrated, pluralistic "source text" grounds the narrative in an indeterminate, heterogeneous, communal past. However, such potentially positive expansions of narrative also bring attendant threats. The negation of a single origin frees us from confinement in a totalizing, monolinear narrative, but the cumulative building of pre-histories could still bind the future to rearticulations of the past. The question—and one crucial to Woolf's revolutionary feminist thinking—is whether one can engage the wholeness of continuum and still allow a space for radical creative freedom to occur.

Such intense hauntings of pre-history escape a defining, deterministic trajectory, however, precisely because the shift from monism to pluralism *makes it possible* to conceive the radically new. By abandoning the construct of a single, unitary origin in one fixed point in time, Woolf's narratives recast beginnings as indeterminate and multiple and hence always pervasively potential. If antecedents of present experience have come into existence in different forms at different times, then the phenomenon of beginning can occur at any future point as well. A new eddy can flow into the stream, a new thread be woven into the cloth, to enter and transform the holistic continuum of ongoing life.

This construct of time as continuous and yet ever changing, repetitive yet never the same, recalls the correspondences, frequently noted, between Woolf's narrative structures and Henri Bergson's concept of duration or durée. It is the late work of William James, however, that most usefully explains the integral tie between narrative pluralism and an open future. James increasingly recognized similarities between his thought and Bergson's, as connections not of influence but affinity. In similar fashion, affinities between Woolf and James help to illuminate the philosophical understandings that Woolf's unconventional beginnings imply.

In his posthumous *Some Problems in Philosophy*, James investigates the philosophical ramifications of positing one "supreme purpose and inclusive story"—the narrative structure he identified with monism—as opposed to numerous stories that "run alongside each other"—the pluralist hypothesis (131). Numerous parallel stories accommodate both oneness and multiplicity; for, as James argues, the physical world manifests "neither absolute oneness nor absolute manyness"; rather, "an infinite hetereogeneity among things exists alongside of whatever likeness of kind we discover" (127, 128). The monistic thesis, which reduces reality to the single attribute of oneness, errs further since it thus circumscribes the future as always "co-implicated with the past" (139). Pluralism, in contrast, conceives an "additive world" in which disparate realities co-exist in loose relations, connected by "the bare conjunctions 'with' and 'and'" (136). It is this loose additive relation between the multiple stories that allows the possibility for genuine novelty to "leak in" (132).

Virginia Woolf's deployment of juxtaposed fragments, lateral associative movements, and multiple simultaneous plots has been well recognised, but we can further link her multiple indeterminate beginnings with the possibilities opened at her narrative ends. Woolf's disjunctive narrative structures disperse the gesture of beginning throughout her texts; the continuous "leaking in" of novelty *dis*orders past perceptions, and such disordering stimulates the forward moving momentum into an increasingly rich, increasingly heterogeneous world. Again James's explanations connect such pluralistic, disjunctive structures with interventions of the radically new. The "classic obstacle to pluralism" and hence to novelty, in James's view, is the "principle of causality" (189). For if all effects proceed from causes, he argues, effect is always inherent in the cause. What is created is always created out of what already exists; nothing can come into existence that is not some manifestation of the old. In contrast, James posits a different perceptual experience of time and motion, one responsive to infinite variety: "Time keeps budding into new moments, every one of which presents a content which in its individuality never was before and will never be again" (148). Our conceptual understandings, which explain by "deducing the identical from the identical," can name new forms, but only in the terms of the already known, so that "if the world is to be conceptually rationalized no novelty can really come" (152). But our own experience, James argues, tells us otherwise: "the perceptual flux is the authentic stuff of each of our biographies, and yields a perfect effervescence of novelty all the time" (151). Transposing James's words to a different medium, Woolf's false starts, multiple starts, radical breaks, and sudden narrative leaps challenge fixed concepts with the shocks of perceptual novelty, making beginning a perpetual possibility, and allowing for additive new stories beyond the end.

If the openings of Woolf's novels adumbrate ghostly and multiple pre-texts, the following narratives function as prologue, framing and shaping the proleptic gestures on the final page. Even *Jacob's Room*, the novel that seems most to end in loss, creates its final impact through the elided presence of beginnings. In the social sphere, Jacob's fate is driven by strong elements of classic causality: the gendered pathways that regulate his life just as much as Florinda's and Fanny's, the forces that send him to his privileged education in Cambridge, and, as an ironic result of that privilege, off to fight in the war. But Woolf's pluralistic narrative structure defies the hegemony of causality, opening itself to the intrusion of multiple pathways through the inscription of broken links. The blank spaces separating textual fragments leave literal gaps on the page, which are widened perceptually by sudden shifts in perspective, abrupt relocations in space, and precipitous leaps forward in time. The passage of time is motion, but it is a motion whose car frequently jumps the rails. And it is this interrupted, zigzag movement—the course, we might say, of repeatedly halting and newly beginning—that brings a genuinely pluralist subject into view. As Woolf wrote in "The Leaning Tower," "A writer has to keep his eye upon a model that moves, that changes, upon an object that is not one object but innumerable objects" (162). Jacob moves, changes, appears in innumerable guises: both the multiplicity of Jacobs, which our outsider's perspective can only intuit in fragmented glimpses, and the adumbrated potentiality of Jacob's becoming, in the future, something other or more than his past. The anti-war protest of this novel is directed not only at the termination of a rich and vibrant life that once existed but, in addition, at the preclusion of the unborn selves that unpredictably could have altered Jacob's life to come. While Jacob's death may logically, though tragically, end the plotted causality, his abandoned and empty shoes—for where would he have walked in them?—recast the novel as prologue to a movement that *might* have been.

While additive beginnings occur throughout Woolf's fiction, the question of post-textual beginning is most urgent in her last two novels, as erupting war gave questions about the future an increasingly ominous ring. Both *The Years* and *Between the Acts* end on the brink of beginnings projected beyond narrative time, perhaps even beyond the language or discourse which has constituted the textual world. Dialogue in *The Years* halts on Eleanor's interrogative, "And now?" (435). In *Between the Acts*, the closing lines recast the entire narrative as prologue to the text about to play: "Then the curtain rose. They spoke" (219). Furthermore, both structurally and thematically, these narratives are fissured with cracks of possibility for novelty to leak in. At the Pargiters' final party, Peggy's fractured phrase about "living... living differently, differently" echoes in her brother's mind, while, in the printed text, the typographical markings open an ever increasing space between the gaps: the punctuation between the repeated "differently"s progresses, in the iterations, from a comma (391) to a dash (422) to an ellipsis (423). The intrusion of discursive difference is then signalled by the entrance of the caretaker's children and their strangely captivating, incomprehensible song. *Between the Acts* calls for an even more radical beginning: the mind at the point "*before* roads were made, or houses" (219; emphasis added), just as Lily cries out, in *To the Lighthouse*, for "the thing itself before it has been made anything," in order to "start afresh" (287).

But (always the word that in Woolf signals complexity), the possibilities at the end of the text are not completely open-ended, for ending too has a ragged edge. To continue our examination of grammatical structures, think about Eleanor's question, "And now?" Capital A making a break with what has gone on before, "and" inserting continuance. The present time "now" and a question mark. The pluralistic world is an additive world; we join the flow even as we break the old with the new.

This dual action of joining and breaking has strong ethical implications for the work of art. The multiple and pluralistic structures that I have been describing go hand in hand with Woolf's objection to didacticism—an objection that was not a matter of prejudice, nor of taste, but of ethics. Excising didacticism was one of Woolf's fervent aims in her revision of *The Years*—and it was perhaps her successful accomplishment of her goal that makes this such an intense and cryptic novel to read.⁴ But Woolf was also a writer with a strong vision to communicate; a writer who posed penetrating and stringent critiques of her society; a writer who probed as far as she could into the depths of reality, on the grounds, again to draw upon *The Years*, that we cannot model a new society if we do not know ourselves. But how do you communicate any system of values without it becoming propaganda? How do you assert a strong coherent vision without the attendant assumption that your vision encompasses all?

In this light, I would argue, the ragged edge establishes a double textual ethics: on the part of the writer, an ethics of interpolation, in which the text is constructed as both provisional and contingent by being inserted into larger ongoing communal flow of thought; on the part of the reader, an ethics of extrapolation, in which the freedom of the future to break out into the new must do so in response to the words of the past. The ethics of interpolation enable the writer to communicate values without their becoming propaganda; the ethics of extrapolation unite the reader's freedom to determine her own values with a responsibility to the text that has been read.

The dynamics I think are easier to explain than to achieve. Ethical writing does not come about without a struggle, and it is this struggle that becomes graphically evident in the playwright Miss La Trobe. For if even La Trobe's pluralistic participatory theatre comes under the threat of being domineering, is Woolf not suggesting that *all* writing is subject to a colonizing desire to impose its own views? Rather than targeting La Trobe for her assertive proclivities (allowing us to distance ourselves from these characteristics as belonging to the enemy), is Woolf not exposing the "subconscious Hitlerism"⁵ that lies in *all* human nature, that is indeed inseparable from the artist's ability to create? That is, is she not showing us something about ourselves? The amazing victory, then, is that La Trobe resists her desire for influence, takes down that fourth wall of the stage, empowers other human beings and even animals as creators, makes the choice, to her own cost, that to lose her audience is better than to win them by authoritative means. La Trobe succeeds in communicating values without writing propaganda through a conscious and heroic effort to give her words to her audience and to take nothing for herself. Furthermore, her play avoids the monist narrative guided by origin and teleology by drawing upon multiple source texts and beginnings, and by transposing into other voices at the end. The closest we get to an originary source is that fertile mud in her mind, but we must also note that the words bubbling out of it are organic transformations of words that have descended into it first. La Trobe was indeed listening to those voices in the pub, and the implication is that those choric voices have sunk deep into her unconscious to mingle with all the cultural detritus that has accumulated in her memory. As Bart Oliver intuits, what La Trobe sought out, at the end of the day, was "darkness in the mud; a whisky and soda at the pub; and coarse words descending like maggots through the waters" (*BA* 203). Linked to the cesspool of the novel's opening words, the fertilizing mud comes close to being a circulating alimentary-excremental paradigm for art's generation, showing once again how those early critics who thought that Woolf eschewed the body were so wrong.⁶ Does not Woolf indeed—to employ another organic metaphor—suggest a paradigm of art as cultural compost: a process of decomposition and composition occurring in the interval between the old and the new? For as part of a continuous process of derivation, assimilation, transformation, and generation, La Trobe's words are interjected into the ongoing flow between inheritance and continuance, just as, in the larger context, the novel as a whole identifies its position as "between."

But just as ethical writing, for Woolf, means positioning the text in the larger dialogic conversation of community, so ethical reading means a two-way relationship with the work of art. Woolf creates for her reader not an absolute freedom but a dialogic freedom, in which the reader must, if reading ethically, respond to what the writer has shown. I don't mean just close textual reading in the way that I've been attempting here. I mean reading in the way Woolf describes it in her essay "Notes on an Elizabethan Play": [We must not forget], she writes, "how great a power the body of a literature possesses to impose itself: how it will not suffer itself to be read passively, but takes us and *reads us*..." (*CR1* 48; emphasis added). Like La Trobe's pageant, Woolf's texts confront us with a mirror.[7] These unpleasant details we encounter in her fiction: we focus on asking what they say about the text, or about "Woolf." But is the text not also asking what they say about *us*?

This reversing temporality—present interrogating past, and past interrogating future—might also explain the recurring figures that make, perhaps not an ending, but a point of arrest in many of Woolf's longer works: a trope of reconciliation, détente, or confrontation between the sexes. Perhaps I am not the only reader who has been puzzled by such seeming conventionality in a writer who so opposed her culture's gendered plots. For Woolf, however, the polarization of entrenched gender identifications marked the site of the most significant conflicts of her generation (remembering all the contesting values that Woolf understood those identifications to imply), so that her hoverings around the traditional sexual plot suggest a constant return to the site where the rip of the cloth must take place. Thus, echoing the end of *A Room of One's Own*, Eleanor Pargiter looks out a window to see an unknown man and woman in a taxi, although the couple in the later work moves out of the taxi and into a house, not—as in the earlier instance—into the taxi and down the street. In *Between the Acts*, Isa and Giles transform from audience members to figures in a play, transforming in this way into emblematic figures, whose dramatic roles remind us of Mrs. Swithin's observation that the Chinese "put a dagger on the table and that's a battle" (142).[8] Functioning at a supra-character level, these figures expand the narrative conflict to the global stage—civilizations at war, humanity divided against itself. The conflict is inherited, and Woolf challenges us to know it, to see it, to face it as she has shown it, even as our own voices are added to her own efforts to transform it. Just as the unknown couple at the end of *The Years* enters a house instead of freely driving off down the street, and the curtain rises, in *Between the Acts* on a continuing performance, there is a structure we must enter in order to play our dialogic role. Woolf avoids propaganda, but she also defines for the future its ethical task, just as in *Between the Acts*, the grammar of the ending moves from repetition through responsibility to possibility: "they *must* fight," "they *would* embrace," "another life *might* be born" (219, emphasis added). Woolf's ragged endings do allow space for novelty to leak in, for thought that has never been thought before. She leaves us free to define a new future as much as we humanly can be free. But she does not let us escape the human condition; she does let us escape her words. The journey's end—whether of Woolf's text or of this conference—marks a site for new beginnings, but in Woolf's vision of human continuance, beginning is both a rupture and part of the on-going flow. Full stop. Capital A and. Now. Question mark. Woolf's legacy, Woolf's challenge, to us.

## Notes

1. For the chapter that provided the foundations for the present paper, see my forthcoming "Virginia Woolf and Beginning's Ragged Edge," *Narrative Beginnings*, ed. Brian Richardson (Lincoln: University of Nebraska Press). I am deeply grateful to Brian Richardson for his helpful comments and support.
2. For the connection of such chiasmic turns to Woolf's "but" clauses, see, for example, Laura Doyle's "The Body Unbound: A Phenomenological Reading of the Political in *A Room of One's Own*," and the critics whom she cites.
3. OED, definition B.2.a.
4. In her diary notes about revising *The Years*, for example, Woolf jotted, "go back: and rub out detail; too many 'points' made; too jerky, and as it were talking 'at'" (*D4* 353).
5. For these words, quoting Lady Astor in the *Times*, see Woolf's "Thoughts on Peace in an Air Raid."
6. Here my thoughts link as afterwords to the earlier conference session on "Trashy Woolf," especially to Sara Crangle's wonderful paper on "Cesspoolage." What I add to her paper is the further connection of the cesspool to the fertilizing mud.
7. "Baedecker [sic] will count the statues," Woolf declared in her 1906 Greece diary, "but we won't write guidebook" (*PA* 319). As one member of my audience commented, the approach I am describing here finds its closer analogue in Rainer Maria Rilke's "Torso of an Archaic Apollo," in which statue and viewer are conjoined in reciprocal gaze, and the reader is both seer and seen.
8. My afterwords here expand upon Thaine Stearne's pertinent suggestion, in his conference paper on Woolf and Imagism, that what distinguishes Woolf's imagism is her incorporation of movement in the image. As we see here, her dynamic images further imply a movement (e.g. battle) that is to come.

## Works Cited

Doyle, Laura. "The Body Unbound: A Phenomenological Reading of the Political in *A Room of One's Own*." *Virginia Woolf Out of Bounds: Selected Papers from the Tenth Annual Conference on Virginia Woolf*. Ed. Jessica Berman and Jane Goldman. New York: Pace UP, 2001. 129-40.
DuPlessis, Rachel Blau. *Writing Beyond the Ending: Narrative Strategies of Twentieth-Century Women Writers*. Bloomington: University of Indiana Press, 1985.
James, William. *Some Problems of Philosophy: A Beginning of an Introduction to Philosophy*. New York: Longmans, Green, 1911.
Oldfield, Sybil, ed. *Afterwords: Letters on the Death of Virginia Woolf*. New Brunswick, N.J.: Rutgers UP, 2005.
Prince, Gerald. *A Dictionary of Narratology*. Lincoln: University of Nebraska Press, 1989.
Woolf, Virginia. *Between the Acts*. New York: Harcourt Brace, 1941.
———. *The Diary of Virginia Woolf*. Ed. Anne Olivier Bell with Andrew McNeillie. 5 vols. New York: Harcourt, 1977-1984.
———. *Jacob's Room*. 1922. New York: Harcourt Brace, 1923.
———. "The Leaning Tower." *Collected Essays*. Ed. Leonard Woolf. Vol. 2. New York: Harcourt Brace, 1967. 162-81.
———. "Mr. Bennett and Mrs. Brown." *Collected Essays*. Ed. Leonard Woolf. Vol. 1. New York: Harcourt Brace, 1967. 319-37.
———. "Notes on an Elizabethan Play." *The Common Reader: First Series*. Ed. Andrew McNeillie. 1925. New York: Harcourt Brace, 1984. 48-57.
———. *Mrs. Dalloway*. New York: Harcourt Brace, 1925.
———. *A Passionate Apprentice: The Early Journals, 1897-1909*. Ed. Michael A. Leaska. London: Hogarth, 1990.
———. *A Room of One's Own*. New York: Harcourt Brace, 1929.
———. "A Sketch of the Past." *Moments of Being*. Ed. Jeanne Schulkind. 2nd ed. San Diego: Harcourt Brace Jovanovich, 1985. 61-159.
———. "Thoughts on Peace in an Air Raid." *Collected Essays*. Ed. Leonard Woolf. Vol 4. New York: Harcourt, Brace and World, 1967. 173-77.
———. *To the Lighthouse*. New York: Harcourt Brace, 1927.
———. *The Waves*. New York: Harcourt Brace, 1931.
———. *The Years*. New York: Harcourt Brace, 1937.

# *Notes on Contributors*

**CHRISTINA ALT** is a DPhil student in English at Lincoln College, Oxford. Her thesis considers changes in the literary representation of nature resulting from late nineteenth- and early twentieth-century developments in the natural sciences, focusing in particular on Woolf's responses to the disciplines of taxonomy, laboratory biology, ethology, and ecology.

**SUZANNE BELLAMY** is an Australian artist and writer, and Director of Mongarlowe Studio Workshops in southern NSW. She exhibits artwork internationally, is a published Woolf and Stein scholar, currently working on a fusion art/writing project about Woolf and the Visual Field, and research into early colonial readings of Virginia Woolf.

**IAN BLYTH** is an AHRC Research Fellow in the School of English, St Andrews. Publications include *Hélène Cixous: Live Theory* (Continuum, 2004), and the Introduction and Explanatory Notes for the Cambridge University Press edition of *The Waves* (forthcoming). He is currently co-editing *The Years*, with David Bradshaw, for Blackwell's Shakespeare Head edition.

**ANNA BURRELLS** is a doctoral candidate at the University of Birmingham, where she is researching the nexus between industrial technology and politics in the inter-war period. She was part of the conference team at the 2006 Woolf conference and presented a paper on Woolf, Wyndham Lewis, and Henri Bergson.

**BEN CLARKE** received his doctorate from the University of Oxford, and has taught at universities in Britain, Taiwan, and the United States. His first book, *Orwell in Context*, will be published by Palgrave this summer. He is currently writing a monograph on political and aesthetic experimentation in the 1930s, and co-writing a study of Richard Hoggart.

**MELBA CUDDY-KEANE** is Professor of English and a Northrop Frye Scholar at the University of Toronto, and the author of *Virginia Woolf, the Intellectual, and the Public Sphere* (2003). She is currently editing *Between the Acts* for Harcourt, and writing a book on Modernism, Globalism, and the Sphere of Tolerance.

**STEVE ELLIS** is Professor of English Literature at the University of Birmingham. He has published many books and articles on medieval and modern literature, including *Virginia Woolf and the Victorians* (Cambridge UP, forthcoming 2007).

**RICHARD ESPLEY** completed his PhD, on Djuna Barnes, at the University of Birmingham in 2005. Since then he has published on various topics, and is currently researching a major project on modernism and London Zoo.

**ALYDA FABER** is Assistant Professor of Christian Theology and Ethics at Atlantic School of Theology in Halifax, Nova Scotia. Her current research interests include Virginia Woolf and religion, as well as religious subjectivity and film spectatorship.

**LARA FEIGEL** is currently completing her doctorate on the influence of cinema on politically engaged literature in Britain 1930-1945 at Sussex University, supervised by Laura Marcus. She is the editor of *A Nosegay: A Literary Journey from the Fragrant to the Fetid* (Old Street Publishing).

**DEBORAH GERRARD** is currently finishing her PhD, *In Dialogue with Modernism: Storm Jameson's Early Formation as a Writer, 1919-1933* at De Montfort University, Leicester. Her essay "'The tempestuous morning energy of a new art': socialism, modernism, and the young Storm Jameson" will be published in Birkett, Jennifer and Chiara Briganti, eds. *Margaret Storm Jameson: Writing in Dialogue* (Cambridge Scholars Press, 2007).

**JANE GOLDMAN** is Reader in English at Glasgow University, General Editor of the Cambridge University Press Edition of the Writings of Virginia Woolf, and author of *The Cambridge Introduction to Virginia Woolf* (2006), *Modernism, 1910-1945* (2004), and *The Feminist Aesthetics of Virginia Woolf* (1998). She is editing *To the Lighthouse* for Cambridge, and writing *Virginia Woolf and the Signifying Dog*.

**RUTH GRUBER** wrote the first doctoral thesis on Virginia Woolf as a twenty-year-old American exchange student at the University of Cologne in 1932, as Adolf Hitler was coming to power. She has now donated Woolf's correspondence to her to the New York Public Library to be with most of Woolf's letters and diaries. In 2007, at the age of 95, she published her nineteenth book called *Witness! One of the Great Correspondents of the Twentieth Century Tells Her Story With 195 of Her Own Photos*.

**BEN HARVEY** is an assistant professor of art history at Mississippi State University. His research focuses on word and image issues, especially as they pertain to the art and literature of both nineteenth-century France and Bloomsbury. He is currently working on several projects concerning Woolf and visual culture.

**MAGGIE HUMM** is a Professor of Cultural Studies, University of East London. She has been a Distinguished Visiting Scholar and professor at many universities including Massachusetts, San Diego State, Stanford, Rutgers, Queen's Belfast, and Karachi. Recent publications include *Snapshots of Bloomsbury: the Private Lives of Virginia Woolf and Vanessa Bell* (Rutgers and the Tate, 2006), and she is currently editing the *Edinburgh Companion to Virginia Woolf and the Arts* (Edinburgh University Press) and researching *Snapshots: a History* for Tate Publishing.

**EMILY KOPLEY** received her BA in English from Yale University in May 2006. This year she is teaching the English language at a high school in southern France. In Fall 2007 she will begin a PhD program in English at Stanford University.

**RANDI SYNNØVE KOPPEN** is Associate Professor of English at the University of Bergen, Norway. She is the author of *Scenes of Infidelity: Feminism in the Theatre* (1995) and has published numerous articles on contemporary theatre, critical theory, and literary modernism. Her current research projects include a study of Woolf's essays and fiction in the context of modern ideas of fashion and anti-fashion.

## Notes on Contributors

**KATIE MACNAMARA** is a doctoral candidate in English Literature at Indiana University in Bloomington, and is working on a dissertation exploring modernist approaches to the essay form. A Chicago native, she studied English and Russian literature at Princeton University and spent two years teaching in Malaysia and Singapore before returning to the Midwest for graduate school.

**WENDY PARKINS** is a Senior Lecturer in the English Department at the University of Otago, New Zealand. She is the editor of *Fashioning the Body Politic: Dress, Gender, Citizenship* (2002) and the co-author of *Slow Living* (2006). She is currently completing a book manuscript entitled *Mobility and Modernity in British Women's Novels, 1850s-1930s*, to be published in 2008.

**DEBORAH PARSONS** is a Senior Lecturer at the University of Birmingham, where she teaches and researches on nineteenth- and twentieth-century literature. She has published widely on modernist women writers, including *Streetwalking the Metropolis* (2000), *Djuna Barnes* (2003) and *Three Thinkers of the Modernist Novel: Joyce, Richardson, Woolf* (2006), and is co-editor of the peer-reviewed online journal *Modernist Cultures* (www.modernist.bham.ac.uk).

**AMBER K. REGIS** is a doctoral student within the Research Institute for Humanities at Keele University, and her PhD research is focused upon gender, sexuality, and genre in experimental Victorian and modernist life writing. She has taught at both Keele University and Wedgwood Memorial College, and is editorial assistant for the *Journal of Victorian Culture*.

**SUSAN REID** is a Postgraduate Research Student at the University of Northampton, completing her doctoral thesis on *D. H. Lawrence and Masculinity*. Her previous papers and articles encompass a range of interests within modernism, including Englishness, the pastoral, the gentleman, nineteenth-century influences, and several studies of gender and sexuality.

**BONNIE KIME SCOTT** is Professor and Chair of the Department of Women's Studies at San Diego State University, where she teaches courses on feminist theory, gender, representation, women writers, and the environment. She is President of the International Virginia Woolf Society. Her latest book is the critical anthology, *Gender in Modernism: New Geographies, Complex Intersections*, a sequel to *The Gender of Modernism*.

**KATHRYN SIMPSON** lectures in English at the University of Birmingham, teaching courses on nineteenth- and twentieth-century fiction and film. Her research interests focus on the interrelationships of sexuality and creativity in the work of Virginia Woolf, H. D., and Gertrude Stein. She is currently writing a monograph on Virginia Woolf, exploring the interrelationships of market and gift economies in relation to desire.

**HELEN SOUTHWORTH** is Assistant Professor at the Clark Honors College, University of Oregon. She has published on various aspects of Woolf's work, most recently on

Woolf's connections to the nineteenth-century British writer George Borrow (*Studies in the Novel*, 2007). She is the author of a study of Woolf and French contemporary Colette (Ohio State UP, 2004) and co-editor of the selected papers from the 2005 Woolf conference.

**ELISA KAY SPARKS** is Associate Professor of English and Director of Women's Studies at Clemson University in South Carolina. A printmaker on the side, specializing in woodcut, she has published articles on Woolf and Georgia O'Keeffe as well as on spaces associated with Woolf, including gardens and aspects of London. She was co-editor, along with Helen Southworth, of *Woolf and the Art of Exploration: Selected Papers from the Fifteenth International Conference on Virginia Woolf*.

**THAINE STEARNS** is Assistant Professor of English at Sonoma State University. He has published articles on Woolf, on Rebecca West and T.S. Eliot, and on Dora Marsden and James Joyce. He is currently working on a book titled *A Visible Chaos: Optics, Status, and Altercations in Anglo-American Modernism, 1913-1938*.

**JIM STEWART** has researched and taught for many years at the University of Dundee, where he has recently assisted with the forthcoming Cambridge UP edition of Virginia Woolf. Modernism, the Renaissance, and theatre are his areas of interest. He is preparing a first book of poetry.

**TARA SURRY** completed her PhD, which focused on Virginia Woolf's essays and forms of urban space, at the University of Western Australia in 2004. Her research interests include modernism, twentieth-century women's writing, nineteenth-century studies, the Gothic, surrealism, and feminist theory. She lives in London and is working on articles based on her research.

**ELIZABETH WRIGHT** is a doctoral student in the School of English, University of St Andrews, where she is writing her thesis on the relationship between Woolf and theatre. Her article, 'Re-evaluating Woolf's Androgynous Mind' appeared on Postgraduate English in 2006 (www.dur.ac.uk/postgraduate.english/journal1.htm).

www.ingramcontent.com/pod-product-compliance
Lightning Source LLC
Chambersburg PA
CBHW021857230426
43671CB00006B/429